Acknowledgements

Writing this book, I received a great deal of support from various advisors, colleagues, and friends, for which I am deeply grateful. Most of the underlying research took shape at the European University Institute (EUI) in Florence. First and foremost, I therefore wish to thank Adrienne Héritier. Without her leadership, this book would have never come into being. The genuine interest and enthusiasm she has dedicated to my research is simply invaluable. I also thank Ulrich Krotz, who helped me present my work in such a way that it became accessible to people other than myself. Furthermore, I am indebted to Amy Verdun, Lucia Quaglia, Douglas Webber, Joachim Schild, Sandra Destradi, Simon Bulmer, William Paterson, and Claus Offe for constructive comments on various aspects of my work. I very much appreciate and value the support of Gerda Falkner and the Centre for European Integration Research (EIF) in Vienna, where I over the last two years have improved and finalized this book. I am also grateful to my colleagues and friends at the EIF, among them Henning Deters, Georg Plattner, Federica Zardo, and Florian Sowa, who contributed with useful feedback and discussions over lunch and coffee. Special thanks go to Olof Karlsson for his assistance with editing and language correction. Next to the friends and colleagues mentioned here, I am hugely indebted to the officials at the EU institutions in Brussels, the German Ministry of Finance, and the European Central Bank who gave their precious time to answer my "ivory tower" questions about their work. Finally, I am grateful to my parents for their unwavering support. My deepest gratitude, however, goes to Katharina for always being by my side.

Contents

Palgrave Studies in European Union Politics

Series Editors
Michelle Egan
American University
Washington, DC, USA

Neill Nugent
Manchester Metropolitan University
Manchester, UK

William E. Paterson
Aston University
Birmingham, UK

Following on the sustained success of the acclaimed European Union Series, which essentially publishes research-based textbooks, Palgrave Studies in European Union Politics publishes cutting edge research-driven monographs. The remit of the series is broadly defined, both in terms of subject and academic discipline. All topics of significance concerning the nature and operation of the European Union potentially fall within the scope of the series. The series is multidisciplinary to reflect the growing importance of the EU as a political, economic and social phenomenon.

More information about this series at
http://www.palgrave.com/gp/series/14629

Magnus G. Schoeller

Leadership in the Eurozone

The Role of Germany and EU Institutions

palgrave
macmillan

Magnus G. Schoeller
Centre for European Integration Research (EIF)
Department of Political Science
University of Vienna
Vienna, Austria

Palgrave Studies in European Union Politics
ISBN 978-3-030-12703-9 ISBN 978-3-030-12704-6 (eBook)
https://doi.org/10.1007/978-3-030-12704-6

Library of Congress Control Number: 2019931745

Cover credit: Magic Lens/Shutterstock

This Palgrave Macmillan imprint is published by the registered company Springer Nature Switzerland AG
The registered company address is: Gewerbestrasse 11, 6330 Cham, Switzerland

Abbreviations

ALDE	Alliance of Liberals and Democrats for Europe
CDU	Christian Democratic party
ECB	European Central Bank
EDIS	European Deposit Insurance Scheme
EFC	Economic and Financial Committee
EFSF	European Financial Stability Facility
EFSM	European Financial Stabilisation Mechanism
EMU	Economic and Monetary Union
EP	European Parliament
EPC	Economic Policy Committee
EPP	European People's Party
ESM	European Stability Mechanism
EU	European Union
EWG	Eurogroup Working Group
IMF	International Monetary Fund
LTRO	Longer-term Refinancing Operations
MEPs	Members of the EP
NGO	Non-Governmental Organisation
OMT	Outright Monetary Transactions
PES	European Socialists
QE	Quantitative Easing
QMV	Qualified Majority Voting
RQMV	Reversed Qualified Majority Voting
SGP	Stability and Growth Pact

SMP	Securities Markets Programme
SRM	Single Resolution Mechanism
SSM	Single Supervisory Mechanism
TFEU	Treaty on the Functioning of the European Union
UK	United Kingdom

List of Figures

List of Tables

CHAPTER 1

Introduction: Explaining Leadership in the Eurozone

Leadership of powerful states and organizations is crucial for the success of regional integration projects (Mattli 1999; Beach 2005; Tallberg 2006). Yet, these collective actors do not always provide successful leadership: they may not even emerge as leaders (leadership vacuum) or they may fail to influence the outcomes of regional integration (failed leadership). The Economic and Monetary Union (EMU) is a case in point. Since the outbreak of the eurozone crisis, neither Germany nor any of the supranational institutions has assumed a permanent leadership role. Instead, according to the issue at stake, we observe three different outcomes: no leadership, failed leadership, and successful leadership. This raises the questions of why and how collective actors emerge as political leaders, and—once in charge—how they influence policy or institutional change. What are the conditions for successful leadership? These questions become particularly relevant in times of crisis. However, despite a large amount of leadership literature, there is no political science approach that systematically theorizes the emergence *and* impact of leadership when exercised by collective actors.

This book therefore offers a causal and generalizable theoretical model to explain leadership of collective actors such as states or international institutions. By applying the model to the case of EMU governance and reform, the book combines innovative theorizing on leadership in regional and international affairs with original empirical research on eurozone politics. Drawing primarily on in-depth interviews with European Union (EU) and government officials, the book helps us

M. G. Schoeller, *Leadership in the Eurozone*, Palgrave Studies in European Union Politics, https://doi.org/10.1007/978-3-030-12704-6_1

understand the behaviour of powerful actors when it comes to leadership, and the extent to which they can contribute to overcoming a crisis and fostering European integration. In particular, the book investigates the under-researched questions of who provided leadership in the eurozone crisis and why, which actor might reasonably be expected to take the lead, and which conditions must be given to achieve successful leadership in the EU.

Research on political leadership is "disparate, under-theorised and under-researched" (Hartley and Benington 2011: 211). The resulting gap in literature is especially striking with regard to collective actors in EU politics (Helms 2017: 3; Tömmel and Verdun 2017: 103–7). In particular, there is no general theoretical model which explains the emergence *and* impact of leadership beyond formal "chairmanship" or specific empirical contexts.[1] Theories of European integration largely neglect the role of leadership, too. According to (liberal) intergovernmentalism, leadership is redundant as negotiation outcomes merely reflect the preferences of the most powerful states, while supranational institutions lack the resources to provide leadership (Moravcsik 1999a, b).[2] Neofunctionalism acknowledges that states and institutions may act as leaders in regional integration, but it leaves the variance in leadership demand and supply undertheorized (Lindberg and Scheingold 1970: 128–33; Niemann and Ioannou 2015: 199). Only Walter Mattli (1999) considers the leadership of powerful states as a crucial explanatory factor of regional integration. Still, he does not elaborate on the theoretical concept of leadership or the distinction between leadership emergence and impact. Moreover, regional integration theory has not taken up Mattli's insights. As Finn Laursen notes: "One can wonder why Mattli's emphasis on leadership has not produced more comparative research over the last ten years" (2010: 8, Footnote 2).

[1] The works of Beach (2005), Tallberg (2006), and Beach and Mazzucelli (2007) are highly exceptional in that regard. However, while the model proposed by Tallberg (2006) addresses only formal leadership in negotiations ("chairmanship"), Beach (2005) and Beach and Mazzucelli (2007) restrict their models to EU institutions and EU constitutional negotiations, respectively. Moreover, they do not make an analytical distinction between a leader's emergence and its actual impact.

[2] Disagreeing with Moravcsik, Beach (2005) and Tallberg (2006) have shown that considerable informational asymmetries and differing institutional positions, which have both been neglected by liberal intergovernmentalism, make a significant difference with regard to negotiation outcomes in EU politics.

With regard to leadership research, we identify two important gaps. First, existing theory-guided work has mainly focused on individual actors, leaving collective actors such as states, supranational institutions, or non-governmental organizations (NGOs) out of the picture (see e.g. Rhodes and 't Hart 2014).[3] Second, "there is no 'rational theory of leadership'" (Shepsle and Bonchek 1997: 380). The few existing rationalist approaches focus on very specific aspects (see Ahlquist and Levi 2011), remain at the level of formal "chairmanship" (Tallberg 2006), or refer to a very concrete empirical scope (Beach 2005). Thus, integrating the leadership factor into rationalist theorizing is still an unresolved issue on the research agenda (Elgie 2001: 8579; Brennan and Brooks 2014: 161).

Hence, there is no specific theory that helps us explain the ambiguous leadership record of eurozone crisis management. Due to its powerful position in EMU, the actor mostly called on to assume leadership was Germany (e.g. Matthijs and Blyth 2011; Paterson 2011; Bulmer 2014). Yet, Germany has not emerged as a constant leader in the eurozone. Depending on the particular issue at stake, it refrained from offering, failed to deliver, or (rarely) succeeded in exercising leadership. This pattern recurs also with regard to other crucial actors in EMU. Especially in cases where Germany did not seek to provide leadership, supranational institutions such as the European Commission, the European Parliament, or the European Central Bank (ECB) had the chance—or were forced—to fill the leadership vacuum. The performance of these actors varied as well, and we observe all three outcomes: no, failed, and successful leadership. To date, however, the causes of this patchy leadership record have not been examined in a systematic and comparative manner.

This book seeks to fill these gaps in the literature. At a theoretical level, it provides a rational institutionalist model to explain the political leadership of collective actors, thereby making a crucial distinction between a leader's emergence and its impact. Although the book applies this model to eurozone governance and reform in times of crisis, it is equally applicable to other instances of formal *and* informal leadership in regional integration and international politics. With regard to its empirical contribution, the book offers an explanation for the ambiguous

[3] An exception is a strand of International Relations literature focusing on the role of powerful states in regional integration (e.g. Destradi 2010; Krapohl et al. 2014; Malamud 2011; Mattli 1999; Schirm 2010). However, even within this literature, the concept of leadership remained largely under-theorized (Laursen 2010: 13f.).

leadership record of the eurozone by analysing cases of crisis management in a systematic and comparative manner. It thus examines under which conditions leaders emerge in EMU and when they are successful. In so doing, the book helps the reader understand when actors are willing and capable to take the lead, how leadership can be a way of driving institutional change, and whether the E(M)U with its multiple access- and veto-points allows for the emergence of leadership at all (see Hayward 2008; Helms 2017; Tömmel and Verdun 2017).

In sum, although many political scientists assign an important role to leadership, there is no generalizable causal model going beyond formal "chairmanship" or specific empirical contexts in explaining the emergence *and* impact of political leadership by collective actors. This is especially striking with regard to European integration and EU governance. The recent example of the eurozone crisis leaves us puzzled in that regard, as there is no theory that can explain why states as well as supranational institutions sometimes refrain from offering, fail to deliver, or succeed in exercising leadership. The research questions arising from this puzzle therefore concern two different aspects of leadership, namely (1) its emergence and (2) its impact:

1. Why and how do collective actors such as states or international institutions emerge as political leaders?
2. How do political leaders influence policy or institutional change? What determines their success or failure?

1.1 The Argument

The book provides a rational institutionalist model of political leadership. It defines "leadership" as a process in which powerful actors use their resources in such a way as to guide the behaviour of others towards a common goal (Chapter 2). The basic argument states that leaders can help a group to enhance collective action when there are no, or only incomplete, institutions[4] to do so (Chapter 3). Leadership is therefore not only a recurrent pattern of political interaction, but also a solution to collective action problems. Thus, especially in times of crisis, leaders can

[4]In this case, "institutions" are understood as man-made rules of behaviour that constrain individual action and thereby shape social interaction (North 1990; Héritier 2007). For the understanding of institutions as used in the theoretical framework, see Sect. 3.1.

act as drivers of policy or institutional change, and may temporarily even function as a substitute for institutions.

By guiding a group of actors to outcomes otherwise not possible, a leader improves the group's way of doing things. On the one hand, a leader can help actors decide between several outcomes and make them choose a collectively beneficial solution. Similarly, a leader can reduce a group's transaction costs, which impede the finding of an outcome that would be better for all (see Beach 2005; Tallberg 2006). On the other hand, a leader can also propose completely new outcomes and thereby act as a game-changer.

However, leaders can also fail. This implies that the emergence of leadership is not sufficient for its impact. The theoretical model therefore introduces a crucial distinction between these two analytical steps. The emergence depends on the would-be leader's expected costs and benefits of leading (leadership supply) and on the status quo costs the group has to bear in case the situation continues without a leader (leadership demand). The impact of leadership, by contrast, depends on the interplay of three factors: a leader's power resources, the distribution of preferences within the group, and the institutional constraint faced by the leader.

1.2 The Evidence

The book tests these propositions by applying them to the context of eurozone crisis management. More precisely, the empirical analysis provides two case studies for each of the three theorized outcomes (no, failed, and successful leadership). In so doing, the analysis includes all relevant leadership candidates in the eurozone.[5] Thus, the theoretical model is applied to Germany's role in the first financial assistance to Greece, the proposal to establish a "super-commissioner", and the shaping of the Fiscal Compact. Moreover, the role of the European Commission and the European Parliament regarding the issue of Eurobonds as well as the ECB's announcement of Outright Monetary Transactions (OMT) are analysed on the basis of congruence tests and process-tracing.

[5] In order to make sure that the different outcomes do not just depend on the different leaders in charge, three of the case studies represent each of the three possible outcomes while focusing on the same actor (Germany).

The empirical analysis corroborates the theoretical model. In all six cases, actors emerged as leaders only if they expected individual benefits from doing so. This was the case despite the strong demand for leadership resulting from the constantly high status quo costs of the eurozone crisis. Once a leader has emerged, she needs to translate her power resources into strategies in order to convince reluctant followers and overcome institutional hurdles for policy change or institutional reform. Thus, the amount of power resources available to the leader partly explains her impact. Moreover, successful leadership becomes more likely if the ex-ante preferences of followers converge on the outcome proposed by the leader, instead of diverging elsewhere, and if the underlying institutional rules provide the leader with enough leeway in decision-making. Hence, no single factor can sufficiently explain a leader's impact. Instead, the interplay of three factors—power resources, preference distribution, and institutional constraint—accounts for the final outcome.

Moreover, the case studies demonstrate that leadership is indeed a solution to collective action problems. In those cases where actors refrained from providing leadership or failed to deliver, the eurozone as a whole was left worse off. By contrast, the case of the ECB's announcement of OMT shows that when a powerful actor decides to bear the costs of leading, this can be to the benefit of the entire group—including the leader herself. Moreover, the analysis unveils new insights with regard to what may be called a "leadership vacuum". On the one hand, such a situation may produce surprisingly weak leaders, who can emerge only because no one else is willing to take the lead. On the other hand, a leadership vacuum can bring about "leaders by default". These are powerful actors that provide leadership only as late as possible because they fear the high costs of leading and therefore attempt to free-ride on the leadership of others.

The single case studies also provide findings that speak to the particular role of single actors in EMU. Germany, as EMU's most powerful member state, enjoys a de facto veto power in EU economic governance. However, its actual shaping power, which is crucial for the exercise of leadership, is much more limited. To put it bluntly, the fact that Germany can block whatever it does not like in current EMU governance and reform does not mean that it also has the power to realize all the things it does like. With regard to the Commission and European Parliament, the analysis shows that although both institutions can be described as power-maximizers, their eventual behaviour differs because they are constrained by their respective institutional roles. Thus, if a solution to a collection action problem in EMU appears politically unfeasible, for instance, the European Parliament may still benefit from taking the lead on it, whereas the Commission would damage its credibility as formal agenda-setter and therefore refrain from taking the lead. The ECB, by contrast, differs from the other two institutions in the sense that it is no institutional power-maximizer in the conventional understanding: if its political independence and its influence are at odds, the ECB refrains from maximizing its influence on outcomes in order to preserve its independence. However, given that the eurozone crisis threatened the ECB's very existence, it could not avoid becoming politicized nevertheless. It therefore emerged as a "leader by default".

1.3 The Method

The book applies a qualitative and comparative methodology. Since the phenomenon of leadership is not externally given, but socially constructed, much can be learned by taking into account the perceptions and evaluations of the actors involved. Moreover, qualitative in-depth analysis opens insights into the interactional dynamics which constitute the process of leadership. Finally, the fine-tuned mechanisms connecting causal antecedents like a leader's resources or institutional constraint to the respective outcomes, can be revealed best by qualitative in-depth investigation (see Conger 1998). The appropriate methodological procedure for these epistemological requirements are case studies as they provide a high level of conceptual validity. They allow for a detailed consideration of contextual factors and further conceptual refinement. Moreover, case studies are a means to explore and prove causal mechanisms, thereby taking into account also those aspects not codified in variables. Finally, case studies are appropriate tools to assess causal complexity such as interaction effects, path dependency, or equifinality (George and Bennett 2005: 19–22).

Hence, case studies of leadership emergence and impact will serve as plausibility probes in the central part of the empirical analysis. These within-case analyses will rely on the congruence method: The researcher formulates a version of the general deductive theory being employed, identifies historical cases whose outcomes enable the researcher to test the theory's explanatory power, and eventually examines whether the predictions of the theory are consistent with the outcomes (George and Bennett 2005: 200f.). Where the empirical material allows for it, the confidence in the findings will be further increased by tracing the underlying causal mechanisms. Given that "there is a growing consensus that the strongest means of drawing inferences from case studies is the use of a combination of within-case analysis and cross-case comparisons within a single study or research program" (George and Bennett 2005: 18), the book will complement the within-case analyses with a cross-case comparison. Going beyond a mere plausibility probe, this allows us to test the theoretical propositions of the book's leadership model.

The universe of cases comprises all events of proposed or realized crisis-management in the eurozone crisis since the end of 2009. These events are contingent with regard to the emergence and impact of leadership: they might be cases of no leadership, failed leadership, or leadership success. The single cases are selected on the basis of their variance along these three outcomes.[6] The actor generally called upon to lead has been Germany (e.g. Matthijs and Blyth 2011; Paterson 2011; Bulmer 2014). Yet, Germany has not emerged as the hoped-for leader in the crisis. Instead, its behaviour reflects all three possible outcomes: no emergence when it came to the first bailout of Greece in late 2009 and early 2010 (Jones 2010); emergence but no impact in the case of the unsuccessful attempt to establish a "super-commissioner" to control national budgets in the eurozone (Karagiannis and Guidi 2014); and successful leadership in the case of shaping the Fiscal Compact (Schoeller 2015). Especially where German leadership was lacking, other collective actors could step in. Again, we find all three outcomes: no emergence when it comes to the Commission's role in dealing with Eurobonds (Hodson 2013); failed leadership in the case of the European Parliament which unlike the Commission took the lead on Eurobonds, but failed to realize them (Héritier et al. 2019, forthcoming, Chapter 7); and successful leadership in the case of the ECB which put a preliminary end to the crisis by announcing OMT (De Grauwe and Ji 2015) (Table 1.1).

In summary, the central part of the empirical analysis consists in a plausibility probe of the theory, which draws on congruence tests and process-tracing within the scope of single case studies (Chapters 4 and 5). These within-case analyses are complemented by a cross-case

[6]In order to avoid truncated variation, the cases must reflect the full variance the dependent variable can possibly have.

Table 1.1 Cases

	Germany	*Institutional actors*
No leadership (=no emergence)	First bailout of Greece	Commission: Eurobonds
Failed leadership (=no impact)	"Super-commissioner"	EP: Eurobonds
Successful leadership (=emergence and impact)	Fiscal Compact	ECB: OMT

Source Own illustration

comparison in order to enhance the external validity of the results, and an overview assessment of leadership in the eurozone crisis (Chapter 6). Next to a variety of sources, which include legislative texts, declarations, speeches, press releases, newspaper articles, and existing empirical research, the analysis draws on 35 semi-structured élite interviews conducted at the German Ministry of Finance, the ECB, the European Commission, the Council of the EU, the European Parliament, and Permanent Representations in Brussels (see Sect. 3.4 for the operationalization of the theoretical propositions and details of data collection).

1.4 The Plan of the Book

The next chapter provides a conceptualization of political leadership (Chapter 2). Based on existing literature, it identifies the basic "ingredients" of leadership (power, common goal, strategies) as well as the parameters of its success. Moreover, the chapter distinguishes two crucial conceptions of leadership, and it concludes by deriving a definition. Chapter 3 builds on this conceptualization in elaborating a causal and generalizable model that combines the basic assumptions of rational-choice institutionalism with current leadership theorizing. While Sect. 3.1 presents the basic theoretical argument, Sects. 3.2 and 3.3 elaborate testable propositions regarding the emergence and impact of leadership. Section 3.4 draws the implications for the empirical research.

Chapter 4 begins the empirical analysis. The chapter offers three in-depth case studies on Germany's role in eurozone crisis management: the first bailout of Greece, the proposal of a "super-commissioner", and the genesis of the Fiscal Compact. By analysing one case for each outcome (no, failed, successful leadership), the chapter probes the plausibility of the theoretical model and explains Germany's ambiguous leadership record in the eurozone. By analogy with Chapter 4, the following chapter (Chapter 5) provides three case studies analysing the role of the EU institutions in eurozone crisis management. The first two sections (Sects. 5.1, 5.2) examine the controversial proposal of Eurobonds. While the Commission did not take the lead on the issue, the European Parliament did so, but remained unsuccessful. The third section explains why the ECB emerged as a leader in declaring "to do whatever it takes to preserve the euro", and which strategies it used to make the announcement a success (Sect. 5.3).

Chapter 6 evaluates the book's leadership model as well as its findings. While Sect. 6.1 presents the comparative results of the empirical analysis, Sect. 6.2 provides an overview assessment of the eurozone's leadership record since the outbreak of the crisis. Chapter 7 concludes by answering the book's research questions and summarizing its results. Finally, this last chapter points to promising avenues for future research and reflects on the broader implications of the book.

References

Ahlquist, John S., and Margaret Levi. 2011. Leadership: What It Means, What It Does, and What We Want to Know About It. *Annual Review of Political Science* 14 (1): 1–24.

Beach, Derek. 2005. *The Dynamics of European Integration: Why and When EU Institutions Matter*. Basingstoke and New York: Palgrave Macmillan.

Beach, Derek, and Colette Mazzucelli. 2007. Introduction. In *Leadership in the Big Bangs of European Integration*, ed. Derek Beach and Colette Mazzucelli, 1–21. Basingstoke: Palgrave Macmillan.

Brennan, Geoffrey, and Michael Brooks. 2014. Rational Choice Approaches to Leadership. In *The Oxford Handbook of Political Leadership*, ed. R.A.W. Rhodes and Paul 't Hart, 161–175. Oxford and New York: Oxford University Press.

Bulmer, Simon. 2014. Germany and the Eurozone Crisis: Between Hegemony and Domestic Politics. *West European Politics* 37 (6): 1244–1263.

Conger, Jay A. 1998. Qualitative Research as the Cornerstone Methodology for Understanding Leadership. *Leadership Quarterly* 9 (1): 107–121.

De Grauwe, Paul, and Yuemei Ji. 2015. Correcting for the Eurozone Design Failures: The Role of the ECB. *Journal of European Integration* 37 (7): 739–754.

Destradi, Sandra. 2010. Regional Powers and Their Strategies: Empire, Hegemony, and Leadership. *Review of International Studies* 36 (4): 903–930.

Elgie, Robert. 2001. Leadership: Political. In *International Encyclopedia of the Social & Behavioral Sciences*, ed. Neil J. Smelser, 8578–8580. Oxford and New York: Elsevier.

George, Alexander L., and Andrew Bennett. 2005. *Case Studies and Theory Development in the Social Sciences*. Cambridge, MA: MIT Press.

Hartley, Jean, and John Benington. 2011. Political Leadership. In *The Sage Handbook of Leadership*, ed. Alan Bryman, David Collinson, Keith Grint, Brad Jackson, and Mary Uhl-Bien, 203–214. London and Thousand Oaks, CA: Sage.

Hayward, Jack (ed.). 2008. *Leaderless Europe*. Oxford and New York: Oxford University Press.

Helms, Ludger. 2017. Introduction: Leadership Questions in Transnational European Governance. *European Political Science* 16 (1): 1–13.

Héritier, Adrienne. 2007. *Explaining Institutional Change in Europe*. Oxford: Oxford University Press.

Héritier, Adrienne, Katharina L. Meissner, Catherine Moury, and Magnus G. Schoeller. 2019, forthcoming. *European Parliament Ascendant: Parliamentary Strategies of Self-Empowerment in the EU*. London: Palgrave Macmillan.

Hodson, Dermot. 2013. The Little Engine That Wouldn't: Supranational Entrepreneurship and the Barroso Commission. *Journal of European Integration* 35 (3): 301–314.

Jones, Erik. 2010. Merkel's Folly. *Survival* 52 (3): 21–38.

Karagiannis, Yannis, and Mattia Guidi. 2014. Institutional Change and Continuity in the European Union: The Super-commissioner Saga. *Acta Politica* 49 (2): 174–195.

Krapohl, Sebastian, Katharina L. Meissner, and Johannes Muntschick. 2014. Regional Powers as Leaders or Rambos? The Ambivalent Behaviour of Brazil and South Africa in Regional Economic Integration. *Journal of Common Market Studies* 52 (4): 879–895.

Laursen, Finn. 2010. Regional Integration: Some Introductory Reflections. In *Comparative Regional Integration: Europe and Beyond*, ed. Finn Laursen, 3–20. Burlington, VT: Ashgate.

Lindberg, Leon N., and Stuart A. Scheingold. 1970. *Europe's Would-Be Polity: Patterns of Change in the European Community*. Englewood Cliffs, NJ: Prentice-Hall.

Malamud, Andrés. 2011. A Leader Without Followers? The Growing Divergence Between the Regional and Global Performance of Brazilian Foreign Policy. *Latin American Politics and Society* 53 (3): 1–24.

Matthijs, Matthias, and Mark Blyth. 2011. Why Only Germany Can Fix the Euro: Reading Kindleberger in Berlin. Foreign Affairs Snapshot, November 17, available online at https://www.foreignaffairs.com/articles/germany/2011-11-17/why-only-germany-can-fix-euro, rev. 2016–05–31.

Mattli, Walter. 1999. *The Logic of Regional Integration: Europe and Beyond*. New York: Cambridge University Press.

Moravcsik, Andrew. 1999a. A New Statecraft? Supranational Entrepreneurs and International Cooperation. *International Organization* 53 (2): 267–306.
Moravcsik, Andrew. 1999b. Theory and Method in the Study of International Negotiation: A Rejoinder to Oran Young. *International Organization* 53 (4): 811–814.
Niemann, Arne, and Demosthenes Ioannou. 2015. European Economic Integration in Times of Crisis: A Case of Neofunctionalism? *Journal of European Public Policy* 22 (2): 196–218.
North, Douglass C. 1990. *Institutions, Institutional Change and Economic Performance*. Cambridge: Cambridge University Press.
Paterson, William E. 2011. The Reluctant Hegemon? Germany Moves Centre Stage in the European Union. *Journal of Common Market Studies* 49 (s1): 57–75.
Rhodes, R.A.W., and Paul 't Hart (eds.). 2014. *The Oxford Handbook of Political Leadership*. Oxford: Oxford University Press.
Schirm, Stefan A. 2010. Leaders in Need of Followers: Emerging Powers in Global Governance. *European Journal of International Relations* 16 (2): 197–221.
Schoeller, Magnus G. 2015. Explaining Political Leadership: Germany's Role in Shaping the Fiscal Compact. *Global Policy* 6 (3): 256–265.
Shepsle, Kenneth A., and Mark S. Bonchek. 1997. *Analyzing Politics: Rationality, Behavior, and Institutions*. New York and London: W. W. Norton.
Tallberg, Jonas. 2006. *Leadership and Negotiation in the European Union*. Cambridge: Cambridge University Press.
Tömmel, Ingeborg, and Amy Verdun. 2017. Political Leadership in the European Union: An Introduction. *Journal of European Integration* 39 (2): 103–112.

CHAPTER 2

Conceptualizing Leadership: What It Is and Why It Matters

In 1978, one of the most influential leadership theorists claimed that "Leadership is one of the most observed and least understood phenomena on earth" (Burns 1978: 2). Almost 40 years later there is not even a consensus to what extent political leadership—be it at the level of individual or composite actors—matters at all.[1] Instead, research on political leadership is disparate and under-theorised (Hartley and Benington 2011: 211). This chapter draws on the fragmented literature in political leadership research to elaborate a coherent conceptualization of political leadership. In doing so, the chapter clarifies crucial questions that emerge from the literature: How does leadership differ from sheer power? Are leaders necessarily successful? How can we conceptualize the many different types of leadership?

The study of leadership is arguably as vast, old, and fuzzy at its borders as political science itself. Therefore, it is indispensable to demarcate the field before assessing it. The following conceptualization limits itself to *political* leadership, thereby excluding insights from psychological or business literature. As it draws on positive political science research, it also leaves out normative or ethical contributions, such as the distinction of good vs. bad leadership (e.g. Kellerman 2004; Nye 2008: 109–45). Moreover, the conceptualization profits from valuable insights on individual leadership, but it omits approaches that focus exclusively on

[1] For two contrasting views in the realm of international relations, see Jervis (2013) (sceptical) and Nye (2013) (affirmative).

M. G. Schoeller, *Leadership in the Eurozone*, Palgrave Studies in European Union Politics, https://doi.org/10.1007/978-3-030-12704-6_2

individual features, since personal traits like intelligence, self-confidence, or social skills cannot explain the leadership of composite actors such as states or organizations. Finally, while "leadership" may denote an actor, a position, a process, or a result (Grint 2005), this book conceives of *leadership as a process.*

2.1 The Basic Ingredients: Power, Common Goal and Strategies

One way of defining a concept is to go through existing definitions and search for common elements or overlaps.[2] In doing so, this section identifies three crucial features of political leadership, which arise from overlaps and common elements in existing definitions. First, leadership requires power resources. Second, leadership is associated with the pursuit of a common goal. Third, a leader guides the behaviour of others by making use of particular strategies.

Power

Arguably the most common element associated with leadership is power. James MacGregor Burns, for instance, came to the conclusion that political leadership consists essentially in "processes and effects of political power" (1978: 434). Power, in turn, is the "ability to affect the behaviour of others to get the outcomes one wants" (Nye 2010: 306) or, in the words of Robert Dahl (1957: 202f.), to make them do something that they would not otherwise do (see Sect. 3.3). Scholars of political leadership have largely agreed that power is based on material, institutional, or purely non-material resources (e.g. Beach 2005: 26–32; Tallberg 2006: 29–31). Hence, power resources constitute a formal or informal position of authority as a necessary condition for the exercise of leadership (Ahlquist and Levi 2011: 5; Burns 1978: 17f.; Endo 1999: 16–26).

However, leadership is not the same as power, but a special form of exercising it (Keohane 2010: 2). In other words, leadership goes beyond the purely structural aspect of possessing power, and comprises also a behavioural aspect (Underdal 1994: 181f.): a leader not only finds

[2] For an overview of some seminal definitions of political leadership, see Elgie (1995: 3).

herself in a position of power, but she translates power into certain outcomes. More precisely, a leader employs power resources in such a way as to reach a common goal (see below). By contrast, there are many other ways of exercising power that have little to do with leadership: blocking innovation in order to enforce one's own interest against others, for instance, requires power, but is generally not considered an instance of leadership. Hence, it is especially the pursuit of a common goal which distinguishes leadership from other possible ways of exercising power (see Malnes 1995: 93, 99–106).

Common Goal

While the issue of power puts emphasis on the leader herself, the notion of a common goal focuses also on the followers. As highlighted by Burns, a common goal is a necessary condition for the exercise of leadership (1978: 18f., 425–32). In the terminology of Kindleberger (1981), this corresponds to the provision of a common good, which on the one hand defines leadership, and on the other distinguishes it from dominance or exploitation. In the words of Joseph Nye, leaders are therefore "those who help a group create and achieve shared goals" (2010: 306).

Yet, the notion of a common goal does not mean that leadership needs to be an altruistic sacrifice (Skodvin and Andresen 2006: 16–8). On the contrary, the existence of a common goal and the pursuit of a leader's self-interest are by no means contradictory. Rational choice approaches have actually emphasized that the willingness to lead depends on the payoffs to the leaders (Shepsle and Bonchek 1997: 381). These payoffs are given if an actor's expected benefits of leading exceed the costs of it (Frohlich et al. 1971: 7). As a consequence, we may expect leadership to emerge precisely in those situations, where there is an overlap of the would-be leader's self-interest and the common interest of potential followers (see Sect. 3.2).

Moreover, the notion of a common goal is not a normative criterion of leadership. It does not mean that the actions of a leader are necessarily "the right thing to do" or "good for each and everyone". Instead, it means that leader and followers jointly aim at an entity or condition that is collectively superior to status quo. However, individual preferences over how to reach that common goal might still diverge. This implies that despite the presence of a leader, there remain relative winners and losers. In the words of Kindleberger: "Leadership may be thought of at first blush as persuading others to follow a given course of action which might not be in the follower's short-run interest if it were truly independent. [...] Without it, however, there may be an inadequate amount of public goods produced" (1981: 243).

Finally, the perception of a common goal is subjective and historically contingent. This implies that something which was perceived of as a common goal at the time leadership emerged can a posteriori turn out to be beneficial only to some actors or even to no one at all. In a similar vein, the notion of a common goal might only be invoked by the potential leader in order to realize her individual goals.

Strategies

In order to invest their resources into the achievement of a common goal, leaders make use of strategies (Baumgartner 1989; Beach 2005: 32–4; Metcalfe 1998). Leadership strategies are thus transmission belts that deploy resources with a view to enhancing collective action. These may be negotiation strategies which enable collective outcomes otherwise prevented by incomplete information, high transaction costs, or free-rider dilemmas (Tallberg 2006: 37–9; Young 1991: 293–8). Such strategies include, for instance, agenda-management, coalition-building or leading by example (Sect. 3.3). But a leader may also define problems, present new ideas, and promote them as solutions. These strategies, which include framing and arguing, provide a group with common knowledge. This of particular importance in situations where beliefs are unsettled by exogenous events like crisis (see below).

Innovation

Leadership is often associated with innovation (Burns 1978: 434; Masciulli et al. 2009: 3; Moon 1995). Especially organizational and business literature emphasizes that it is the creation of something new which distinguishes leadership from management (Grint 2005: 15; Northouse 1997: 9). Also in political science, leaders have been described as those who change the equilibrium ways of doing things or—more metaphorically—as "agents of change" (Hargrove 1989: 57; see Schofield 2002). However, if we want to avoid the methodological pitfall of measuring leadership by its effects, the criterion of innovation can apply only to those leaders who turn out to be successful. This implies that innovation is a target condition of leadership—a leader is supposed to innovate—but not a defining feature, as leaders can also fail.

2.2 Leadership and Success

This section points out that leadership is not successful by definition. Three parameters determine a leader's success: the leader's position ("trait approach"), behaviour ("style approach") and environment ("situational approach"). These three factors lay the groundwork for the theoretical model outlined in Chapter 3.

The question of whether leadership is intrinsically successful,[3] or whether there might also be unsuccessful leaders, is ultimately a definitional one and may therefore give rise to endless debates. However, from a methodological point of view, there is a clear answer. If we conceive of leaders as successful by definition, we not only measure leadership by its effects, which might easily result in a tautological pitfall, but we are also forced to assess leadership only *ex-post*, once we know about success or failure. If we instead conceive of leadership as not successful by definition, the question arises as to when it is successful: what determines a leader's success or failure? While a theory-guided answer to this question is provided by Chapter 3, this section summarizes the major aspects emerging from the existing literature in political leadership research.

The determinants of a leader's success can be differentiated into a positional, a behavioural, and an environmental dimension. This basic division is reflected in the three leadership approaches which dominate the literature: the trait approach (positional), the style approach (behavioural), and the situational approach (environmental) (see Northouse 1997: 13–73). A leader's success can therefore be described as a function of these three factors.

The *positional* factor consists in a leader's traits and, in most cases, the corresponding power resources. One may expect, for instance, that

[3] In the context of politics, and based on the criteria elaborated above, "success" is understood as the attainment of a policy or institutional change that is supposed to contribute to a common goal.

the stronger a leader's position, or the greater her resources, the more likely her success (Elgie 1995: 204). However, as already Karl Deutsch has pointed out with regard to individual leaders in international relations, a leader's success depends not only on her resources, but also on other factors such as the support of the followers (Deutsch 1988: 71–3; see below).

With regard to the *behavioural* factor, the literature suggests that a leader must actively choose the appropriate means (or strategies) to win the support of followers and influence the outcomes (see Masciulli and Knight 2009: 92; Metcalfe 1998; Underdal 1994: 181f.). The fact that a strong position does not suffice to be a successful leader as long as it is not complemented by a certain behaviour was pointed out by Philip Selznick already in 1957 (see Helms 2012: 3). In political science literature, however, it has remained unclear what exactly the appropriate means are. Moreover, as stressed by Baumgartner (1989), for example, the successful employment of means or strategies depends not least on the environmental setting of a leader.

Although highlighted by many authors (e.g. Jones 1989a: 13; Cole 1994: 468; Elgie 1995; Hargrove 2004), the *environmental* factor, or a leader's situation, is still the most neglected one in the study of political leadership. On the one hand, this dimension concerns the followers' preferences or their support for the leader's action: the smaller their support, the less likely a leader's success (see Deutsch 1988: 72). On the other hand, it concerns the institutional setting. Although the relationship between leadership and institutions is still under-researched (Elgie 2001: 8579), one can state as a general rule: the more favourable a leader's institutional environment, the more likely her success (see Blondel 1987: 148–80; Tallberg 2010: 246).

The interplay of these three parameters not only allows for estimating a leader's success (Fig. 2.1), but also provides an explanation for the alleged paradox of weak, but successful leaders on the one hand, and strong, but unsuccessful leaders on the other. Leader that are equipped with few power resources can still be successful if they actively employ the right measures to reach a common goal and if followers' preferences and the institutional environment constitute only small constraints. Vice versa, the most powerful leaders can fail if they choose the wrong means, the followers withhold their support and/or the institutional environment is unfavourable.

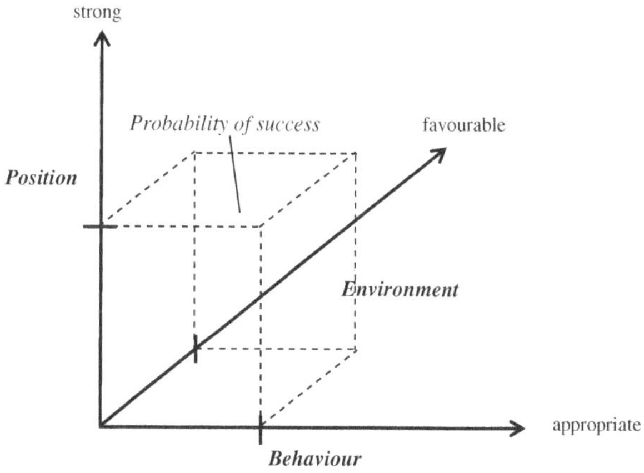

Fig. 2.1 Probability of a leader's success as determined by its position, behaviour, and environment (*Source* Own illustration)

2.3 Two Conceptions of Leadership

Political science literature suggests countless types of leadership. This section argues, however, that they can be differentiated according to two basic conceptions: providing common knowledge and enhancing collective action. First, a leader can provide actors with common knowledge should their collectively shared beliefs as well as their individual preferences be unsettled by exogenous events like crises. Second, a leader can enhance collective action by helping a group to overcome problems arising from imperfect or incomplete information, high transaction costs, or free-rider dilemmas.

Structural, entrepreneurial, intellectual, problem-solving, positional, directional, ideational, or innovative leadership are just a few of the leadership types that can be found in political science literature. However, there is one basic typological distinction that is more pervasive and persistent than the others, which is Burns' (1978) seminal distinction between transactional and transformational leadership (see Nye 2014). In its original meaning, transactional leadership refers to the "exchange of valued things" (Burns 1978: 19); there is no higher, continuing purpose and the preferences of leader and followers remain stable. Instead, in the case of transformational leadership "leaders and followers raise one

Table 2.1 Two basic conceptions of political leadership

	Providing common knowledge	*Enhancing collective action*
Burns (1978)	Transformational leadership	Transactional leadership
Jones (1989b)	Leadership in ambiguous and changing systems	Leadership under unambiguous rules
Young (1991)[a]	Intellectual leadership	Entrepreneurial leadership
Malnes (1995)	Directional leadership	Problem-solving leadership
Nye (2013, 2014)	Inspirational leadership	Transactional leadership

Source Own illustration

[a]A third type singled out by Young is "structural leadership" and refers to the mobilization of power resources. In conceptualizations according to which all types of leadership are to a certain extent based on power resources, this type becomes redundant (Malnes 1995)

another to higher levels of motivation and morality" (Burns 1978: 20). This implies that leader and followers mutually affect their preferences, which is why this kind of leadership "has a transforming effect on both" (Burns 1978: 20).

This basic distinction between reaching certain outcomes within a given game and changing the game itself has been put forward by many authors without explicitly referring to the work of Burns (see Table 2.1). Bryan Jones (1989b), for example, distinguishes between leadership under unambiguous rules and leadership in ambiguous and changing systems; and Raino Malnes (1995) separates problem-solving from directional leadership. In a similar vein, most of the existing distinctions between leadership types are based on two basic conceptions, which somewhat reflect Burns' original categories. In this book, they are labelled 'providing common knowledge' and 'enhancing collective action'.

According to the first conception of leadership, a leader acts as a provider of common knowledge. Common knowledge is a collectively shared set of beliefs, which constitutes the basis for the actors' interests and preferences. However, a group's collective knowledge can be unsettled by exogenous events like crises. In these cases, uncertainty rises and the group experiences pressure to adapt (Boin and 't Hart 2003; Schofield 2002). As opposed to most collective action problems (see below), the problem in this case is not caused by divergent preferences over solutions, but by the actual lack of solutions. In this situation a leader can provide new common knowledge by exposing the drawbacks of the status quo, coming up with new interpretations and ideas, and promoting them as solutions to the defined problems (see Eberlein and Radaelli 2010: 791f.; Keohane 2010; Stiller 2010: 34–9; Tucker 1981: 18f.). The innovation of this kind of leadership is not only given by the "solution" of a collective action problem, but by the creation of a completely new situation. This conception of leadership corresponds to what has been labelled "intellectual" (Young 1991: 298–302), "innovative" (Sheffer 1993), or "ideational leadership" (Stiller 2010) in the literature (Table 2.1).

Following the second conception, a leader "simply" enhances collective action. Actors who engage in a collective endeavour face a variety of problems leading to suboptimal outcomes. These problems comprise coordination and distributional problems and are based on imperfect or incomplete information and communication, high transaction costs, or free-rider dilemmas. By using certain strategies such as agenda-managing or coalition-building (see Sect. 3.3 for a detailed list), a leader can help a group overcome these problems and thereby enhance collective action. These leaders bring about innovation by solving problems, but they do not change the group's common knowledge and, by extension, the actors' (meta-)preferences. Therefore, this type roughly corresponds to Oran Young's concept of the "entrepreneurial leader"[4] who uses negotiation strategies to shape deals that "solve or circumvent the collective action problems that plague the efforts of parties seeking to reap joint gains in processes of institutional bargaining" (Young 1991: 285, 293–8; see also Beach 2005: 17–20; Fiorina and Shepsle 1989; Frohlich et al. 1971; Tallberg 2006: 19–29; Wilson and Rhodes 1997).

2.4 Defining Political Leadership

A look at the state of the art reveals, that there is no coherent research agenda on political leadership. Instead, "much of the work on political leadership is [...] either focused on highly specific aspects of leadership or consists of collections of essays. [...] the general phenomenon of political leadership is still understudied" (Peele 2005: 190). Still, based on the overlap of central criteria in different conceptualizations, political leadership can be defined as a *process where an actor in a formal or informal position of power employs her resources in such a way as to guide the*

[4] To be precise, the category of entrepreneurial leadership as proposed by Young refers only to individuals, not to composite actors such as states or organizations.

behaviour of others towards a common goal. In the case of success, this process results in innovation; namely policy or institutional change.

In line with this definition, the chapter first concludes that leadership is not the same as power. Instead, it is a special form of exercising power aimed at the achievement of a common goal. While powerful actors may block any decision that would make the entire group better off on the grounds that this is not in their individual interest (obstructionism; veto-players), or strive for innovation that exclusively serves their self-interest, leaders pursue a common goal by aiming at innovation and employing strategies to the benefit of themselves *and* their followers. Second, a leader is not necessarily successful. Instead, success depends on a leader's position, her behaviour, and her environment. Third, the chapter argues that most types of leadership can be classified according to the two basic conceptions of 'enhancing collective action' and 'providing common knowledge'.

References

Ahlquist, John S., and Margaret Levi. 2011. Leadership: What It Means, What It Does, and What We Want to Know About It. *Annual Review of Political Science* 14 (1): 1–24.

Baumgartner, Frank R. 1989. Strategies of Political Leadership in Diverse Settings. In *Leadership and Politics: New Perspectives in Political Science*, ed. Bryan D. Jones, 114–134. Lawrence, KS: University Press of Kansas.

Beach, Derek. 2005. *The Dynamics of European Integration: Why and When EU Institutions Matter*. Basingstoke: Palgrave Macmillan.

Blondel, Jean. 1987. *Political Leadership: Towards a General Analysis*. London: Sage.

Boin, Arjen, and Paul 't Hart. 2003. Public Leadership in Times of Crisis: Mission Impossible? *Public Administration Review* 63 (5): 544–553.

Burns, James MacGregor. 1978. *Leadership*. New York: Harper & Row.

Cole, Alistair. 1994. Studying Political Leadership: The Case of François Mitterrand. *Political Studies* 42 (3): 453–468.

Dahl, Robert. 1957. The Concept of Power. *Behavioral Science* 2 (3): 201–215.

Deutsch, Karl W. 1988. *The Analysis of International Relations*, 3rd ed. London: Prentice-Hall International.

Eberlein, Burkhard, and Claudio M. Radaelli. 2010. Mechanisms of Conflict Management in EU Regulatory Policy. *Public Administration* 88 (3): 782–799.

Elgie, Robert. 1995. *Political Leadership in Liberal Democracies.* Basingstoke and London: Macmillan.
Elgie, Robert. 2001. Leadership: Political. In *International Encyclopedia of the Social & Behavioral Sciences*, ed. Neil J. Smelser, 8578–8580. Oxford and New York: Elsevier.
Endo, Ken. 1999. *The Presidency of the European Commission Under Jacques Delors: The Politics of Shared Leadership.* Basingstoke, London and New York: Macmillan and St. Martin's Press.
Fiorina, Morris, and Kenneth Shepsle. 1989. Formal Theories of Leadership: Agents, Agenda-Setters, and Entrepreneurs. In *Leadership and Politics: New Perspectives in Political Science*, ed. Bryan D. Jones, 17–40. Lawrence, KS: University Press of Kansas.
Frohlich, Norman, Joe A. Oppenheimer, and Oran R. Young. 1971. *Political Leadership and Collective Goods.* Princeton, NJ: Princeton University Press.
Grint, Keith. 2005. *Leadership: Limits and Possibilities.* Basingstoke: Palgrave Macmillan.
Hargrove, Erwin C. 1989. Two Conceptions of Institutional Leadership. In *Leadership and Politics: New Perspectives in Political Science*, ed. Bryan D. Jones, 57–83. Lawrence, KS: University Press of Kansas.
Hargrove, Erwin C. 2004. History, Political Science and the Study of Leadership. *Polity* 36 (4): 579–593.
Hartley, Jean, and John Benington. 2011. Political Leadership. In *The SAGE Handbook of Leadership*, ed. Alan Bryman, David Collinson, Keith Grint, Brad Jackson, and Mary Uhl-Bien, 203–214. London: Sage.
Helms, Ludger. 2012. Introduction: The Importance of Studying Political Leadership Comparatively. In *Comparative Political Leadership*, ed. Ludger Helms, 1–24. Basingstoke: Palgrave Macmillan.
Jervis, Robert. 2013. Do Leaders Matter and How Would We Know? *Security Studies* 22 (2): 153–179.
Jones, Bryan D. 1989a. Causation, Constraint, and Political Leadership. In *Leadership and Politics: New Perspectives in Political Science*, ed. Bryan D. Jones, 3–14. Lawrence, KS: University Press of Kansas.
Jones, Bryan D. 1989b. Two Conceptions of Political Leadership Revisited. In *Leadership and Politics: New Perspectives in Political Science*, ed. Bryan D. Jones, 289–294. Lawrence, KS: University Press of Kansas.
Kellerman, Barbara. 2004. *Bad Leadership: What It Is, How It Happens, Why It Matters.* Boston: Harvard Business School Press.
Keohane, Nannerl O. 2010. *Thinking About Leadership.* Princeton: Princeton University Press.
Kindleberger, Charles P. 1981. Dominance and Leadership in the International Economy: Exploitation, Public Goods, and Free Rides. *International Studies Quarterly* 25 (2): 242–254.

Malnes, Raino. 1995. 'Leader' and 'Entrepreneur' in International Negotiations: A Conceptual Analysis. *European Journal of International Relations* 1 (1): 87–112.
Masciulli, Joseph, and W. Andy Knight. 2009. Conceptions of Global Leadership for Contextually Intelligent, Innovatively Adaptive Political Leaders. In *The Ashgate Research Companion to Political Leadership*, ed. Joseph Masciulli, Mikhail A. Molchanov, and W. Andy Knight, 89–122. Farnham and Burlington, VT: Ashgate.
Masciulli, Joseph, Mikhail A. Molchanov, and W. Andy Knight. 2009. Political Leadership in Context. In *The Ashgate Research Companion to Political Leadership*, ed. Joseph Masciulli, Mikhail A. Molchanov, and W. Andy Knight, 3–27. Farnham and Burlington, VT: Ashgate.
Metcalfe, David. 1998. Leadership in European Union Negotiations: The Presidency of the Council. *International Negotiation* 3 (3): 413–434.
Moon, Jeremy. 1995. Innovative Leadership and Policy Change: Lessons from Thatcher. *Governance* 8 (1): 1–25.
Northouse, Peter G. 1997. *Leadership: Theory and Practice*. Thousand Oaks, CA: Sage.
Nye, Joseph S. 2008. *The Powers to Lead*. Oxford: Oxford University Press.
Nye, Joseph S. 2010. Power and Leadership. In *Handbook of Leadership Theory and Practice*, ed. Nitin Nohria and Rakesh Khurana, 305–332. Boston, MA: Harvard Business Press.
Nye, Joseph S. 2013. *Presidential Leadership and the Creation of the American Era*. Princeton: Princeton University Press.
Nye, Joseph S. 2014. Transformational and Transactional Presidents. *Leadership* 10 (1): 118–124.
Peele, Gillian. 2005. Leadership and Politics: A Case for a Closer Relationship? *Leadership* 1 (2): 187–204.
Schofield, Norman. 2002. Evolution of the Constitution. *British Journal of Political Science* 32 (1): 1–20.
Selznick, Philip. 1957. *Leadership in Administration: A Sociological Interpretation*. New York: Harper & Row.
Sheffer, Gabriel (ed.). 1993. *Innovative Leaders in International Politics*. Albany, NY: State University of New York Press.
Shepsle, Kenneth A., and Mark S. Bonchek. 1997. *Analyzing Politics: Rationality, Behavior, and Institutions*. New York: W. W. Norton.
Skodvin, Tora, and Steinar Andresen. 2006. Leadership Revisited. *Global Environmental Politics* 6 (3): 13–27.
Stiller, Sabina. 2010. *Ideational Leadership in German Welfare State Reform*. Amsterdam: Amsterdam University Press.
Tallberg, Jonas. 2006. *Leadership and Negotiation in the European Union*. Cambridge: Cambridge University Press.

Tallberg, Jonas. 2010. The Power of the Chair: Formal Leadership in International Cooperation. *International Studies Quarterly* 54 (1): 241–265.
Tucker, Robert C. 1981. *Politics as Leadership*. Columbia, MO and London: University of Missouri Press.
Underdal, Arild. 1994. Leadership Theory: Rediscovering the Arts of Management. In *International Multilateral Negotiation: Approaches to the Management of Complexity*, ed. I. William Zartman, 178–197. San Francisco: Jossey-Bass.
Wilson, Rick K., and Carl M. Rhodes. 1997. Leadership and Credibility in N-Person Coordination Games. *Journal of Conflict Resolution* 41 (6): 767–791.
Young, Oran R. 1991. Political Leadership and Regime Formation: On the Development of Institutions in International Society. *International Organization* 45 (3): 281–308.

CHAPTER 3

Theorizing Leadership: Emergence and Impact

This chapter elaborates a model of leadership that combines the basic assumptions of rational-choice institutionalism with current leadership theorizing. The model is causal, conditional, and generalizable (see Tallberg 2006: 18). It is causal because it makes testable cause-effect propositions on a leader's emergence and impact. Moreover, it is conditional in the sense that it determines the circumstances that may impede a leader's emergence or impact. Finally, the model is generalizable as it is not restricted to the empirical scope of this book, but formulated in abstract theoretical terms. In principle, this makes the model applicable to all instances in which collective actors refrain from offering, fail in delivering, or succeed in exercising political leadership. While Sect. 3.1 presents the basic theoretical argument, Sects. 3.2 and 3.3 elaborate testable propositions regarding the emergence and impact of leadership. Section 3.4 draws the implications for the empirical research.

3.1 A Rational Theory of Political Leadership

Basic Assumptions: Actors and Institutions

This leadership model assumes actors to be boundedly rational. Actors seek to maximize their utility by making consistent rank orders of possible interaction outcomes (preferences). Thus, they act according to a logic of consequentiality and make decisions by balancing the expected costs and benefits of a certain action (Lake and Powell 1999: 7). In

M. G. Schoeller, *Leadership in the Eurozone*, Palgrave Studies in European Union Politics, https://doi.org/10.1007/978-3-030-12704-6_3

doing so, their basic interests consist in their self-preservation, autonomy, and growth (Scharpf 1997: 64). However, actors are neither 'human computers' nor omniscient. In making their decisions, they are bound by cognitive constraints as well as imperfect and incomplete information.[1] Moreover, actors do not operate in a social vacuum, but in the context of institutions.

Institutions are man-made rules of behaviour that constrain individual action and thereby shape social interaction (North 1990; Héritier 2007). As they form expectations about the behaviour of others, institutions reduce uncertainty that otherwise might inhibit collective undertakings. While formal institutions are written down and subject to courts and sanctions in case of non-compliance, informal institutions are not legally enforceable. Usually, they are neither written nor created within official channels of rule-creation (Helmke and Levitsky 2004: 725, 727; Stacey and Rittberger 2003: 861). Institutions thus exist prior to actors' behaviour. As they are subject to man-made change, however, they can also be the outcome of social interaction (Héritier 2007: 5–7).

Theoretical Argument

Leaders are drivers of policy or institutional change. If there is a collective action problem and a lack of institutions to deal with it, there will be an enhanced demand for a powerful actor to help the group compensate for the lack of institutions. This situation can lead to three possible outcomes. First, there are no actors that make a leadership offer (*leadership vacuum*). Second, if a powerful actor emerges as a leader, she may not be able to realise the desired institutional or policy change (*leadership failure*). Third, a leader emerges *and* successfully influences policies or institutions (*leadership success*).

As Fig. 3.1 illustrates, the three outcomes correspond to two different analytical steps: the emergence of leadership on the one hand, and its impact on the other. With regard to the first step, the theory posits that a leader emerges if there is a demand for leadership and a supply of it (see

[1] *Perfect* information means that the actor is aware of all the relevant events that have previously occurred. This regards primarily the actions that other actors have chosen. *Complete* information, by contrast, means that the actor is aware of the strategies and payoffs (expected utilities) available to other actors and thus of all possible interaction outcomes.

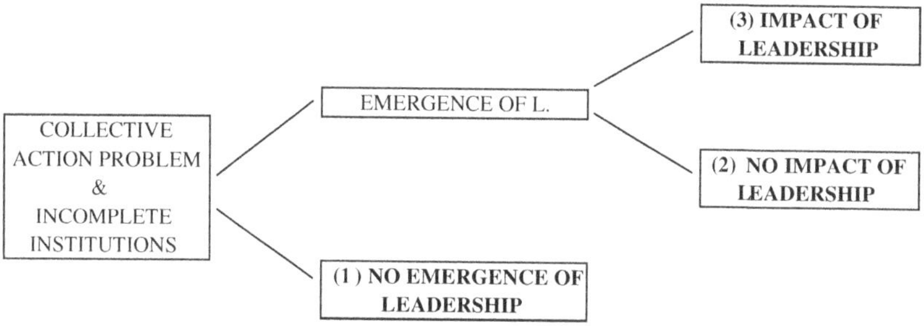

Fig. 3.1 Possible outcomes (*Source* Own illustration)

Sect. 3.2 below). The demand for leadership arises from the costs that a group has to suffer if the status quo (without a leader) continues. If these "status quo costs" are high, there will be a high demand for leadership. In this situation, powerful actors consider whether to supply leadership: they weigh the expected costs of leading against their benefits. If an actor finds that leading would be profitable ("leader's surplus"), she will supply leadership. Finally, if there is more than one leadership candidate on the supply-side, the most powerful candidate will emerge as a leader.[2]

However, the fact that a leader has emerged does not tell us anything about her success or failure. Thus, a second analytical step focuses on the impact of leadership (see Sect. 3.3 below). A leader's impact depends on the distribution of preferences among her followers: If preferences converge on the outcome proposed by the leader, it will be relatively easy for her to reach the desired institutional or policy change. The same is true if the institutional constraint on the leader is low: If the leader can decide by herself, for instance, it is much easier to influence outcomes than if the followers need to be included in the decision-making process (by majority or even unanimity). However, even in the most adverse environment, when the followers' preferences diverge from those of the leader and the institutional hurdles for change are high, a leader might still be able to have an impact. This is the case if the leader has sufficient power resources, which can be invested in strategies to overcome

[2]This does not apply to formal elections, in which a leader must be appointed even if there is no actual demand for leadership. In this case, other factors come into play and the group may deliberately agree on a weak leader.

Table 3.1 Two analytical steps—emergence and impact of political leadership

	Emergence of leadership	*Impact of leadership*
Highlighted aspect	Structural (position, followers)	Behavioural (strategies)
Dependent variable	Presence vs. absence of leadership	Policy or institutional change
Independent variables	Leader's surplus Status quo costs	Leader's power resources Preference distribution Institutional constraint

Source Own illustration

the followers' resistance or the institutional constraint. Hence, a leader's impact depends on her power resources, the preference distribution among the followers, and the institutional constraint (Table 3.1).

3.2 The Emergence of Political Leadership

A leader emerges if there is a demand for leadership and a supply of it. The demand for leadership arises from status quo costs that a group has to suffer because of suboptimal collective action outcomes (see Tallberg 2006: 19–29). These costs are either already present or imminent if the status quo persists. If they are high, the actors involved perceive a strong pressure for action. In this situation, powerful actors weigh the expected costs of leading against its benefits. If an actor comes to the conclusion that she would be better off leading, she will offer leadership. This is done by expressing preferences with regard to a policy or institutional change. The other actors notice this expression of preferences and at least some of them object.[3] The powerful actor can then react by

[3] If all actors agree on what to do, there is no need for a leader since each actor could simply do what she wants without preventing the group from reaching its common goal. However, as pointed out in Sect. 2.1, the fact that there is a common goal does not mean that everyone agrees on *how* to reach it. Only in the case of diverging preferences on how to achieve a common goal, a leader is needed. This leader usually employs strategies (Sect. 3.3) to persuade her followers of one particular way of reaching the common goal (see Kindleberger 1981: 243). This is even true for mere coordination problems. Take the example of traffic coordination: if there were no ex-ante rule determining on which side of the road to drive, traffic participants would have different preferences on whether to take the right or the left side. This would result in traffic chaos. In such a situation, in which all actors have a common goal (smoothly running traffic) but diverging preferences (left or

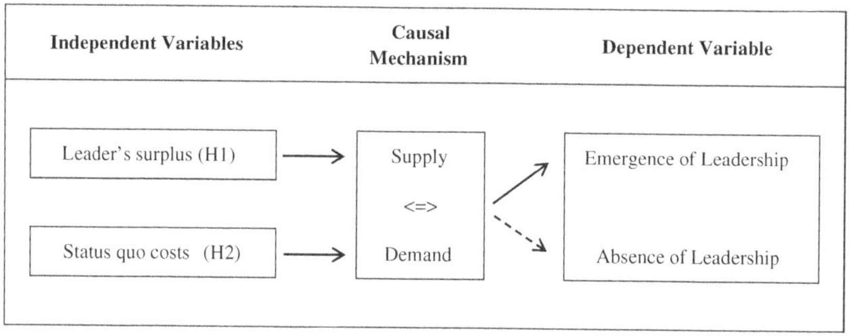

Fig. 3.2 The emergence of political leadership (*Source* Own illustration)

employing strategies (Sect. 3.3) to reach an outcome as close as possible to her preferences. In this case, she takes over leadership, which is the dependent variable of this first analytical step (see Fig. 3.2).

With regard to the supply-side, leadership is offered if at least one actor is willing to take the lead. Willingness, in turn, depends on the pay-offs to potential leaders, which implies that the leader must prefer the expected outcome of leading to the status quo. However, given that leadership is costly, this is a necessary but not sufficient condition for the supply of leadership. In order to invest in costly leadership strategies, the leader's expected benefits in case of success must also exceed her costs of leading. In other words, there must be a "*leader's surplus*" (Frohlich et al. 1971: 7).

H1 If the expected benefits of leading exceed the perceived costs of it, political leadership will be offered and—on condition that there is a demand for it—emerge.

This conjecture can also explain the case of a "leadership vacuum", where we observe a collective demand for leadership, but no supply of it. Following the above-stated propositions, a leadership vacuum is a

right side), a leader deciding for one side would be highly welcome. By contrast, if all road users shared the same preference for one side ex ante (e.g. because of existing rules), there would be no traffic chaos and no leader would be needed.

situation in which the collective would benefit from a leader, but no single actor could benefit to the extent that her costs of leading would be covered by the outcomes.

With regard to the demand-side, a leader can serve followers as a solution to collective action problems. On the one hand, this may be the case in coordination problems, where the best outcome (or common goal) is reached through cooperation, but actors fail due to a lack of information, communication, or distributional consequences. The same is true for free-rider problems, where the common goal is jeopardized by stronger individual incentives to defect. In these cases, a leader can enhance collective action by removing the status quo costs caused by suboptimal outcomes (see Beach 2005: 17–20; Tallberg 2006: 19–29; Young 1991: 293–8). On the other hand, a leader can also serve as a provider of common knowledge in cases where exogenous events like crises cause pressure for adaptation (see Young 1991: 298–302). Especially under conditions of bounded rationality regarding alternative courses of action, a leader can provide new common knowledge which helps actors adapt to the new situation (see Spender 2008: 99). Hence, in both cases the demand for a leader results from a group's *status quo costs*, which are caused by suboptimal collective outcomes or by non-adaptation to exogenous change.

H2a If the aggregate status quo costs are high, there will be a strong demand for leadership, and—on condition that there is a supply of it—political leadership will emerge.

H2b Vice versa, if the aggregate status quo costs are low, there is a low demand for leadership, and no political leadership emerges.

It is important to distinguish between costs and benefits of leading on the one hand, and status quo costs on the other. While status quo costs are aggregate and become manifest in the case of non-action, costs of leading are individual and become manifest in the case of action. Moreover, the benefits of leading not only consist in the removal of status quo costs, but also in the leader's individual gains if one particular solution (as opposed to others) is applied to a collective action problem.

Both benefits of leading and status quo costs are partly determined by the institutional environment. Institutions are behavioural prescriptions that have the same function as a leader: they enable collective action and provide common knowledge. Therefore, the less complete they are with regard to the prevention or regulation of collective action problems, the higher the need for a leader to compensate for the insufficient rules and to help the group fill the institutional gap. Hence, institutional incompleteness is a precondition for the emergence of leadership (see Fig. 3.2).

Once the demand for leadership matches the supply of it, leadership emerges. If the supply contains more than one candidate, a selection must take place. The current state of the art in leadership research suggests that the selection of a leader among different candidates depends primarily on the available ex-ante resources of a candidate (Ahlquist and Levi 2011: 19). However, the underlying mechanism has not yet been explicated. This model assumes that if there is more than one candidate, the most powerful actor emerges as a leader because her absence in the final agreement would cause the highest costs. This is because leaders not only pursue collective goals, but also self-interest: if the common solution proposed by a leader does not match the preferences of any concerned actor, this actor can still decide not to cooperate; the more powerful this reluctant actor is, the more costs she can cause for the others; thus, as no leader proposes a solution that contravenes her own interests, the selection of the most powerful leadership candidate avoids the highest possible costs. Moreover, given that the exercise of leadership requires power resources (Sect. 2.1), the most powerful candidate has the best prospects of success. Therefore, the selection of the most powerful candidate maximizes the expected utility of the entire group.

3.3 The Impact of Political Leadership

Jean Blondel once pointed out that "there is little point in analysing leaders if we do not know how great their impact is or whether they have any impact at all" (1987: 80). As elaborated in Chapter 2, a leader's impact crucially depends on her power resources. Power can be understood as the capacity to influence the behaviour of others, or, in the words of Robert Dahl (1957: 202f.), to make them do something that they would not otherwise do.[4] This may happen in different ways, ranging from making binding decisions (Dahl 1957) via setting the agenda (Bachrach and Baratz 1962) through to shaping others' preferences (Lukes 1974). In any case,

[4]This includes also the option of making others not do something they would otherwise do.

Table 3.2 Power resources

Material	*Institutional*	*Ideational*
Economic capabilities Military capabilities	Procedural rights, e.g. Agenda management Veto rights Executive competences etc.	Information (incl. expertise) Credibility Legitimacy

Source Own illustration, based on Krotz and Schild (2013: 22–4)

the capacity to influence the behaviour of others cannot only be reduced to an actor's fall-back options, as negotiation theory often has it, but it is essentially based on resources (see also Tallberg 2006: 14f., 221).

Power resources can be differentiated into material, institutional, and ideational resources.[5] A type of leadership that is primarily based on material power resources has also been labelled "structural leadership" (Young 1991: 288–93), emphasizing thereby the positional advantage of the leader compared to her followers. Generally speaking, material resources comprise military and economic capabilities. Institutional resources, in contrast, refer to procedural advantages, which are formal and informal rights of agenda-setting, decision-making, implementation, and evaluation. Ideational resources, finally, vest the leader with non-material advantages, namely privileged information (including expertise), credibility and legitimacy (see Beach 2005: 27–9; Parker and Karlsson 2014: 586f.) (Table 3.2).

There are two ways a leader's *power resources* can take effect. First, the leader translates them into strategies to influence outcomes (see below). Thus, the more resources can be invested into the employment of strategies, the more likely it is that a leader affects the outcomes. Second, the leader does not actively use her resources, but influences the outcomes through the "rule of anticipated reaction(s)" (Friedrich 1963: 199–215). In this case, followers anticipate that the resources might be deployed to their disadvantage if they do not behave as the leader wants them to. In both cases, the following conjecture applies:

[5] A slightly different classification is proposed by Derek Beach, who distinguishes between material, informational, and reputational resources, while conceptualizing institutional aspects as an external variable determining a leader's impact (2005: 26–9).

H3a If a leader possesses many power resources (in relation to the resources of the followers), she will *ceteris paribus* have a strong impact on the outcomes.

H3b Vice versa, if a leader possesses few power resources (in relation to the resources of the followers), she will *ceteris paribus* have a weak impact.

However, a leader's impact not only depends on her individual capacity, but also on her environment. In an unfavourable environment, even huge power resources might not suffice to reach the desired goal (see Sect. 2.2).

The first environmental factor determining a leader's impact is the *distribution of preferences.* If all actors have the same preferences over outcomes and how to reach them (homogeneous preferences), there is no problem to find a common solution, and indeed no leader is needed. If, in contrast, the followers' preferences diverge, some actors have to depart from their preferred outcomes in order to find an agreement. These actors have to bear the respective costs, which can be described as the difference between the utility of their preferred outcome and the utility of the outcome they finally obtain. The stronger the divergence of preferences, the more actors have to bear costs or the higher are the costs of those who have to relinquish their preferred outcomes. With regard to collective action problems, these costs can be distributional consequences ('battle of the sexes') or the opportunity costs of no free-riding ('prisoner's dilemma'). A leader can ease distributional consequences, for example by giving incentives, and overcome free-rider problems, for instance by signalling credible commitment through 'leading by example' (see below). Generally, a leader can compensate the losers, find a solution where all followers win—for instance by adding a further outcome through the provision of common knowledge—or, if the institutional circumstances allow, make certain actors accept the costs. In the case of 'anticipated reaction' by the followers, instead, already the sheer possession of power resources may suffice to overcome the divergence of preferences.

Hence, if preferences are only slightly heterogeneous and converge around the leader's preferred outcome, distributional consequences and opportunity costs of non-free-riding are relatively small. This makes it easy for a leader to find an agreement by compensating potential losers or proposing a win-win solution. If preferences are distributed around the whole preference space and are thus maximally heterogeneous, instead, it is more difficult to find a solution. But at the same time it is also very difficult to build a successful opposition against the leader.[6] However, if the followers' preferences converge on an outcome different from that preferred by the leader, a powerful opposition can be built against her and leadership failure is most likely. This leads to the following conjecture:

H4a If preferences converge around the outcome preferred by the leader, she will *ceteris paribus* have a strong impact on the outcomes.

H4b Vice versa, if preferences converge on an outcome different from that preferred by the leader, she will *ceteris paribus* have a weak impact.[7]

The second environmental factor accounting for a leader's impact is the institutional setting (see Blondel 1987: 148–80; Elgie 1995: 195–203) or, more precisely, the *institutional constraint* faced by the leader (Endo 1999: 19f.). The institutional constraint determines a leader's latitude in decision-making and is defined by the underlying institutional rules (Tallberg 2006: 34–6). It is lowest if the leader enjoys full discretion in making decisions. Instead, if the leader needs the consent of a majority or even of all her followers, the institutional constraint is considerably higher. It is even higher where not only the followers' final consent is needed, but where they participate in the decision-making progress from the beginning. In this case, it makes a further difference whether a simple majority, a qualified majority, or even unanimity is needed to pass a decision. The institutional constraint is highest if certain actions are straight out prohibited.[8] Hence, provided that preferences are not completely homogeneous,[9] this leads to the following conjecture:

[6] This is why Principal-Agent theory forwards the thesis that latitude, shirking, and slacking of the agent is highest when the principals' preferences are heterogeneous.

[7] The three values of the independent variable thus are: convergence on the leader's preferred outcome (strongest influence) ⇔ heterogeneity of preferences ⇔ convergence elsewhere (weakest influence) (see Sect. 3.4).

[8] For methodological reasons, it is important to clearly distinguish between a leader's institutional resources and her institutional constraint. While the resources refer to positive rights of agenda-management, decision-making, implementation, or evaluation, the institutional constraint describes the negative restraints a leader faces when trying to use her resources. For instance, Germany's institutional resources are, among others, its voting weight in the Council; the institutional constraint is that a certain initiative has to go through the Council in the first place.

[9] If preferences are completely homogeneous, the institutional constraint does not matter anymore because even if unanimity is needed to make a certain decision, all followers will agree.

H5a If the institutional constraint is low, the leader will *ceteris paribus* have a strong impact on the outcomes.

H5b Vice versa, if the institutional constraint is high, the leader will *ceteris paribus* have a weak impact.

Moreover, Beach has argued that the number of issues and actors involved can raise the level of complexity and thus reduce a leader's impact (2005: 30f.). However, given that leaders often times modify these factors to increase their impact (e.g. through agenda-setting or coalition-building, see below), this model treats them as strategic components explaining *how* a leader affects outcomes rather than as independent variables (see Fig. 3.3).

Leadership Strategies

Apart from anticipated reaction, where followers pre-emptively behave as the leader wants them to, a leader influences outcomes by actively translating her resources into strategies. Based on the two conceptions of leadership presented in Sect. 2.3, the following typology of leadership strategies distinguishes between "providing common knowledge" and "enhancing collective action" (Table 3.3). Although this distinction is inherent in many studies on leadership, it is rarely made explicit.

The first set of strategies (Enhancing Collective Action) corresponds roughly to what has been labelled "entrepreneurial leadership" by Oran Young (1991: 293–8)[10] and comprises a leader's negotiation strategies which serve to enable collective action outcomes that otherwise are prevented by imperfect information or communication, high transaction costs, or free-rider dilemmas.

Agenda-management is a strategy that relies on the alteration of issues or proposals for solutions. It can be differentiated into agenda-setting, agenda-structuring, and agenda-exclusion (Blavoukos et al. 2006: 146;

Only when a certain policy or institutional change is forbidden, which is the highest degree of institutional constraint, could one argue that even unanimity is insufficient for the respective decision to pass.

[10] Young's concept of entrepreneurial leadership refers only to individuals, though. Unlike this model, it does therefore not include composite actors.

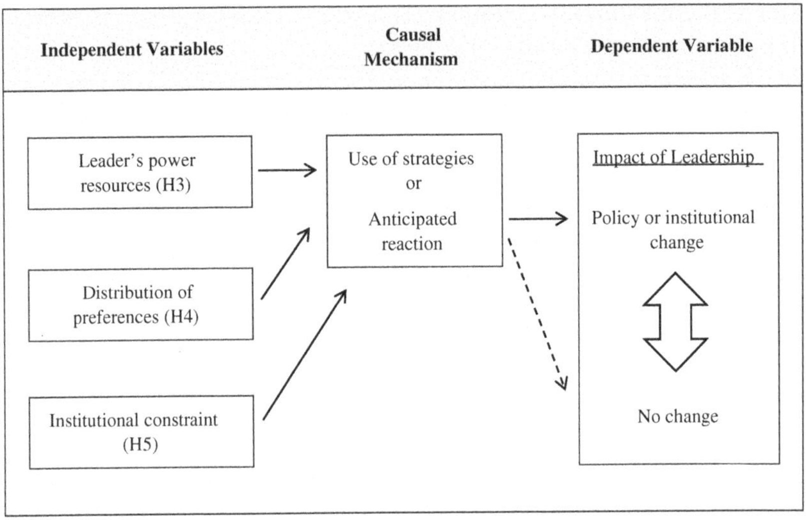

Fig. 3.3 The impact of political leadership (*Source* Own illustration)

Table 3.3 Leadership strategies

Providing common knowledge	*Enhancing collective action*
Problem definition	Agenda-management
Presentation of new ideas	Arena-shifting/-linking
Promotion of new ideas	Coalition-building
	Pre-negotiations
	Unilateral action
	Leading by example

Source Own compilation

Tallberg 2006: 24). In particular agenda-setting and agenda-exclusion may serve as leadership strategies. Agenda-setting can widen the zone of agreement: by adding differently valued or related issues to the agenda, a leader can facilitate the finding of a solution. This is the case when package deals or side-payments are made (Lax and Sebenius 1986: 218–20). By directly tabling solutions to controversial issues, instead, a leader provides a focal point around which a solution can be found. In doing so, the leader helps followers to choose one equilibrium among several options (Fiorina and Shepsle 1989: 29–32; Scharpf 1997: 159f.).

Agenda-exclusion, finally, refers to the subtraction of a particularly divisive issue from the agenda in order to reach consensus on other issues (Odell 2009: 279), whereas the exclusion of possible solutions serves to concentrate the support of followers on one alternative only.

A second strategy that serves to enhance collective action is *coalition-building*. While agenda-managing concerns the adding and subtracting of issues and solutions, coalition-building refers to adding and subtracting actors. A leader can facilitate the finding of an agreement by adding actors that have an interest in a settlement. Vice versa, the leader can exclude reluctant actors to form a group which allows for the finding of a common solution. Moreover, a leader can add actors to a group in order to spread the risks of a common enterprise or to increase the gains of each single actor (e.g. "economies of scale"). By contrast, the exclusion of actors can also lead to an agreement if it reduces certain costs (e.g. for monitoring or enforcement) or increases the individual shares in a given profit (Lax and Sebenius 1986: 228–30).

Two further negotiation strategies at a leader's disposal consist in the *linking and shifting of arenas*. An arena is an institutional setting which determines the participants and the rules of decision-making. First, by linking two arenas, a leader can use the actors' interest in finding a solution in arena A to overcome deadlock in arena B. This strategy is most promising if the leader can make the outcome in one arena dependent on the outcome of another arena, which, for instance, can be done by relying on a blocking minority or a veto in one of the two arenas. Second, instead of linking arenas, a leader can also shift them: "If agreement on an issue cannot be reached in one territorial or functional arena, moving the issue to a different arena, with a different set of participants and/or different decision rules, may help to alleviate conflict" (Eberlein and Radaelli 2010: 789).

Arena-shifting can be combined with coalition-building in the form of *pre-negotiations*: a leader can start negotiations outside the central bargaining arena with a few crucial actors to shape a compromise which can subsequently be presented to the other actors in the actual negotiations. This facilitates communication and coordination among the actors, reduces transaction costs, enables the leader to split opponents into different bargaining rounds, and enables her to pool power resources—such as voting weights or economic resources—in the central bargaining arena (Héritier 1999: 21; Schild 2013: 36; Schoeller 2018: 5).

If a leader's power resources heavily outweigh those of her followers, she can also have recourse to *unilateral action*. According to Arild

Underdal, unilateral action "is exercised whenever one moves to solve a collective problem by one's own effort, thereby setting the pace for others to follow" (1994: 183). There are two ways unilateral action can contribute to the exercise of leadership. First, unilateral action may have an impact on the options available to other actors (thereby providing the leader with a first-mover advantage). Second, it may reduce uncertainty, as this is the case when an actor leads 'by example'.

Leading by example refers to the attraction and co-optation of other actors to the leader's way of doing things (Nye 2010). There are two mechanisms through which this happens. First, actors switch to the leader's practice because it is less costly for them. This is the case if the leader pursues a more efficient policy, for example (Mattli 1999: 55). Second, the leader actively contributes resources to a common project, thereby signalling credible commitment to her followers (Hermalin 1998; Güth et al. 2007).

The second set of strategies (Providing Common Knowledge) refers to what has been labelled "intellectual" (Young 1991: 298–302), "innovative" (Sheffer 1993) or "ideational leadership" (Stiller 2010). In that case a leader comes up with completely new beliefs about which policy instrument or institutional arrangement works best in certain situations. In doing so, the leader defines a problem, proposes a solution to it, and promotes this solution towards her followers (see Sect. 2.3).

Note that the use of one or the other set of strategies has different effects on the followers' preferences. In the case of "enhancing collective action", the followers' preferences over outcomes are already given, but influenced by the leader's action. In other words, the leader *modifies* the followers' subjective rank order of possible outcomes. In the case of "providing common knowledge", in contrast, the leader adds new possible outcomes previously unknown to the folliowers. Thereby, the leader *extends* the followers' rank order of outcomes. However, while the two types of strategies are clearly distinguishable in theory, they might occur simultaneously in practice.

3.4 Implications for the Empirical Research

As outlined in Sect. 1.3, the book adopts a qualitative and comparative methodology. Drawing on congruence tests and process-tracing, the theoretical model will thus be tested against six cases of eurozone crisis management. This section outlines how to operationalize the abstract theoretical propositions, and what kind of data is needed to test them.

Operationalization

The *explanandum* of the first analytical step is the *emergence of leadership*. It is conceptualized as a binary variable with the values "presence" and "absence" of leadership (see Table 3.1). In order to assess this variable, we can draw on the definition of leadership elaborated in Chapter 2: political leadership is a process where an actor in a formal or informal position of power employs her resources in such a way as to guide the behaviour of others towards a common goal. This definition provides three indicators for the emergence of leadership: (1) an actor in a position of power; (2) the employment of resources by translating them into strategies or provoking an anticipated reaction (Sect. 3.3); and (3) the existence of a common goal. There are two ways of assessing an actor's position of power: first, a resource-based power index can be used (see below); second, expressions of other actors may indicate a predominant position of one particular actor. The use of leadership strategies or the mechanism of anticipated reaction can only be revealed through the reconstruction of the decision-making process. A common goal, finally, is given if all actors involved agree on a yet unreached entity or condition in their interest.

With regard to the explanatory factors for a leader's emergence, the first independent variable is a candidate's expected *surplus*. This is given if the expected benefits of leading exceed the costs of it. The three possible values of this ordinal variable are (1) benefits > costs (surplus), (2) benefits = costs, and (3) benefits < costs (no surplus). However, as opposed to economics, cost-benefit analyses in political science can be conducted only under certain conditions. A first condition is given if there are no significant costs or benefits. If one of the two parts of the subtraction is zero, the respective other automatically prevails. A second situation that enables a cost-benefit analysis is given if the benefits of leading consist in the potential leader's (institutional) survival. Given the theoretical assumption that no actor risks institutional suicide (Sect. 3.1), the benefits of leading always exceed the costs in this case. Vice versa, if the costs of leading involve the institutional death of the potential leader, they exceed all possible benefits. A third option of comparing the expected benefits of leading against the costs is to determine a common currency in which the two variables are assessed (e.g. electoral votes, GDP/capita). Given that they are always expected and subjective, costs and benefits of leading must be assessed by the expressions of single actors while assuming an ex-ante perspective.

The second variable accounting for the emergence of leadership are the *status quo costs* caused by a collective action problem. As opposed to the costs of leading, these costs are aggregate and already present or imminent in the case of status quo. They are conceptualized as a continuous variable and, like in the case of a leader's surplus, they must be assessed on the basis of subjective expressions. Since status quo costs cannot be evaluated directly, "perceived pressure for action" is used as a proxy in the data collection.[11] In the context of the eurozone crisis, the relative development of government bond spreads can be used as a complementary proxy for status quo costs since these spreads partly reflect the perceived fragmentation risk in the eurozone in case of non-action—and thus the gravity of the crisis.

In the second analytical step, the *explanandum* is the *impact of leadership*. It is conceptualized as a continuous variable ranging from the absence to the complete realisation of the desired leader-initiated policy or institutional change. Change is given if there is a difference between the *ex-post-* and the ex-ante situation. The benchmark for the desirability of a given change is the leader's most preferred outcome (preference attainment). Whether the change is really leader-initiated can be assessed by tracing the strategies used by the leader.

The first independent variable of this second step are a leader's *power resources*. These resources must be measured as relative to those of the other actors (followers). We can distinguish between material, institutional, and ideational resources (Sect. 3.3). In the context of eurozone crisis management, the most relevant indicators for material resources are the aggregate GDP of member states, their current account balance, public debt, and their government bond yields.[12] As regards non-state actors (e.g. EU institutions), material power resources can be measured by those budgetary capacities which they can deploy to influence EU economic governance. Institutional resources include all legislative

[11] This means, for instance, that interviewees were not asked about their status quo costs, but how they perceived the pressure for action in a certain situation.

[12] The aggregate GDP determines a member state's capacity to contribute to financial stability in the eurozone and to bail out other countries. Moreover, a member state's current account balance indicates its saving potential, government bond yields reflect the credibility in the financial markets and thus the refinancing options, and gross public debt indicates the long-term solvency.

and executive competences, namely agenda-managing, voting- and veto-rights, and rights of implementation. Ideational resources, finally, comprise information, expertise, credibility, and legitimacy. While credibility and legitimacy need to be assessed on the basis of actors' perceptions, information and expertise can also be measured by auxiliary indicators such as the number of relevant administrative staff. The assessment of power resources can be complemented by appropriate power indices (e.g. Janning 2013: 7–9).

The second variable accounting for the impact of leadership is the *distribution of preferences*. It is useful to distinguish between real and strategic (or situational) preferences. Real preferences are an actor's subjective evaluation and ranking of all conceivable interaction outcomes. They may be deduced from theoretical assumptions about actors' basic interests (here: survival, autonomy, growth), or, if this is not possible, they need to be determined inductively (Frieden 1999: 54, 61–6; Scharpf 1997: 66). Strategic preferences, by contrast, are an actor's ranking of interaction outcomes once she has taken into account the preferences of other actors and further situational circumstances. Given that this book examines political leadership as an issue-specific phenomenon (i.e. case by case), the actors' strategic preferences at the beginning of each case study are the unit of interest, because these are the ones the leader faces when trying to bring about change. The distribution of preferences is conceptualized as an ordinal variable with the values (1) strong convergence around the leader's preferred outcome, (2) weak convergence around the leader's preferred outcome, (3) divergence of preferences (heterogeneity), (4) weak convergence elsewhere, and (5) complete convergence elsewhere (Fig. 3.4). Finally, it is important that the assessed preferences always reflect the actors' ex-ante perspective on the respective outcome (Frieden 1999: 60).

The third and last explanatory variable for a leader's impact is the degree of *institutional constraint*, understood as the extent to which given institutional rules limit a leader's latitude in making decisions. Institutional constraint is an ordinal variable with the values (1) discretion, (2) consent, (3) participation and (4) interdiction. Full discretion is given if a leader can decide autonomously without having to take the preferences of followers into consideration. The discretion is slightly restricted if the leader needs to consult followers before deciding. By contrast, the institutional constraint is considerably higher if the leader needs the followers' formal

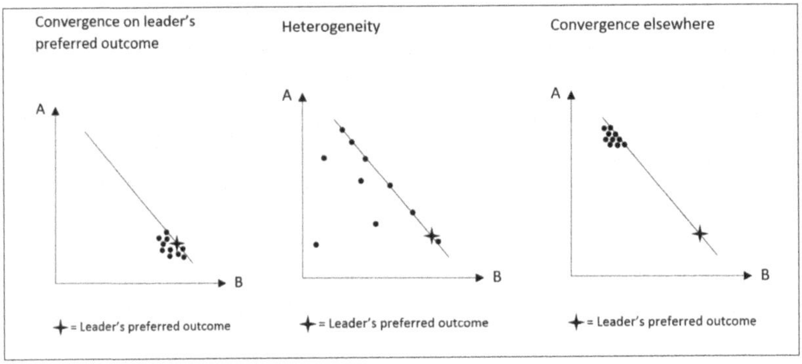

Fig. 3.4 Distribution of preferences (*Source* Own illustration)

consent to make a decision. The share of followers required to obtain this consent can vary. Thus, the institutional constraint is higher if consent by unanimity is required than if only a simple or qualified majority needs to agree (see Tallberg 2006: 35). An even higher level of institutional constraint is given if the followers can participate in the decision-making process from the outset. Also in this case, the institutional constraint is lower if a final decision can be reached by simple majority than if qualified majority or even unanimity is required. Finally, it may be forbidden to make certain decisions, which is the highest possible degree of institutional constraint. Table 3.4 illustrates the different degrees of institutional constraint and gives empirical examples from the EU context.

Data Collection

In order to obtain relevant data to assess the single variables and test the theoretical model, this book relies on a variety of sources. Firstly, primary sources such as legislative texts, rules of procedure, declarations, speeches, press releases, and first-hand accounts are used. Secondly, where no other information could be found, newspaper articles and journalistic accounts are consulted. Thirdly, data is drawn from existing empirical research and secondary literature in the field. Still, the book's most important data source are semi-structured interviews with officials who have been involved in the cases of interest. As for instance Brian Rathbun has pointed out:

Table 3.4 Degrees of institutional constraint

Degree of institutional constraint	*Theory*	*Empirical examples (EU)*
	1. Discretion	
	Complete	Commission acting alone (special legislative procedure based on Art. 45(3) and 106(3) TFEU) ECB's monetary policy decisions
	Consultation	Consultation procedure
	2. Consent	
	Simple	
	Qualified majority	Consent procedure
	Unanimity	(e.g. international agreements)
	3. Participation	
	Simple	
	Qualified majority	Ordinary legislative procedure Intergovernmental treaty[a]
	Unanimity	Treaty amendment
	4. Interdiction	Ex post facto law Legislation violating the principles of conferral, proportionality, or subsidiarity etc.

Source Own illustration

[a]Intergovernmental treaties require formal unanimity. However, as opposed to EU treaty amendments, reluctant actors can be excluded from the treaty. This implies that single actors cannot prevent the others from adopting the treaty by exercising a veto. Therefore, the institutional constraint of intergovernmental treaties is lower than that of EU treaty amendments

> Interviewing is often necessary for establishing motivations and preferences. […] Without an understanding of desires, even the most rigorous rationalist argument will not be falsifiable if it simply infers preferences from observable behavior and a posited set of situational constraints. […] Desires and beliefs must be measured independent of action. In some instances, interviewing is the only way to do so. (2008: 690f.)

Next to being an efficient way of gathering data and obtaining valid results (Bogner et al. 2009: 2), interviews are often the only possible way to collect certain information. Thus, they are especially valuable "when influence over the outcome of interest was restricted to a few select decision-makers, creating a bottleneck of political power that increases the importance of agency in the story" (Rathbun 2008: 690).

Conducting the interviews, I guaranteed the respondents strict confidentiality. If the respondents agreed, I recorded the interviews. Otherwise I took notes. In total, I thus conducted 35 semi-structured interviews. 17 interviews were conducted in November 2014 in Brussels with mostly high-ranking officials from the Commission, the Council of the European Union and European Council, and two Permanent Representations. All of the interviewees were closely involved in at least one of the six cases that are analysed in the following. In February 2015, I conducted another eight interviews with several officials of the EP's permanent staff and a Member of the EP. In March 2015, I conducted seven interviews with officials of the ECB in Frankfurt who either dealt with the drafting of the Outright Monetary Transactions or were involved in the ECB's decision-making of summer 2012. In the same month, I interviewed three high-ranking state officials in the German Ministry of Finance who were involved in the three cases that deal with Germany's role in the eurozone crisis. The questions enquired about the values of the predefined variables, but they did not suggest any causal relation. Based on 23 recordings and 12 transcripts, I finally coded the data according to the values of the single variables.

References

Ahlquist, John S., and Margaret Levi. 2011. Leadership: What It Means, What It Does, and What We Want to Know About It. *Annual Review of Political Science* 14 (1): 1–24.

Bachrach, Peter, and Morton S. Baratz. 1962. Two Faces of Power. *American Political Science Review* 56 (4): 947–952.

Beach, Derek. 2005. *The Dynamics of European Integration: Why and When EU Institutions Matter*. Basingstoke: Palgrave Macmillan.

Blavoukos, Spyros, Dimitris Bourantonis, and Panayotis Tsakonas. 2006. Parameters of the Chairmanship's Effectiveness: The Case of the UN Security Council. *The Hague Journal of Diplomacy* 1 (2): 143–170.

Blondel, Jean. 1987. *Political Leadership: Towards a General Analysis*. London: Sage.

Bogner, Alexander, Beate Littig, and Wolfgang Menz. 2009. Expert Interviews—An Introduction to a New Methodological Debate. In *Interviewing Experts*, ed. Alexander Bogner, Beate Littig, and Wolfgang Menz, 1–13. Basingstoke: Palgrave Macmillan.

Dahl, Robert. 1957. The Concept of Power. *Behavioral Science* 2 (3): 201–215.

Eberlein, Burkhard, and Claudio M. Radaelli. 2010. Mechanisms of Conflict Management in EU Regulatory Policy. *Public Administration* 88 (3): 782–799.

Elgie, Robert. 1995. *Political Leadership in Liberal Democracies*. Basingstoke and London: Macmillan.

Endo, Ken. 1999. *The Presidency of the European Commission Under Jacques Delors: The Politics of Shared Leadership*. Basingstoke, London, and New York: Macmillan and St. Martin's Press.

Fiorina, Morris, and Kenneth Shepsle. 1989. Formal Theories of Leadership: Agents, Agenda-Setters, and Entrepreneurs. In *Leadership and Politics: New Perspectives in Political Science*, ed. Bryan D. Jones, 17–40. Lawrence, KS: University Press of Kansas.

Frieden, Jeffry A. 1999. Actors and Preferences in International Relations. In *Strategic Choice and International Relations*, ed. David A. Lake and Robert Powell, 39–76. Princeton, NJ: Princeton University Press.

Friedrich, Carl J. 1963. *Man and His Government*. New York: McGraw-Hill.

Frohlich, Norman, Joe A. Oppenheimer, and Oran R. Young. 1971. *Political Leadership and Collective Goods*. Princeton, NJ: Princeton University Press.

Güth, Werner, M. Vittoria Levati, Matthias Sutter, and Eline Van der Heijden. 2007. Leading by Example With and Without Exclusion Power in Voluntary Contribution Experiments. *Journal of Public Economics* 91 (5–6): 1023–1042.

Helmke, Gretchen, and Steven Levitsky. 2004. Informal Institutions and Comparative Politics. *Perspectives on Politics* 2 (4): 725–740.

Héritier, Adrienne. 1999. *Policy-Making and Diversity in Europe: Escaping Deadlock*. Cambridge: Cambridge University Press.

Héritier, Adrienne. 2007. *Explaining Institutional Change in Europe*. Oxford: Oxford University Press.

Hermalin, Benjamin E. 1998. Toward an Economic Theory of Leadership: Leading by Example. *The American Economic Review* 88 (5): 1188–1206.

Janning, Josef. 2013. *State Power within European Integration: On the Limits and Context of Germany's Power in the Union*. DGAPanalyse kompakt 1/2013, Berlin.

Kindleberger, Charles P. 1981. Dominance and Leadership in the International Economy: Exploitation, Public Goods, and Free Rides. *International Studies Quarterly* 25 (2): 242–254.

Krotz, Ulrich, and Joachim Schild. 2013. *Shaping Europe: France, Germany, and Embedded Bilateralism from the Elysée Treaty to Twenty-First Century Politics*. Oxford: Oxford University Press.

Lake, David A., and Robert Powell. 1999. International Relations: A Strategic-Choice Approach. In *Strategic Choice and International Relations*, ed. David A. Lake and Robert Powell, 3–38. Princeton, NJ: Princeton University Press.

Lax, David A., and James K. Sebenius. 1986. *The Manager as Negotiator: Bargaining for Cooperation and Competitive Gain*. New York and London: Free Press and Collier Macmillan.

Lukes, Steven. 1974. *Power: A Radical View*. London: Macmillan.

Mattli, Walter. 1999. *The Logic of Regional Integration: Europe and Beyond*. New York: Cambridge University Press.

North, Douglass C. 1990. *Institutions, Institutional Change and Economic Performance*. Cambridge: Cambridge University Press.

Nye, Joseph S. 2010. Power and Leadership. In *Handbook of Leadership Theory and Practice*, ed. Nitin Nohria and Rakesh Khurana, 305–332. Boston, MA: Harvard Business Press.

Odell, John S. 2009. Breaking Deadlocks in International Institutional Negotiations: The WTO, Seattle, and Doha. *International Studies Quarterly* 53 (2): 273–299.

Parker, Charles F., and Christer Karlsson. 2014. Leadership and International Cooperation. In *The Oxford Handbook of Political Leadership*, ed. R.A.W. Rhodes and Paul 't Hart, 580–594. Oxford: Oxford University Press.

Rathbun, Brian C. 2008. Interviewing and Qualitative Field Methods: Pragmatism and Practicalities. In *The Oxford Handbook of Political Methodology*, ed. Janet M. Box-Steffensmeier, Henry E. Brady, and David Collier, 685–701. Oxford: Oxford University Press.

Scharpf, Fritz W. 1997. *Games Real Actors Play: Actor-Centred Institutionalism in Policy Research*. Boulder, CO: Westview Press.

Schild, Joachim. 2013. Leadership in Hard Times: Germany, France, and the Management of the Eurozone Crisis. *German Politics and Society* 31 (1): 24–47.

Schoeller, Magnus G. 2018. The Rise and Fall of Merkozy: Franco-German Bilateralism as a Negotiation Strategy in Eurozone Crisis Management. *Journal of Common Market Studies* 56 (5): 1019–1035.

Sheffer, Gabriel (ed.). 1993. *Innovative Leaders in International Politics*. Albany, NY: State University of New York Press.

Spender, J.C. 2008. Can Simon's Notion of "Bounded Rationality" Give Us New Ideas About Leadership? *Leadership* 4 (1): 95–109.

Stacey, Jeffrey, and Berthold Rittberger. 2003. Dynamics of Formal and Informal Institutional Change in the EU. *Journal of European Public Policy* 10 (6): 858–883.

Stiller, Sabina. 2010. *Ideational Leadership in German Welfare State Reform*. Amsterdam: Amsterdam University Press.

Tallberg, Jonas. 2006. *Leadership and Negotiation in the European Union*. Cambridge: Cambridge University Press.

Underdal, Arild. 1994. Leadership Theory: Rediscovering the Arts of Management. In *International Multilateral Negotiation: Approaches to the Management of Complexity*, ed. I. William Zartman, 178–197. San Francisco: Jossey-Bass.

Young, Oran R. 1991. Political Leadership and Regime Formation: On the Development of Institutions in International Society. *International Organization* 45 (3): 281–308.

CHAPTER 4

Analysing Leadership I: Germany in the Eurozone Crisis

When the Economic and Monetary Union (EMU) found itself in crisis, the actor mostly called on to assume leadership was Germany.[1] Maybe most impressively, even Poland's foreign minister made a plea for German leadership:

> I demand of Germany that, for its own sake and for ours, it help the eurozone survive and prosper. [...] I fear German power less than I am beginning to fear its inactivity. You have become Europe's indispensable nation. You may not fail to lead: not dominate, but to lead in reform. (Sikorski 2011)

This strong focus on Germany has been reflected by a considerable amount of academic literature, which refers to Germany as a (reluctant) leader or hegemon.[2] Based on three case studies, the following analysis contributes to this literature. The chapter not only tests the book's leadership model, but also provides a theory-guided and generalizable explanation of Germany's ambiguous leadership record in the eurozone. While others have argued that Germany's behaviour in EMU is largely

[1] See e.g. *Financial Times* (2012), Jacoby (2015: 189f.), Jones (2010: 33), Matthijs (2016b: 136), Matthijs and Blyth (2011), Morisse-Schilbach (2011: 33f.), Steinmeier and Steinbrück (2010), Techau (2014), *The Economist* (2013).

[2] See e.g. Bulmer (2014), Bulmer and Paterson (2013), Jacoby (2015), Matthijs (2016a, b), Matthijs et al. (2016), Newman (2015), Otero-Iglesias (2017), Paterson (2011).

M. G. Schoeller, *Leadership in the Eurozone*, Palgrave Studies in European Union Politics, https://doi.org/10.1007/978-3-030-12704-6_4

determined by ordo-liberal ideas (e.g. Matthijs 2016a) or domestic constraints (e.g. Bulmer 2014), this chapter submits that Germany's (non-)leadership is primarily driven by its material interest to shift the adjustment costs of the crisis to the national level and thus to the "debtor states". Whether Germany succeeds in doing so depends on the preferences of other eurozone actors and the respective institutional constraint.

The first case study (Sect. 4.1) deals with the first possible outcome of the theoretical model (Fig. 3.2): a leadership vacuum. When the eurozone put together the *first bailout package for Greece* in spring 2010, Germany did not emerge as a leader. Although the status quo costs created a high demand for leadership, Germany's expected costs of leading exceeded the benefits. Most critically, the German government feared that by taking the lead it would become the permanent "paymaster" of the eurozone.

The second case study, by contrast, is an instance of failed leadership (Sect. 4.2). In the case of the so-called "*super-commissioner*" proposal, Germany emerged as a leader, but failed to influence the outcomes. The emergence of leadership can be explained with the benefits that a super-commissioner would have brought Germany and the high status quo costs. The lack of impact results from an unfavourable preference constellation in the eurozone combined with high institutional constraint (treaty change).

In the third case study, finally, the model is applied to an instance of successful leadership (Sect. 4.3). In shaping the *Fiscal Compact*, Germany did emerge as a leader and successfully influenced the outcomes. A high demand for leadership based on unprecedented spreads in government bonds and the looming collapse of the eurozone met with Germany's interest in sending an effective signal to the financial markets and German voters. Moreover, the favourable preference distribution in the eurozone helped Germany overcome the high institutional constraint by translating its power resources into classic leadership strategies.

Before proceeding with the single case studies, however, some preliminary notes on the eurozone's twofold lack of institutions are needed.

Incomplete Institutions in the Economic and Monetary Union

It is a central argument of this book that leaders can act as substitutes for *incomplete institutions* (Sect. 3.1). Institutions are behavioural prescriptions that constrain single actors and enable collective action. If they are incomplete, collective action may fail or result in suboptimal outcomes. In these cases, a leader can step in, enhance collective action and bring about institutional change. In so doing, the leader acts as a driver of institutional change. Institutional incompleteness has therefore been conceptualized as a pre-condition for the emergence of leadership.

The eurozone crisis exposed a twofold lack of institutions. First, institutions to contain EMU's inbuilt free-rider problem turned out to be incomplete. Second, there were no institutions regulating EMU's distributional problem, which consists in the mutualisation of risk and costs associated to a common currency. On the one hand, non-optimal currency areas face the problem of moral hazard. Less competitive member states are tempted to borrow "cheap money" in order to finance public spending. In so doing, they may exceed sustainable limits because even in the case of bankruptcy they can expect to be bailed out by the central bank or other members, which have an interest in preserving the single currency. Thus, states with high deficit or debt levels might free-ride at the expense of fiscally more solid members. In order to avoid this free-rider problem, fiscal rules are needed. On the other hand, however, such rules tie the hands of states when it comes to fighting economic crises through counter-cyclical spending. Maintaining a balanced budget in hard times, or applying austerity measures, worsens the economic situation and can result in a self-reinforcing process that might spill over to other members of the currency union. Therefore, a common backstop is needed to assist member states in times of crisis. Such a backstop can take different forms, ranging from a central bank acting as lender of last resort, via a fiscal capacity or the issuance of common debt, through to a permanent transfer union. This creates a distributional problem which, if not regulated by institutions, might jeopardize the existence of the single currency. In other words, institutions providing for both fiscal restraint (free-rider problem) and risk-sharing (distributional problem) are needed in the eurozone; austerity and solidarity are two sides of the same coin (see Bénassy-Quéré et al. 2018; Beach 2013: 123–5).

One of EMU's two collective action problems—namely its *free-rider problem*—was anticipated at the outset and institutional arrangements were laid down by the Treaty on the Functioning of the European Union (TFEU) in articles 123–126. Article 123 prohibits monetary financing by the ECB; article 124 denies member states privileged access to financial institutions; article 125 is the so-called "no-bailout clause" which prohibits the Union and its members to assume financial commitments of other members; article 126 contains provisions to avoid excessive deficit (max. 3% of GDP) and debt levels (max. 60% of GDP).

Since 1997, the Stability and Growth Pact (SGP) specifies the operationalization of these rules in secondary legislation (Heipertz and Verdun 2010).

However, these "anti-free-rider" institutions proved to be incomplete when in 2009 the sovereign debt crisis broke out in Greece (Buti and Carnot 2012: 900–5). First, there was a lack of surveillance: member states did not comply with the rules and neither the Commission nor any other supranational body had the means to properly monitor compliance. Second, the institutions lacked credible enforcement mechanisms. This is especially true since member states themselves decide in the Council whether rules have been breached and if an excessive deficit procedure should be launched. In particular after Germany and France succeeded in making the Council suspend the excessive deficit procedure against them in 2003, the institutions lost credibility. Third, the "no-bailout clauses" (Art. 123 and 125 TFEU) did not have the desired effect on the financial markets. Instead of exerting disciplining pressure on financially less solid members through higher risk premiums, the markets treated all government bonds as virtually risk-free. Finally, the rules were incomplete in the sense that they targeted only governments. However, fiscal risks stem not only from government spending, but also from unsustainable private behaviour. Even if member states are perfectly disciplined as regards their public expenditure, they might still be forced to bail out their national banks. This may result in the (in)famous "doom loop" or "vicious circle", where excessive public debt leads to the need to bail out banks that hold bonds of their highly indebted sovereigns, which in turn raises public debt even more, and so forth (Véron 2011). In sum, although decision-makers had anticipated EMU's free-rider problem, the institutions to deal with it turned out to be incomplete.

For EMU's *distributional problem*, the situation is another. While anti-free-rider institutions to prevent moral hazard were just incomplete, institutions to regulate risk sharing were almost entirely absent. The ECB is legally prohibited from assuming the role of lender of last resort (De Grauwe 2013: 9–11, 16–8). An alternative would be a federal budget with redistributive features (Drudi et al. 2012: 894). More far-reaching solutions could consist in the issuance of common debt or a supranational fiscal authority with tax and spending powers (Schelkle 2012: 31–3; Verdun 2015: 224f.). However, at the onset of the crisis there were no such instruments, and those that were built up as a crisis response turned out to be insufficient.[3]

In sum, while the institutions to prevent a crisis by regulating the eurozone's free-rider problem were incomplete and thus enabled the outbreak of the crisis in the first place, there were no institutions to deal with the ensuing distributional problem of allocating the adjustment costs. According to the theoretical model, a leader would thus have to enhance the incomplete institutions against fiscal free-riding ("austerity") and come up with institutional solutions to the underlying distributional problem ("solidarity"). Consequently, the cases analysed in this book concern either the enhancement of institutions ensuring fiscal restraint (Super-commissioner, Fiscal Compact) or the establishment of institutions regulating the mutualisation of risk (Greek bailout, Eurobonds, Outright Monetary Transactions).

4.1 No Leadership: The First Financial Assistance to Greece

When it came to the first financial assistance package granted to Greece in spring 2010, Germany did not emerge as a leader. Although the feared collapse of the eurozone created a high demand for leadership and Germany would have been the ideal leadership candidate, the expected costs of leading clearly exceeded the benefits. Thus, Germany refrained from taking the lead and left the eurozone as a whole worse off. After the case description, which presents the relevant events, actors and preferences, the values of the dependent variable (absence of leadership) and the explanatory factors (leadership surplus, status quo costs) are assessed. The section concludes by summarizing the results of this case study.

Case Description: Shaping the Eurozone's First Bailout

In October 2009, the newly elected Greek government revealed that its fiscal deficit was roughly twice as high as previously reported and its debt level for 2009 even three times higher (Featherstone 2011: 199).

[3]In the wake of the first financial assistance package to Greece, temporary rescue funds (EFSF, EFSM) were created and later replaced by a permanent fund (ESM). However, this permanent fund also turned out to be insufficient, thereby forcing the ECB to step in with the announcement of Outright Monetary Transactions in 2012 (Sect. 5.3).

This raised fears in the financial markets that Greece would no longer be able to service its debt in the long run. As a consequence, Greek government bond yields started to rise rapidly and thus jeopardized the eurozone's financial stability and coherence. Although there was an early consensus among decision-makers that a Greek default would not be a solution because of its dire economic and political consequences, no significant action was taken until February 2010. Only after the Greek government had announced a first austerity plan, did the European Council at an informal meeting on 11 February agree to "take determined and coordinated action, if needed, to safeguard financial stability in the euro area as a whole" (European Council 2010). However, in doing so the member states avoided committing themselves in any substantive way. First, the main part of the statement emphasized that each member state is responsible for its own finances. Second, as a German government official stated, there were "no concrete plans" (Euractiv 2010c) for financial assistance to Greece. Moreover, in the run-up to the February summit the German Chancellor even rejected a more far-reaching draft statement, which had been prepared by the Eurogroup as a calming signal to the financial markets (Ludlow 2010c).

By mid-February, the Greek government made clear that it would need financial assistance, possibly ranging from guarantees by other member states to external refinancing through the International Monetary Fund (IMF) (Ludlow 2010b: 11f.). Nevertheless, other eurozone members—and in particular Germany—denied such requests. On 3 March, the Greek government announced a second far-reaching austerity programme (Euractiv 2010e). This was the precondition for the other eurozone member states to agree at their summit of 25 March "to contribute to coordinated bilateral loans" (Euro Summit 2010). However, although this second official statement was more concrete than the February statement, it still did not mean that a decision on financial assistance was taken. As the statement made clear, financial assistance "has to be considered ultima ratio, meaning in particular that market financing is insufficient" (Euro Summit 2010).

Through the Eurogroup agreement of 11 April, the eurozone finance ministers made the Euro summit statement of 25 March fully operational (Eurogroup 2010). Nevertheless, the defined goal was still to calm the financial markets and to avoid activating the rescue mechanism. On 23 April the Greek government officially requested financial assistance. Although this request did not come as a surprise since informal consultations had already taken place weeks before the official request (Interview 15), there was no immediate answer by the other member states. As the German Finance Minister stated two days later: "The fact that neither the EU nor the German government have taken a decision [on providing aid] means that the response can be positive as well as negative" (Euractiv 2010d). Indeed, on 29 April the Greek government agreed for the third time in three months on even tougher austerity measures in order to receive the requested financial help. Eventually, on 2 May 2010, the eurozone finance ministers and the IMF agreed on the first 'Economic Adjustment Programme for Greece': conditional on an austerity programme supervised by the so-called 'Troika' (IMF, Commission, ECB), the member states and the IMF committed themselves to bilateral loans to be disbursed in tranches and amounting to a total of 110bn.

Hence, the first bailout of Greece was a purely intergovernmental endeavour. Although the Commission and ECB were present and provided expertise in the run-up to the bailout, they were not in the role of decision-makers. Thus, apart from the IMF, the relevant actors were only eurozone member states. Their preferences converged in the sense that they all preferred financial assistance to Greece over a Greek default or a "Grexit" (Interview 5; Ardagna and Caselli 2014: 296–9). The reason for this convergence were the feared consequences a Grexit would bring.[4] Economically, a Greek default would have triggered a bank run in the highly indebted peripheral member states and considerable losses for the exposed banks in the northern member states.[5] The result would have been a Europe-wide banking crisis and massive bailouts. Next to a dramatic rise of public debt through bailouts, such a banking crisis would have spilled over to the real economy, resulting in capital flights

[4]While it is true that especially in the beginning of the Greek debt crisis, there was a lot of uncertainty and therefore different opinions regarding the consequences of a potential default, there was an early consensus among governments that a Greek default, or even "Grexit", would in any case do considerable harm to the eurozone. Even sceptical decision-makers like German Finance Minister Wolfgang Schäuble, who later adopted a more favourable stance towards "Grexit", "considered the damage of a default of a euro country to be incalculable and more costly than the rescue" (Schimmelfennig 2015: 182).

[5]As regards the banks of "creditor countries" like Germany, there was no systemically relevant exposure to Greece alone, but given that a Greek default would most probably have spilled over to other countries like Spain and Italy, the overall exposure was enormous (Ardagna and Caselli 2014: 297; Thompson 2013: 8).

from the eurozone, bankruptcies, a collapse of internal demand, and a profound recession. Moreover, in the absence of a banking union or a central rescue mechanism, a Greek default would have led to a contagion of Italy or Spain, which were considered too big to be bailed out. Hence, a default might even have triggered the collapse of the eurozone. Politically, a default or Grexit could have ended up as a precedent for further disintegration. For Germany in particular, a fragmentation of the eurozone would furthermore result in a slump of exports, a loss of its price competitiveness, and a heavy setback as regards its global leadership aspirations (Bonatti and Fracasso 2013: 1033).

Thus, since all member states preferred a bailout over a default, the former would have taken place also without any particular actor taking the lead. The question of leadership, therefore, did not concern the bailout as such, but rather the shape this bailout would take. The two ideal-typical options were either an early and full commitment to the integrity of the eurozone, which would lead to more lenient conditions for Greece and less instability and contagion risk for the rest of the eurozone, or, by contrast, a bailout as "ultima ratio", resulting in better conditions for the creditors, but less stability and a higher contagion risk (see below). As opposed to the question whether there should be a bailout at all, the preferences over the type of bailout diverged. While Greece and a group of mainly southern member states (Italy, Portugal, Spain, Belgium, France) preferred an early commitment and thus a more "generous" bailout, Germany, followed by the Netherlands, Finland and Austria, preferred the ultima ratio type of bailout, which would allow them to minimize their liabilities (see Schimmelfennig 2015: 182f.).

No German Leadership

The *explanandum* of the model's first analytical step is the emergence of leadership. Leadership is given if there is (1) a common goal and (2) an actor in a position of power who (3) uses her resources in such a way as to guide a group towards the achievement of the common goal.

With regard to the first criterion, a common goal, Erik Jones (2010) has pointed out that an early commitment to bail out Greece would have calmed the financial markets, meaning less trouble for Greece in refinancing its debt. This would have limited the risk of contagion, government bond yields would have remained low, banks would have maintained sounder balance sheets, economic stability would have been restored, and an eventual bailout of Greece would have been cheaper (also Featherstone 2011: 194). Thus, whereas an early commitment to financial assistance implied several disadvantages for the so-called "creditor states" (see below), it would have contributed to the common goal of protecting the common currency and maintaining stability in the eurozone.

Next to a common goal, there was also an actor in an extraordinary position of power as Germany has been the eurozone's most powerful member state (Sect. 4.2). However, as the following analysis shows, Germany did not take the lead by translating its power resources into strategies and making an early commitment to a bailout. Instead, Germany denied the need for financial assistance until the very last moment on the brink of a Greek default. By pursuing these "politics of the ultima ratio" (Ludlow 2010b: 13), Germany delayed any decision in favour of financial assistance. In Chapter 2, this strategy has been conceptualized as the exact opposite of leadership, namely acting as a veto player and defending the status quo.

Already at the European Council of 10–11 December 2009, when Greek Prime Minister George Papandreou emphasized the need for cooperation, German Chancellor Angela Merkel replied that "the Stability Pact [...] remains the essential reference point for EU policy" (Ludlow 2010a: 12). After the German Chancellor had rejected a draft declaration of the Eurogroup by the beginning of February, considering it too committing with regard to an eventual bailout, she stated: "Greece is a part of the European Union and won't be left on its own, but there are rules and these rules need to be adhered to" (Euractiv 2010a). When the EU finance ministers met on 16 February to discuss how to proceed further with the Greek sovereign debt crisis, the "Irish Finance Minister Brian Lenihan told journalists that some member states – notably Germany – were unwilling to spell out in detail what member states would be expected to do to prop up the Greek economy" (Euractiv 2010b).

Even after Greece had announced its second austerity programme on 3 March, the German Chancellor reiterated: "I want to say clearly that it is not about aid measures for Greece" (Euractiv 2010e). When asked again about financial assistance after a meeting with Greek Prime Minister Papandreou, Merkel answered that "'this is a question that we do not have to face today' [and that] Europe was not 'going to face in the future'" (Ludlow 2010b: 12). On 15 March, Merkel prevented the

EU finance ministers once again from finalizing a deal in favour of a Greek bailout (Ludlow 2010b: 47). Even after the Greek Prime Minister had openly urged his colleagues to make a decision about the conditions of financial assistance to Greece on 18 March, Merkel insisted:

> Greece is not insolvent and therefore we do not have to discuss the question of help now […] It is the best solution for the euro if Greece solves its problems alone; of course, with the political support of the European heads of state and government.[6] (Tagesschau 2010)

While German Finance Minister Schäuble on 24 March still claimed that financial aid would not be on the agenda, the German Chancellor agreed on bilateral loans only one day later, although this had "to be considered ultima ratio, meaning in particular that market financing is insufficient" (Euro Summit 2010). This meant that a final decision had once again been delayed until the very moment Greece would become virtually insolvent. In the beginning of April, as the situation had become increasingly pressing and Greek sovereign bonds interests raised to unprecedented levels, Papandreou informally asked for immediate help. However, whereas ECB President Trichet as well as French President Sarkozy pushed for an immediate mobilization of funds, the German government insisted on several formal steps to be concluded before financial assistance would actually be granted (Ludlow 2010b: 24f.). Thus, it took until 23 April for Greece to officially request financial assistance, which was subsequently agreed on 3 May.[7]

The unambiguous media coverage regarding Germany's delaying attitude towards a bailout decision has not been challenged by any of the interviewees. EU officials observed that Germany waited until the market pressure forced it to react and that "Germany and others were hesitating for a long time" (Interview 10): "they were essentially … quoting the good old treaty stuff and then … acting very lately" (Interview 12).

[6] Translated by the author from the original: "Griechenland ist nicht zahlungsunfähig und deshalb ist die Frage der Hilfen auch nicht die, die wir jetzt diskutieren müssen […] Die beste Lösung für den Euro ist, wenn Griechenland alleine seine Probleme löst, natürlich mit der politischen Unterstützung natürlich [sic] der europäischen Staats- und Regierungschefs".

[7] Due to the devastating signalling effect to the financial markets, Greece could make an official request for financial assistance only when it was assured that help would definitely be granted.

Somehow surprisingly, the most corroborating answer came from a German government official recognizing that at the end, Germany was the only member state still hesitating (Interview 25).

In sum, by making an early commitment to bail out Greece, Germany would have used its power resources in such a way as to guide the other member states towards a common goal, namely a cheaper bailout and more stability in the eurozone. In other words, Germany would have assumed leadership. Yet, Germany did not emerge as a leader, but opted for the alternative option: despite becoming increasingly isolated, the German Chancellor denied any need for financial assistance to Greece until the very last moment before Greek default ("politics of ultima ratio").

Explaining Germany's Lack of Leadership: Leadership Surplus and Status Quo Costs

As outlined above, there was an early consensus that "Grexit" was no viable option. If really necessary, a bailout would thus have taken place also without any particular actor taking the lead. Therefore, the costs and benefits of leading ("leader's surplus") did not concern the bailout as such, but rather the shape it would take. From a German perspective, there were two ideal-typical strategies: First, an early and unambiguous commitment to do whatever it takes to keep Greece in the eurozone and to help whenever Greece would not be able to service its debt anymore; second, no commitment at all and delaying any decision as long as possible. The preceding section showed that Germany opted for the second strategy and thereby refused to provide leadership.

The first explanatory variable accounting for the supply of leadership is the leader's surplus, which is defined as the difference between the expected benefits of leading and the perceived costs of it. Table 4.1 provides an overview of relevant interview answers regarding Germany's costs and benefits of leading in bailing out Greece. As can be seen at first glance, there is a striking asymmetry between the mentioned benefits of leading, on the one hand, and the costs of it, on the other. Those interviewees who were particularly strongly involved in the events leading to the first Greek bailout are printed in bold. Those representing the German government are italicised.

The most frequently mentioned cost of leading was the causation of moral hazard in Greece and other peripheral member states.

Table 4.1 Germany's costs and benefits of leading according to interviewees (Greek bailout)

Interview	*Benefits*	*Costs*
		MORAL HAZARD
5		Taking the lead by making an early commitment creates moral hazard in Greece and other member states
7		**Moral hazard, see above**
10		**Risk setting a precedent with regard to other member states (= wrong signal)**
12		Moral hazard, see above
15		**Wrong signal to other member states ("bailout as a cheap solution")**
26		*Wrong signal*
27		***Achieving only weak consolidation programme in Greece (yet, pressure on Greece needed to be high to adopt "sustainable" adjustment measures)***
		ELECTORAL COSTS
1	German business profits from economic prosperity in Greece	Acting against public opinion
8		Acting against public opinion
15		**Lack of legitimacy: early commitment would run counter to the expectations of German voters**
25		***Taking the lead would have implied electoral costs***
26		*Electoral costs, see above*
		BARGAINING POSITION
13		**Low pressure on Greece, leading to a worse bargaining position of Germany**
15		**Wrong signal to Greece ("structural reform is dispensable")**
26		*"Bad" consolidation programme ("bargaining position needs to be built up along the extremes")*
27		***No effective conditionality (as no incentives for reform)***
		UNCERTAINTY
10		**Uncertainty re. outcomes of leading** **Uncertainty re. tools and design of bailout**
15		**Uncertainty re. outcomes of leading**

Source Own compilation

The German government feared that an early commitment to bail out Greece would be perceived as a signal that painful fiscal discipline is not rewarding because in the end there would always be a lender of last resort in the eurozone. Thus, the "no-bailout clause" (Article 125 TFEU) would be de facto neutralised and the eurozone would become a system in which free riding by "fiscal sinners" at the expense of the fiscally more solid "creditor states" would be rewarding. Especially (but not exclusively) for Germany this would become very costly. The only way to avoid such a result was to make sure that an eventual bail-out would not be a "cheap solution" for the respective debtor state. In other words: if a bailout was really inevitable, it needed to be a costly one. Taking the lead on this, however, would have lowered the costs for Greece, thereby creating moral hazard in Greece and other potential debtor states of the euro area.

A second aspect regarded the electoral costs the German government would have had to face if it had taken the lead on the Greek bailout. The public opinion at the time was perceived as predominantly against financial assistance to Greece. In general, there has been little understanding of the complex interdependence among eurozone member states. The conventional wisdom, which has also been fostered by the German Chancellor,[8] was that the Greek people had lived beyond their means and thereby created a huge amount of debt. Thus, it was considered their exclusive responsibility to make the necessary cost-cutting efforts in order to consolidate their budget. Financial assistance by other eurozone member, instead, was seen as paying someone else's debts. Therefore the German government feared that by even assuming a pro-active role in a possibly inevitable bailout, it would lose a significant share of electoral votes.

In addition, the German government feared that taking the lead by signalling an early commitment to Greece would have worsened its bargaining position with regard to a consolidation programme. From a German perspective, a strict programme of austerity measures was needed for at least three reasons: firstly, a tough programme would make sure that a bailout would not be perceived as a cheap solution to a

[8] See e.g. Merkel's press conference after the European Council of 11 and 12 December 2009, in which she refers to the responsibility of Greece to implement structural reforms as a solution to its financial problems, instead of financial assistance by the other Eurozone member states (Merkel 2009).

member state's financial difficulties; secondly, such a programme would reduce the electoral costs of a bailout as it would signal that the problem will not turn up again in the future and that Greece will be able to return the loans; thirdly, far reaching structural reforms and cost-cutting efforts have been regarded as an essential condition for a sustainable solution to a sovereign debt crisis. However, a programme could not simply be imposed on Greece, but needed to be negotiated. In this context, an early commitment by Germany would have provided a comfortable fall-back position for the Greek government as it would have been assured of the financial assistance by other member states irrespectively of the programme design. Vice versa, the later Germany would act, the stronger the pressure on Greece would be, and the more costly its access to the financial markets would become. As one very closely involved interviewee put it: In the extreme case of Greece not being able anymore to place its bonds on the markets, its fall-back position would be sovereign default with all its consequences (Interview 13). For Germany, by contrast, precisely this situation would provide the best bargaining position, because it would allow the German government to achieve the toughest programme possible. Hence, Germany's perceived costs of leading included also a worsening of its bargaining position and thus a more lenient consolidation programme for Greece.

Finally, the uncertainty about the design and possible outcomes of a bailout constituted a further cost of leading. Until Greece was de facto not able anymore to refinance itself on the markets, it had never been absolutely certain whether and when a bailout would become necessary (Interview 10). Moreover, at a technical level, the legal and financial tools for a bailout still needed to be invented. As long as it was not completely clear what the financial assistance would actually look like, the costs of an early commitment could hardly be estimated. This regarded especially the role of the IMF. While German Finance Minister Schäuble, with the support of the ECB, was strictly against an involvement of the fund in order to preserve the integrity of the eurozone, Chancellor Merkel eventually decided to include the IMF because of her mistrust in the ultimate rigour of the Commission. Since the Commission was perceived as being more interested in the cohesion of the eurozone than in the fiscal discipline of single member states, Merkel shared the Dutch view that the Commission alone could not credibly represent the creditor countries. Taking the lead without having sorted out such crucial questions would have been a risky undertaking.

In stark contrast to all the costs of leading, only one interviewee mentioned also a potential benefit, namely that German business would profit from economic prosperity in Greece. The underlying rationale is in line with the argumentation of Jones (2010) that an early commitment by Germany would have immediately calmed the financial markets. This would have had the effect that investors would feel safe to invest in the Greek economy. Moreover, a more lenient adjustment programme might have done less damage to the growth in Greece. Also the German banks holding Greek bonds would have suffered less depreciation in their balance sheets. These effects would not only have applied to Greece, but to all potential "debtor states" in the eurozone. Thereby a recession could have been mitigated in these countries, which would have been in the interest of both German banks and German export industry.

Yet, how to compare the mentioned costs of leading against its benefits? As pointed out in Sect. 3.4, this is only possible if (1) there are no significant costs or benefits, (2) one of the two elements implies the institutional survival or death of the potential leader, or (3) we find a "common currency" for the cost-benefits analysis. Options (1) and (2) do not apply: neither were the benefits of an early commitment to bail out Greece insignificant—let alone the costs—nor was any side of the cost-benefit balance of vital significance for Germany. Hence, the only option left is a common currency to compare cost against benefits. Given that the benefits consist in the material savings an early commitment would bring about, this is the only currency eligible for a proper analysis.

To be sure, the material savings of an early commitment cannot be compared against the uncertainty over outcomes or the electoral costs of leading. However, they can be compared against the material costs which a worse bargaining position for Germany and moral hazard in Greece and other member states would have caused. An early commitment might have helped to avoid the short- and medium-term costs of a bailout (lower volume of loans, less risk of contagion, less damage to German banks' balance sheets), but it would not have resolved the persisting fiscal and economic problems of Greece. Thus, from a German perspective, the real problem would only have been postponed (Interview 27). This postponement, however, would have come at a cost: there would be no (or only a very lenient) adjustment programme in Greece due to the worse bargaining position of Germany, and there would be no (or only weak) incentives for fiscal discipline in Greece and other member states. Germany would have de facto neutralised the "no-bailout clause" which hitherto functioned as a safeguard against fiscal profligacy. These *long-term costs* would by far exceed the short- and medium term costs caused by the German hesitance. The scenario of much bigger bailouts at a later point in time, not only of Greece, but also of other eurozone members, was perceived as very realistic by the German government at the time (Interviews 10, 27). As long as Germany and other creditor states would be willing and able to finance such bailouts, the feared costs would consist in Germany becoming the "paymaster" of the eurozone. Once Germany would or could not shoulder the financial transfers anymore, the long-term costs would consist in the break-up of the eurozone.

Thus, the costs of a late commitment to bail out Greece could not be more expensive for Germany than a de facto Transfer Union or even a break-up of the eurozone. To put it bluntly, the question was whether to have a costly, but quantitatively limited bailout of Greece (and possibly a few other small member states), or systematic and unlimited transfers in the long run. The electoral costs and the risk caused by the high degree of uncertainty come only on top of this calculation. In sum, the expected benefits of leading, namely a cheaper bailout or even no bailout for the time being, were clearly outweighed by the much higher costs consisting in the moral hazard created by a German commitment and the perceived consequence of either becoming the "paymaster of the eurozone" or having provoked its collapse. Hence, according to the model's first theoretical proposition (Sect. 3.2, H1), we would not expect Germany to supply leadership as there was no leadership surplus.

Indeed, Germany's solution to the dilemma of having to send two opposed signals at the same time—namely "there won't be a sovereign default of Greece" in the direction of the markets and "fiscal profligacy is not rewarding" towards the other member states—consisted in acting as late as possible. By acting only when Greece was already in deep trouble with only the option of sovereign default left, Germany could still signal to the markets that sovereign default remained off the table and that speculating against a eurozone member would not be rewarding. At the same time, it signalled to other potential debtor countries that fiscal profligacy was not rewarding either, given that financial assistance would take place in the last moment only, thereby making a bailout a very costly undertaking. As a high-level official of the German Treasury stated when asked about a trigger point enabling the final agreement: "No, there was no trigger point. The critical factors were Greece's readiness to accept an adequate programme and Germany's readiness to commit itself to the actual financial assistance. Both was only possible because it was the very last moment [before default]"[9] (Interview 27).

The second factor accounting for a leader's emergence are the status quo costs of all actors involved. Although status quo costs were relatively high throughout the crisis, they were especially high when it came to the first bailout of Greece. Of the 19 interviewees who answered the question when the perceived pressure for action during the crisis was highest, 13 named spring 2010, when the Greek bailout and the establishment of the European Financial Stability Facility (EFSF) took place. In the case of the first Greek bailout, most of the status quo costs had not materialised yet, but were expected in case a lack of action would result in a sovereign default of Greece.

These costs regarded, firstly, other member states' bank exposure to Greece. Although the exposure to Greece alone was not big enough to be systemically relevant, the exposure to other member states which were seen at risk of contagion in the case no bailout was to take place (namely Ireland, Portugal, Spain and eventually Italy) was so big that a new banking crisis would have been inevitable (Ardagna and Caselli 2014: 296f.; Mayhew et al. 2011: 21; Thompson 2013: 7–9). Moreover, actors feared that such a banking crisis would have been accompanied by a macroeconomic crisis affecting stability and growth in the entire eurozone (Interviews 5, 11, 25, 26).

What is more, however, maintaining the status quo would have put the eurozone as such at risk as a sovereign default of Greece would have spilled over to other member states. This might have happened directly through an explosive surge of interest rates on government bonds and, in the case of highly indebted countries, the complete loss of access to the financial markets. More indirectly, contagion could have also taken place through the banking crisis that would have followed once the sovereign debt crisis had spread beyond Greek borders. In this case the governments would have been forced to bail out their banks, thereby accumulating huge amounts of public debt, which in turn would have worsened the banks' balance sheets even more ("vicious circle" or

[9] Translated by the author from the original: "Nein, es gab keinen Trigger-Moment. Ausschlaggebend waren Griechenlands Bereitschaft zu einem entsprechenden Programm und Deutschlands Bereitschaft zur tatsächlichen Finanzhilfe. Beides war möglich weil das der letzte Moment war."

"doom loop"). Further attacks by the financial markets accompanied by negative self-fulfilling market sentiments would have only come on top. Thus, already at the European Council of 10 and 11 December 2009, "everybody was aware that Greece's difficulties constituted a threat to the euro area as a whole" (Ludlow 2010a: 9; also Interviews 1, 5, 8, 11, 25, 26).[10]

This assessment was corroborated by the short-term development of eurozone government bond spreads at the time. Government bond spreads partly reflect the perceived fragmentation risk of the eurozone in case of non-action: the higher the spreads, the stronger the expectation that single member states will default on their debt and, in case of status quo, redenominate and leave the eurozone. Therefore, government bond spreads can be used as a proxy for status quo costs in the eurozone crisis. As can be seen from Fig. 4.1, since October 2009 the spread between Greek and German bonds had been dramatically increasing. Ever since the introduction of the common currency, this was a phenomenon unheard of. Moreover, given that the eurozone members, and in particular Germany, did not commit themselves to assist each other in case of need, also Portuguese, Italian, and Spanish bonds yields started to increase in relation to German bond interests. Thus, by the beginning of 2010, status quo costs had reached unprecedented levels in the eurozone.

Apart from the economic consequences, there was the fear that a Greek default accompanied by the country's exit from the eurozone could become a precedent as regards the irrevocability of EMU (Ardagna and Caselli 2014: 297). The underlying idea is that the common currency is not just an economic project, but another crucial step of European integration with historical and political implications. Thus, the ultimate rationale of EMU is not only economic prosperity, but peace and stability in Europe. A failure of this project could be a precedent with regard to other integration projects that so far have never been contested. In the most extreme case, it was feared that a failure of EMU could ultimately result in the failure of European integration as such. As German Chancellor Merkel put it at a later point in the crisis: "I have chosen for Europe and the euro, and thus for Greece [...] If the euro

[10]This is also shown by the fact that the German Ministry of Finance was "cluttered" at the time with policy proposals outlining alternatives to the existing Monetary Union, such as a split into a northern and a southern eurozone (Interview 26).

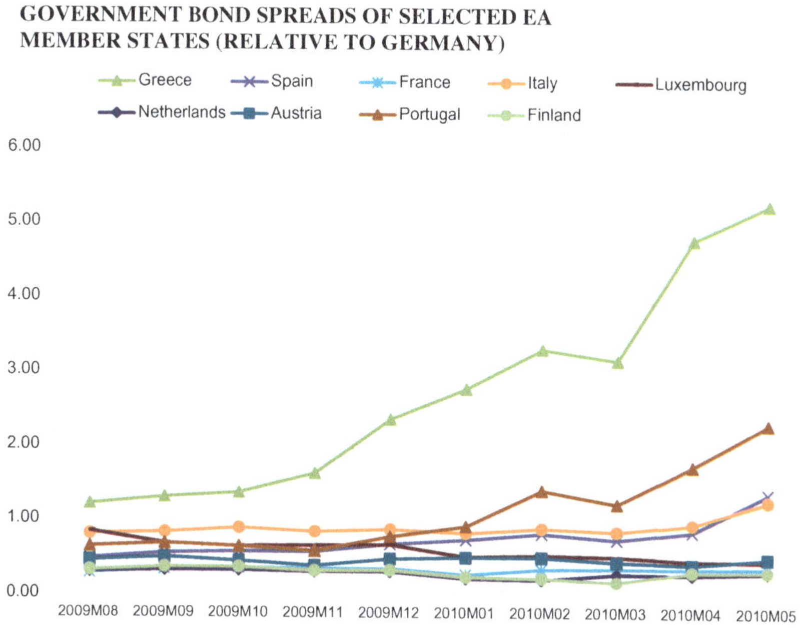

Fig. 4.1 Government bond spreads relative to German bond yields, August 2009–May 2010 (*Source* Eurostat)

falls, then Europe falls" (Spiegel 2014). Hence, the status quo costs were extraordinarily high, which, according to our second theoretical proposition (H2) should lead to a strong demand for leadership. However, given that there was no offer (see above), the result was a "leadership vacuum".

Results

Although only one of the two theoretical propositions could be assessed on the basis of the congruence method (H1), the theoretical model appears plausible since it can deliver an explanation as to why Germany did not emerge as a leader in the case of the first Greek bailout. The high costs caused by the status quo created a demand for leadership with regard to a swift bailout of Greece. Given that Germany would have to shoulder the biggest share of this bailout, it was the most powerful actor and thus the most likely leadership candidate. While it was beyond doubt that Germany would ultimately have to agree to some kind of bailout in order to preserve the common currency, it could either wait until the very last moment before a Greek default ("politics of ultima ration") or take the lead by moving first and shaping a bailout closer to the Pareto frontier. Although the latter option would have produced a collectively better outcome (see below), it would have been further away from Germany's individual preferences. Therefore, as predicted by the rationalist model of this book, Germany decided not to take the lead, thereby leaving the eurozone worse off.

Thus, this case study corroborates the basic assumption that leadership functions as a solution to collective action problems. Given that Germany did not emerge as a leader, we would expect only a suboptimal solution. Indeed, this can be clearly seen by the fact that the bailout came too late: when it finally took place, the crisis had already spread to Portugal and Spain, and the markets' confidence into Greece's long-term solvency could not be restored anymore. In addition, it is highly plausible that an earlier and thereby more generous programme for Greece would have led to a collectively better outcome for the entire eurozone. As for instance Ardagna and Caselli argue:

> this was a political-economy equilibrium in the sense that, for each of its signatories, it was *individually rational* to agree to it. [...]. However, this does not necessarily mean that the agreement of May 2010 was the best possible deal available to European leaders, or that it was *collectively rational.* We speculate that a program more generous towards Greece, particularly one that gave Greece more time before having to return to borrowing on private markets, might have made everyone better off. (2014: 292)

According to this argument, leadership in the form of an early commitment by Germany to support Greece would have resulted in a collectively better outcome. While Germany might have set a precedent which would have pushed it closer to the feared role of the eurozone's "lender of last resort", the contagion risk for the rest of the eurozone and the enduring recession in many southern member states could have been restrained. Thus, although Germany as a single actor would have been worse off, the eurozone as a whole would have profited if Germany had taken the lead.

4.2 Failed Leadership: The Super-Commissioner

In the case of the "super-commissioner" proposal, Germany emerged as a leader, but failed to influence the outcomes in the desired way. The benefits a super-commissioner would have brought Germany as a "creditor state", together with the persistently high status quo costs in the eurozone, can explain Germany's emergence as a leader. As regards its impact, Germany's leadership failure can be traced back to the unfavourable preference constellation and the high institutional constraint, which consisted in a treaty change. The following section describes the case of the super-commissioner and singles out the relevant actors and their preferences. After that, both *explananda*—Germany's emergence as a leader as well as its (lack of) impact—are assessed. The subsequent sections explain the outcome (failed leadership) by examining the respective explanatory factors and tracing the causal mechanisms. The last section draws the conclusions of this case study.

Case Description: Promoting the Super-Commissioner

In autumn 2011, the Dutch government suggested a considerable empowerment of the European Commissioner for Economic and Monetary Affairs (at the time Olli Rehn) as a measure to overcome the crisis. This idea was coined "super-commissioner" or "budget-tsar". The proposal was supported by the German government and most notably by its Finance Minister Schäuble (Interview 11; Spiegel and Schäuble 2011). However, although Rehn's position was slightly strengthened, the crucial features of the plan, namely full discretion in the College of Commissioners and a veto on national budgets, were not realised.[11]

In the beginning of October 2012, Schäuble therefore started a new initiative with the same demands. After bilateral talks with his Dutch colleague Jan Kees de Jager, who had made the original proposal in 2011, Schäuble presented the idea to the media and mentioned it repeatedly in the Eurogroup meetings at the time (Euractiv 2012b; Interviews 2, 7, 8, 11, 13, 25). In doing so, the German Finance Minister represented the German government and was clearly backed by Chancellor Merkel. However, after Commission President Barroso at the European Council of 18 and 19 October 2012 publically declared that he had already done

[11] See also Schäuble (2014) and Lamers and Schäuble (2014).

everything which could be done without Treaty change to strengthen the Economic and Monetary Commissioner, the idea was quietly abandoned again (see section 'Failed Leadership' below).

As opposed to other proposals in crisis management, the super-commissioner idea did not originate from the European institutions, but was developed in the Dutch (and later also German) Finance Ministry. The proposal was discussed internally in the Eurogroup and at the European Council and Euro Summits as well as in the form of a public debate. Although the member states were thus the key players in this case, the Commission played a prominent role in both the internal and the public debate. On the one hand, the proposed changes directly concerned the institutional structure of the Commission, which is why its reaction to the proposal got immediate public attention (e.g. Bohne 2012; Riegert 2012; Spiegel 2012b). On the other hand, the Commission was crucial in the internal debate, too, because it had the necessary expertise with regard to the legal requirements and the feasibility of the proposed changes. To a lesser extent, also the opinions of ECB and EP played a role in the public debate (*Telegraph* 2012). The preferences of these actors differed considerably, though. While the northern "creditor states" strongly supported the idea, southern member states preferred the status quo or a super-commissioner in conjunction with further risk-sharing mechanisms such as Eurobonds (see Sects. 5.1 and 5.2). While the Commission strongly rejected the proposal, the ECB was clearly in favour of it (see below).

Failed Leadership

The *explanandum* of the model's first analytical step is the emergence of political leadership. This is given if there is (1) a common goal and (2) an actor in a positon of power who (3) uses her resources to guide a group towards the achievement of this common goal. In the context of eurozone crisis management, the common goal consisted in overcoming the crisis and preserving the common currency. Given that a common goal is always subjective, a leader can invoke the notion of a common goal by framing a proposal as a measure to overcome the crisis (Sect. 2.1). Indeed, Germany presented the super-commissioner proposal as an anti-crisis measure and a way to stabilize the common currency. Regarding the second criterion, Germany was also in an ideal position to take the lead in this issue, being the eurozone's most powerful member state (see below).

With regard to the third indicator for leadership emergence (use of strategies), the German government employed a twofold approach: internally, it interacted with other member states "behind closed doors"; externally, it used the media to promote the idea publically. German Finance Minister Schäuble coordinated the German initiative in bilateral talks with his Dutch colleague Jan Kees de Jager (Interview 11). This type of coalition-building ahead of multilateral negotiations or discussions is a typical leadership strategy (see Sect. 3.3). Moreover, Schäuble promoted the super-commissioner proposal *vis-à-vis* his other eurozone colleagues and the presidents of Commission, European Council, Eurogroup, and ECB (Böll 2012). Next to all relevant EU fora, the idea was primarily promoted in the Eurogroup. As an eye witness of the Eurogroup meetings stated:

> It was more Mr Schäuble saying it from time to time in the Eurogroup. [...] As a politician he has learned [...] that by simply repeating something, especially if you are a powerful politician, [...] it develops a life of its own and gets on to other people's agendas. (Interview 13)

Externally, Germany used the press as a "multiplier" of the super-commissioner idea. Due to the resistance faced in the Eurogroup, not least by then President Juncker, the media were considered the "only effective channel" by some officials in the German government (Interviews 11, 25). This strategy is part of what has been conceptualized as the provision of common knowledge (Sect. 3.3).

Although the super-commissioner initiative was primarily driven by Schäuble, there was no doubt that he represented the German government in doing so. The German Finance Minister was explicitly backed by the Chancellor who advocated the proposal herself at the European Council of 18 and 19 October 2012 (Interview 2; BBC 2012; Böll 2012; Euractiv 2012b; Spiegel 2012b; Tagesschau 2012). However, the German government did not engage in the more expensive employment of negotiations strategies, because it anticipated that there would be "a very significant counter-price paid" (Interview 10; also Interviews 13, 27). Instead, Germany restricted itself to the provision of common knowledge and thus provided a "light version" of leadership, which did not exploit the entire spectrum of leadership strategies.

The *explanandum* of the second analytical step is the impact of leadership. It is conceptualized as a continuous variable ranging from the absence to the full realisation of the desired leader-initiated policy or institutional change. Although Schäuble's proposal was even mentioned in the European Commission's "Blueprint for a Deep and Genuine Economic and Monetary Union" (2012: 38f.), the super-commissioner saga is "a case of attempted, but ultimately unsuccessful, institutional change" (Karagiannis and Guidi 2014: 177). The trigger point for abandoning the idea was Commission President Barroso's statement at the European Council of 18 and 19 October that without Treaty change nothing else can be done to further strengthen the position of the Economic and Monetary Commissioner. In anticipation of these institutional requirements, combined with the high counter-price demanded by the southern member states (see below), Germany stopped the initiative before it could come to an open defeat.

In sum, Germany provided a "light" version of leadership: it emerged as a leader, but restricted itself to the provision of common knowledge, thereby avoiding the more expensive employment of negotiation strategies; as regards the impact, Germany failed as a leader: the government abandoned its initiative because it anticipated a politically costly defeat.

Explaining Germany's Leadership Emergence: Leadership Surplus and Status Quo Costs

The first variable accounting for the emergence of leadership is the expected surplus of a leadership candidate, which consists of the expected costs and benefits of leading. As pointed out by Schimmelfennig (2015), there are two ideal-typical options how to distribute the adjustment costs caused by the common goal of preserving the euro and overcoming the crisis: first, the adjustment costs can be allocated nationally through fiscal restraint in the highly indebted states ("austerity"); second, they can be allocated at the European level through the mutualisation of risk or debt ("solidarity"). Thus, the more an outcome of EU crisis management shifts the adjustment costs towards the "debtor states" (e.g. by implying austerity measures), the more beneficial this is for the "creditor states". *Vice versa*, the more of these adjustment costs are allocated at the European level (e.g. through common funds), the more costly it is for states like Germany.

Therefore, the most obvious benefit Germany would have if it managed to lead the other member states towards the establishment of a super-commissioner would be a further institutionalization of fiscal discipline in the eurozone. A commissioner with particular discretion within the *College* of Commissioners and a real veto-right over national budgets would considerably strengthen the enforcement of the SGP and thereby foster national consolidation (instead of mutualising debt or stimulating growth). As a result, the adjustment costs of the eurozone crisis would be further allocated to the debtor states. A feature which was emphasized in particular by German government officials is the intended effectiveness of such a commissioner: by enabling a "more *effective* control over fiscal sinners"[12] (Interview 25), the super-commissioner would be an "*effective* means to consolidate national budgets"[13] (Interview 27).

A second benefit, which Germany expected from a super-commissioner, was a calming effect on the financial markets contributing to the stabilization of the eurozone. As market players would understand the super-commissioner as a means to make sure that single member states keep solid budgets and thereby remain capable of paying back their debts, government bond spreads and fragmentation risks in the eurozone would be expected to decline. Finally, the proposal would have added to Schäuble's pro-European agenda and received electoral approval at home (Interviews 8, 25, 27).

As regards Germany's costs of leading, instead, there was a large consensus among the interviewees that there were no relevant costs. This is mainly because the German government never committed itself to any concessions in exchange for the other member states' approval of the super-commissioner. Only one interviewee mentioned that Schäuble's proposal led to an internal debate in the government and the Christian Democratic party (CDU), where certain groups rejected a further conferral of national competences to the European level (Interview 2).

As elaborated in Sect. 3.4, a cost-benefit analysis is possible if there are either no significant costs or no benefits. As can clearly be seen from Table 4.2, this applies to the super-commissioner case. Germany's benefits of leading clearly outweighed the costs, which resulted in a leadership surplus. According to our first theoretical proposition (H1), we therefore expect Germany to offer leadership and, under the condition that there was a demand for it, to emerged as a leader.

[12] Translated by the author from the original: "effektivere Kontrolle über Fiskalsünder".

[13] Translated by the author from the original: "effektives Mittel zur Haushaltskonsolidierung".

Table 4.2 Germany's costs and benefits of leading according to interviewees (super-commissioner)

Interview	*Benefits*	*Costs*
1, 25, 26, 27	Institutionalization of fiscal discipline	
8, 27	Calming financial markets/Stabilizing euro area	
8, 25	Realization of Schäuble's pro-European agenda	
8	Electoral approval	
2		Internal debate?

Source Own compilation

The confidence in this explanation can be further strengthened by evidence for the underlying causal mechanism. Thus, with regard to the supply of leadership, we should find expressions that emphasize the leader's preferences for changing the status quo in such a way that the aggregate costs of the entire group would be reduced (Sect. 3.2). In other words, the alleged leader should frame the proposed institutional innovation as something all parties involved would ultimately profit from, thereby invoking the notion of a common goal. While such evidence cannot eliminate alternative explanations, it increases our confidence that the explanation based on the leader's surplus (H1) is actually valid. By contrast, if we do not find any such evidence, this would eliminate our hypothesis ("hoop test"; see Collier 2011).

Germany has always presented the super-commissioner as a way of preserving the common currency and overcoming the crisis. Thus, when Schäuble made the proposal public, this was perceived as a German "master plan for the euro" (Böll 2012). Both German Chancellor Merkel and her Finance Minister Schäuble emphasized that this would be a necessary step "in the direction of a fiscal union" and a "lasting solution" (Euractiv 2012b). Moreover, Schäuble framed the proposal as a chance for the entire eurozone that must be used. As his spokesman said: "A strengthened currency commissioner could stand for greater confidence in the implementation of measures and greater confidence in the euro zone itself" (Euractiv 2012b). Also the German Chancellor presented the proposal as a chance to increase the markets' confidence in the common currency and thus to provide for financial stability in the eurozone. She therefore expressed incomprehension about the other member states' reluctance when reporting to the German Parliament on this: "This is not how we build a credible Europe" (BBC 2012). A leading official in the Treasury even described the proposal as a "guarantee" for other member states, that also in the future when powerful countries like Germany might have incentives not to comply with the SGP anymore, there would be an apolitical supranational body to enforce the common rules. Moreover, he named stability in the eurozone and the consolidation of national budgets as expected consequences of a super-commissioner from which every member would profit in the long run (Interview 27).

Next to a leader's surplus, also the status quo costs suffered by the entire group account for the emergence of leadership (H2). When Schäuble revisited the Dutch proposal of a super-commissioner in October 2012, the peak of the eurozone crisis was already overcome. One month earlier, the ECB had presented its "Outright Monetary Transactions", with the effect that government bond spreads decreased and speculations about a collapse of the eurozone came to an end (Sect. 5.3). However, in autumn 2012, actors were not yet aware that the peak of the crisis might already have been overcome. The announcement of Outright Monetary Transactions was perceived as an attempt to buy time for member state reforms and a further enhancement of the eurozone's institutional framework. Thus, the effect of the ECB's measures was perceived as temporary and contingent on the willingness of governments to implement structural reforms at home and undertake common steps at the European level (e.g. banking union). Although the perceived pressure for action was therefore not as high as in the preceding summer, there was little confidence that the measures already taken would actually suffice. Thus, the actors involved still considered themselves to be in a crisis and the perceived status quo costs were relatively high (Interview 6).

This assessment is confirmed by the development of government bond spreads at the time (Fig. 4.2). While the effect of the ECB's announcement of Outright Monetary Transactions in July 2012 is clearly visible, the spreads (and thus the perceived fragmentation risk) were almost as high as in the months before when Schäuble presented the super-commissioner proposal in October 2012. Moreover, they were still much higher than before the sovereign debt crisis had started by the end of 2009. In line with the second theoretical proposition of the model (H2), we would therefore expect that there was a high demand for leadership and, under the condition that Germany as the most powerful actor offered leadership, it emerged as a political leader.

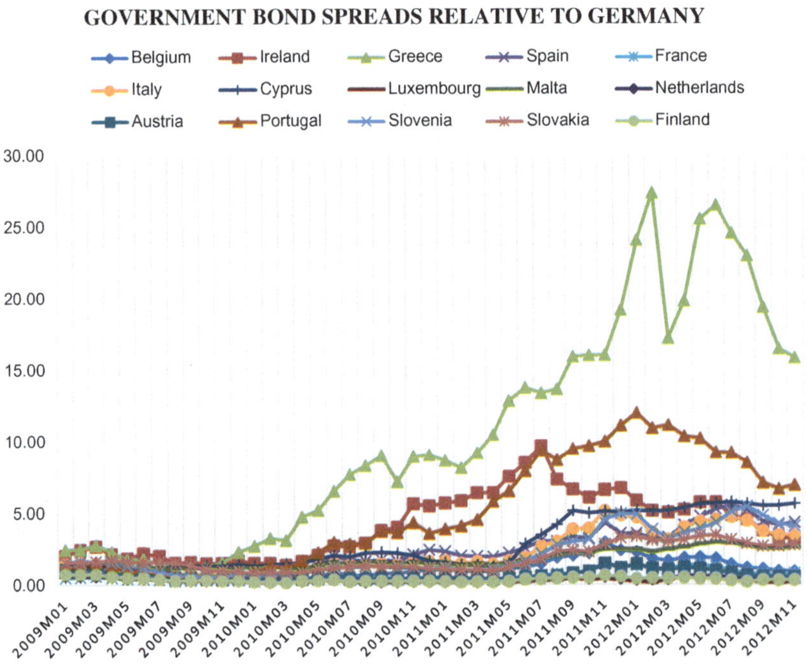

Fig. 4.2 Government bond spreads relative to German bond yields, January 2009–November 2012 (*Source* Eurostat [own illustration])

Also this second theoretical proposition can be corroborated further with process-tracing evidence. While on the side of the leader we search for expressions in favour of changing the status quo to the benefit of the entire group, on the side of the followers we should find evidence that they perceived the offer of leadership and that at least some of them objected to it. Again, such evidence cannot eliminate alternative explanations, but as it does increase our confidence in the underlying hypothesis. By contrast, evidence that all potential followers agreed on Germany's proposal ex ante would disconfirm our explanation.

Evidence for the expected causal mechanism was given by the German Chancellor herself when she complained in front of the German Parliament that "some EU member states were not ready for such a step" (BBC 2012). When the French President Hollande was interviewed ahead of the European Council in October 2012, he was well aware of the German proposal, but he directly rejected it as a "topic [which] is not on the agenda" (BBC 2012). Also the Italian Prime Minister Mario Monti rejected the idea, arguing that by proposing always new proofs of fiscal discipline, one would leave the impression to the markets that the already existing instruments do not work. Also Spanish Prime Minister Rajoy said that he was against the proposal. He added that the super-commissioner would only have a chance if it were part of a larger package deal on a closer eurozone union. After a pre-summit lunch of leaders affiliated to the European Socialists (PES), including among others the Prime Ministers of France, Denmark, and Slovakia, the leader of the EP group of Socialists and Democrats, Hannes Swoboda, said that they were united against the German proposal of a super-commissioner (Euractiv 2012a, b, c). The Commission rejected Schäuble's proposal, too (Spiegel 2012b; Interviews 7, 27). However, a few actors perceived the German proposal as a step towards the common goal of stabilizing the Eurozone. Most prominently, ECB President Mario Draghi backed Schäuble's proposal by stating: "I am certain: if we want to restore confidence in the eurozone, countries will have to transfer part of their sovereignty to the European level" (*Telegraph* 2012).

In sum, the first step of the leadership model can plausibly explain Germany's emergence in the case of the super-commissioner. Against the background of relatively high status quo costs (H2), Germany emerged as a leader because its expected benefits—primarily the institutionalization of fiscal discipline and the allocation of adjustment costs at the national level—clearly outweighed the costs, which, due to Germany's limited commitment, were virtually inexistent (H1). Both theoretical propositions passed a congruence test and are corroborated by additional evidence on the underlying causal mechanisms. Still, the emergence of a leader is not sufficient for her impact. The following section will therefore explain the failure of Germany's leadership attempt.

Explaining Germany's Leadership Failure: Resources, Preferences and Institutional Constraint

According to the theoretical model, the first variable which accounts for a leader's impact are her power resources (H3). They are differentiated into material, institutional, and ideational resources. While most of the literature has put emphasis on Germany's economic resources in the context of eurozone crisis management, few accounts consider also institutional or ideational resources (Krotz and Schild 2013: 22–9; Matthjis 2016b: 140–3).

The most important economic indicator for Germany's position of power in the eurozone is its aggregate GDP. The size of a member state's economy determines its capacity to contribute to financial stability in the eurozone. In 2011,[14] Germany's GDP amounted to 2699bn euro, or 27.7% of the entire eurozone's GDP, and was thus the largest GDP of the eurozone. However, in the context of a sovereign debt crisis, not only the overall size of member state's economy, but also its credibility in the financial markets and thus its refinancing options play an important role. Also on this score, Germany ranked first among all eurozone members. With an average interest rate of 2.61% on 10 years government bonds in 2011, and a constantly falling trend at the time, Germany paid the lowest interest rates in the eurozone. Also as regards the member states' current account balance, which is not only an indicator for an economy's overall performance, but also for its savings potential, Germany ran the biggest surplus in absolute terms. Finally, gross public debt is an important indicator since it reflects a country's long-term solvency. Although Germany's government debt in 2011 amounted to 77.9% of its GDP and was thus considerably higher than the Maastricht criterion of 60%, it was still lower than the Eurozone's average public debt of 86.0% (Table 4.3).

A leader's power resources must be assessed in relation to those of the other actors (Sect. 3.4). One way of assessing Germany's material resources as compared to those of the EU institutions, is to compare the available budgetary capacities the respective state or institution can deploy to influence the eurozone's economic governance. In October 2012, Germany was exposed to Greece through the Greek loan facility with 15,165bn euro (Dor 2015) and to Greece and other eurozone members through the EFSF with 54,448bn euro (EFSF 2011, 2015). Moreover, Germany subscribed to 190,025bn euro of the European Stability Mechanism (ESM), which was established in September 2012 (ESM 2012, Appendix II). In total, Germany's actual commitment to EMU amounted to 259,638bn euro.

[14] Data from 2011 is most appropriate because these are the figures that were known at the time of Germany's super-commissioner initiative.

Table 4.3 Indicators for Germany's economic power (2011)

	GDP		*Government bond yields*	*Current account balance*		*Public debt*
	Million EUR	*% of EU-17*	*%*	*Million EUR*	*% of GDP*	*% of GDP*
Germany	**2,699,100**	**27.7**	**2.61**	**164,550**	6.1	77.9
France	2,059,284	21.1	3.32	−21,245	−1.0	85.2
Italy	1,638,857	16.8	5.42	−50,387	−3.1	116.4
Spain	1,075,147	11.0	5.44	−34,040	−3.2	69.2
Netherlands	642,929	6.6	2.99	58,579	**9.1**	61.3
Belgium	379,915	3.9	4.23	−4067	−1.1	102.0
Austria	308,675	3.2	3.32	5058	1.6	82.1
Greece	207,752	2.1	15.75	−20,634	−9.9	171.3
Finland	196,869	2.0	3.01	n/a	n/a	48.5
Portugal	176,167	1.8	10.24	−10,616	−6.0	111.1
Ireland	171,042	1.8	9.60	n/a	n/a	111.2
Slovakia	70,160	0.7	4.45	−3497	−5.0	43.4
Luxembourg	42,410	0.4	2.92	2461	5.8	19.1
Slovenia	36,868	0.4	4.97	84	0.2	46.5
Cyprus	19,487	0.2	5.79	n/a	n/a	66.0
Estonia	16,404	0.2	n/a	222	1.4	**6.0**
Malta	6903	0.1	4.49	n/a	n/a	69.7
Euro Area (EU-17)	***9,748,036***	***100.0***	***4.34***	***n/a***	***n/a***	***86.0***

Source Eurostat (own compilation)

The Commission does not have a budget which it could deliberately use to influence crisis management. However, through the European Financial Stabilisation Mechanism (EFSM) it can raise 60bn euro on the financial markets in order to lend assistance to eurozone members in financial difficulties (European Commission 2015). The EP, in contrast, has neither budgetary capacities to influence crisis management, nor does it have any control over the funds provided by the member states. Finally, the ECB's material capacity to influence economic and monetary policy in the eurozone is theoretically unlimited. Although this material capacity is strictly limited by the ECB's mandate, it still exceeds the budgetary resources Germany could mobilize (Sect. 5.3). In sum, Germany's economic resources exceeded those of all other member states as well as those of the Commission and the EP. Only the ECB had even more material capacities.

The second type of power resources are institutional resources. They comprise an actor's legislative and executive competences, such as agenda-managing, voting- and veto-rights, and rights of implementation. In the EU polity, the official forum where Germany exercises its institutional power, is the Council of Ministers. In economic governance, the respective configuration is the ECOFIN Council which formally decides by qualified majority and, if it comes to fiscal matters, by unanimity. The corresponding configuration for the euro area is the Eurogroup, but formal voting on Eurogroup decisions takes place in the ECOFIN Council under exclusion of non-eurozone member states. In 2012, Qualified Majority Voting (QMV) based on the Treaty of Nice was still in place. According to this voting system, Germany had 29 out of a total of 345 voting weights. Thereby Germany's voting weight corresponded to 8.4% of all votes and to 31.9% of the blocking minority. In terms of population, which also played a role in order to pass a decision, Germany had the biggest share of circa 16.5% (of 62% needed). However, in the ECOFIN Council "there is a strong sense to come to joint, common solutions" (Interviews 15). Not least due to its economic resources, Germany thus enjoyed a de facto veto in the ECOFIN Council and the Eurogroup. As one high-level official in Brussels put it: "Germany practically has a veto on whatever is happening at present. And if they don't like it, they don't take it. So you need to rewrite, and rewrite, and rewrite, until the Germans are in agreement" (Interview 13; also Interviews 10, 11).

In spite of its de facto veto, Germany's shaping power in the eurozone should not be overrated. Firstly, many decisions of EU crisis management were made outside the Council. Secondly, in the case of OLP, the additional participation of Commission and EP diminishes the significance of a member state's institutional resources within the Council. Thirdly, many other factors that go beyond the formal competences of single member states determine decision-making in the Council. For instance, the work of preparatory bodies, pre-negotiations among single member states, preferences of the Council Presidency, mutual anticipation of voting behaviour, side-payments and package-deals lead to decisions that do not merely reflect formal voting rights. In sum, if it comes to the shaping of new policies or rules, Germany had only few institutional resources in the eurozone. Only if it comes to the prevention of certain decisions, Germany could rely on its de facto veto ("Germany was often saying 'no'", Interview 10). This permits to avoid unpleasant decisions, but as regards policy or institutional change, it enables only little more than agreements on the lowest common denominator.

Finally, a leader can draw on ideational resources. A proxy for Germany's information and expertise is the number of the administrative staff who works primarily and specifically in the area of European economic governance (including fiscal or budgetary matters). According to the written answers of the German Chancellery and Treasury on respective requests from June 2015, the *German government* employs a total of *117* staff members dealing with issues of European economic governance.[15] The *Commission's* DG ECFIN, in contrast, employs *391* staff members in its relevant directorates according to an information obtained from Europe Direct on 5 August and referring to July 2015. The *EP* communicated on 13 and 17 July 2015 that it has about *40* staff members closely dealing with the relevant issues in its Secretariat of the ECON Committee (~25) and the Economic Governance Support Unit (~15), ranging from Head of Unit to trainees. The EP emphasized in its answer that there are another 149 staff members employed in the Directorate for Economic and Scientific Policies, whose work is less closely related to the relevant issues, though, and that external services provide the EP with expertise. The *ECB*, finally, answered on 9 July 2015 that it employs *523* staff members in its relevant divisions.

Thus, taking the number of administrative staff as proxy, the ECB is the actor with most expertise if it comes to the eurozone's economic governance. The figures were strongly corroborated by the interviews. Based on its generally acknowledged expertise, the ECB has assumed the role of an advisory body for member states and other EU institutions[16] (Interviews 14, 21, 22, 24). Besides the ECB, only the Commission with its thematic and geographical units has both the legitimacy and the technical means to provide the latest facts and figures about the situation in single member states, which are of extraordinary importance in the context of crisis management. Thus, while Germany has less informational resources than the ECB and the Commission, it has roughly the same resources as other member states, and clearly more than the EP.

[15]Information obtained from the Chancellery on 16 June and from the Treasury on 3 July 2015.

[16]As a background talk with a strongly involved ECB official revealed, for instance, it was the ECB which before the onset of the eurozone crisis alerted the Commission several times to disconcerting irregularities in the Greek data on sovereign debt and deficit.

Yet another ideational power resource is an actor's credibility. Being an actor pursuing national interests by nature, Germany's credibility cannot be as high as that of supranational institutions. As regards the Commission, it is in its own interest to preserve its role and reputation as an honest broker that can be trusted by the member states (Interview 17). In a similar vein, the EP is interested in preserving its role as promoter of the EU's common good representing all EU citizens. However, as compared to the Commission, the EP is more exposed to political pressures and thus less "technocratic". The ECB has an inherent interest to remain politically independent and, by fulfilling its primary objective of ensuring price stability, preserve its position as a provider of the common good in the Eurozone (Interviews 2, 5, 8, 13, 18, 20, 22). Thus, the innate institutional interests of all three bodies, Commission, EP, and ECB, provide them with a degree of credibility which is necessarily higher than that of any member state.

As compared to other member states, however, Germany enjoyed relatively high credibility. There are two different sources of this credibility. First, Germany's solid economic and fiscal position serves as a source of credibility as "it is the interest of the other member states to borrow from the credibility of Germany in the capital markets" (Interview 15). A second type of credibility derives from the strong position of the German Parliament (*Bundestag*) and Constitutional Court (*Bundesverfassungsgericht*). The fact that on many issues the German government depends on the approval of its parliament and court functions as credible commitment and thus strengthens Germany's position in Eurozone negotiations (see Bulmer 2014; Bulmer and Paterson 2013: 1398f.). As a German government official put it: "The others were sick of hearing the word 'Karlsruhe',[17] although it was not used explicitly [as bargaining chip]"[18] (Interview 25). In sum, due to the roles of the German Parliament and Constitutional Court, Germany's bargaining position was more credible than that of most other member states.

What applies to Germany's credibility, also applies to its legitimacy. On the one hand, Germany's legitimacy to direct EU crisis management has generally been perceived as lower than that of the supranational

[17] Karlsruhe is the city where the Federal Constitutional Court is located and has thus become a synonym for the Court.

[18] Translated by the author from the original: "Die andern konnten das Wort 'Karlsruhe' nicht mehr hören, auch wenn es nicht explizit eingesetzt wurde".

institutions, which had been established precisely for such purposes and, as opposed to Germany, are regarded as primarily interested in the common good of the Eurozone (Interview 13, 17). On the other hand, Germany is perceived to have the biggest claim to a hearing among the member states because of its economic weight (Interview 2). As German Finance Minister Schäuble once admitted: "At some Council meetings I ask myself, why is it always me who should speak first. Also the others could begin once in a while [...]" (Spiegel and Schäuble 2011).

In sum, Germany scores highest on economic resources. Only the ECB possessed even more material capacity. As regards its institutional resources, however, Germany is much weaker: While enjoying a de facto veto based on its economic resources and the (informal) decision-making rules in economic governance, the eurozone's biggest economy lacks institutional shaping power. With regard to Germany's ideational resources, the assessment is mixed. Germany has roughly the same information and expertise as other member states, but less than the Commission and the ECB. Although its credibility and legitimacy is higher than that of other member states, it cannot reach the EU institutions in that regard. Germany is thus clearly the most powerful member state, but its position is not dominating (see Janning 2013).[19] Nevertheless, Germany's position of power in the eurozone is unprecedented. As one EU official put: "One country leading so much at the back is something which is new by EU standards" (Interview 17). This assessment is shared by the German government officials themselves: "Germany has become the hegemon of Europe – what we never wanted to be"[20] (Interview 26). The reason for this new role in Europe is not only seen in Germany itself, but also in the apparent weakness or passiveness of other member states (see Matthijs 2016b: 137).

[19] This assessment is confirmed by Janning's "power calculator", according to which Germany scores highest with 60 points, but is closely followed by France (53) and Italy (43). The index includes indicators which go beyond the three categories considered by the present work. It comprises size of population, contribution to EU budget, military strength, status in international affairs, geographic location, net contribution position, opt-outs (Schengen, EMU), good governance, capacity for coalition building, and public opinion (Janning 2013: 7–9).

[20] Translated by the author from the original: "Deutschland ist zum Hegemon Europas geworden – was wir nie sein wollten".

This regards, first of all, France, which from a German perspective "fail[ed] completely" (Interview 15) in the eurozone crisis. According to some senior EU officials, this had (inter-)personal reasons. First, the French and German Ministers of Finance, Christine Lagarde and Wolfgang Schäuble, collaborated very well until Lagarde took up the post as Managing Director of the IMF in July 2011. The collaboration with her successors, especially with socialist Pierre Moscovici was less successful, though (Interview 2). The same is said about German Chancellor Angela Merkel and the French Presidents: while the collaboration with former President Sarkozy worked very well, even earning them the nickname "Merkozy", the relationship with his successor François Hollande was described as a failure (Interview 10). Other interviewees, in contrast, stressed domestic problems as reason for France's lack of power (Interview 15). In particular, political weakness to reform, economic weakness to enhance growth and competitiveness, and, as a consequence, financial weakness to consolidate the national budget, were mentioned in this context (Interviews 25, 26).

Also other member states contributed to Germany's position of power through their own weakness. As regards Italy, former President Silvio Berlusconi, who resigned in November 2011, and the traditionally unstable political system are seen as reasons for its weakness at the European level. Spain was in a weak position because of its own financial problems, for which it had to accept a bailout programme. The UK, finally, assumed an outsider role not only because it was not a eurozone member, but also because of the strong Eurosceptical tendencies at home. Although a Eurosceptical attitude at home does not automatically weaken a member state's power, the UK remained virtually "absent from the debate" (Interview 2).

Hence, a differentiated empirical analysis reveals that Germany's score on the variable "power resources" is located in the upper range of variation, but not at its upper extreme. In none of the categories does Germany have the highest score of all actors involved. With regard to the theoretical model, this undistinguished value should have the effect that the other two variables' impact is more decisive. In other words, given that Germany's power resources are not so high that strategic and institutional obstacles could easily be wiped away, we expect that the distribution of preferences among the actors and/or the institutional constraint on the leader make the substantial difference with regard to the outcome.[21]

The model's second explanatory factor for a leader's impact is the distribution of preferences (H4). As outlined above, eurozone member state governments seek to distribute the adjustment costs of the crisis in such a way that their individual share is as small as possible. This means that "solvent northern countries prefer national adjustment [while] heavily indebted southern countries prefer mutualized adjustment" (Schimmelfennig 2015: 181). Given that the super-commissioner would be a tool to better enforce EMU's fiscal rules and thus ensure fiscal discipline, it would foster national adjustment in the primarily southern "debtor states", while reducing the risk of debt mutualisation for the "creditor states". A secondary cleavage separated those states principally in favour of further integration through treaty change from those unwilling to accept further losses of sovereignty (Interviews 2, 25).

As can be seen from Table 4.4, of the twelve eurozone member states on which empirical information could be gathered, only four were in favour of both fiscal restraint at the national level and further integration. These were also the states which, according to the interview material, were in favour of a super-commissioner. Thus, the preference distribution roughly represented the North-South cleavage between "creditor" and "debtor states" in the eurozone. Still, some member states like Finland, Ireland, or France were primarily against a super-commissioner because they felt that "having a supranational body or single politician governing over the public finances of member states is not something that [their] societies [were] ready to accept" (Interview 2).

France was most clearly opposed to the German proposal (Interviews 5, 25). But also the other two big eurozone members, Italy and Spain, were very sceptical, although rather because of their fiscal position than their sovereignty concerns. The only thing that could have changed their strategic preferences would have been a package deal including a shift of adjustment costs to the European level through

[21] Thus, the value of the independent variable is "neutral" with regard to a (dis)confirmation of the theoretical model: while the confidence in the theoretical proposition on power resources (H3) cannot be increased by means of the congruence method or process tracing (because the value on the independent variable is not perfectly congruent with the outcome), it does not diminish the plausibility of the causal model either.

Table 4.4 Preference distribution regarding the super-commissioner[a]

		Allocation of adjustment costs	
		National level (Austerity)	*European level (Solidarity)*
Further Integration	Pro	**Germany** Netherlands Austria Estonia	Portugal Cyprus[b]
	Contra	Finland	France Italy Spain Ireland Greece[b]

Source Own illustration
[a]No reliable information could be obtained on the preferences of Belgium, Slovakia, Luxembourg, Slovenia, and Malta
[b]The interview material does not provide evidence on this country in particular, but on a group of countries to which this country belongs

solidarity instruments such as a eurozone budget, a fiscal capacity, or the establishment of permanent transfer and insurance mechanisms. As a close observer put it:

> There is very little appetite in other countries for this. You can imagine how our French colleagues see this. And it will only fly if there is a very significant counter-price paid. But just to have the rigour without the incentives, I guess the Italians, the Frenchs, and others will not buy it. (Interview 10)

With regard to the smaller member states, Finland would have been in favour of a further institutionalisation of fiscal discipline in the eurozone. However, because of the right-wing faction in its parliament, the Finnish government was very sceptical towards further integration of national powers. Similarly, also the Irish government is normally very sceptical when it comes to further sharing of sovereignty because of "problems with its parliament" (Interview 25) and because EU treaty changes usually require amendments to the Irish constitution and thus a referendum. Portugal is usually not opposed to further integration, but due to its own financial problems it preferred the mutualisation of risk to national adjustment. Thus, only the Netherlands, Austria, and Estonia remained in Germany's camp in favour of a super-commissioner.

As regards the EU institutions, the Commission was most firmly against a super-commissioner as proposed by Schäuble, although it would have been in favour of getting more ex-ante influence on the shaping of national budgets. Thus, the Commission stuck with its official position that the topic was not on its agenda at the time (Interviews 10, 12). Even when journalists took the spokeswoman of the Commission by surprise asking her about Schäuble's proposal even before she had been informed about it, she replied that "[t]his is not an issue, which, as far as we're concerned, is something that is up for decision, or even central to the discussion this week" (Riegert 2012). When asked what the Commission's position would be if the topic came on the agenda, a high-ranking Commission official said this would depend on the bargaining context and the concrete institutional design. In other words, the Commission would make its position conditional on the package deal Germany would have to propose and on the competences that would be assigned to it (Interview 6).

Internally, the Commission was even more hostile towards Germany's proposal. According to a senior official in the German Treasury, the Commission rejected the idea out of hand, stating that it already had a "super-commissioner" as Olli Rehn had been made Vice-President and could decide discretionary as long as there was no written objection by his colleagues (Interview 27). This was confirmed by senior officials of the European Council and the Commission (Interviews 2, 7). A Commission official gave more detailed reasons for the Commission's attitude: Firstly, the Commission considered the idea as not suitable in terms of legitimacy as it was convinced that a super-commissioner would provoke further euro-scepticism. Secondly, in the light of the adopted "Sixpack-" and the initiated "Twopack" legislation and lowered market pressure at the time, the German proposal was perceived as redundant (Interview 2). There are two further possible reasons for the Commission's outright rejection of the idea. According to a German government official, the Commission was actually in favour of a super-commissioner because it would have implied a gain in power, but it did not want to take a stand for an unpopular issue (Interview 25). According to a Dutch official, by contrast, the resistance came directly from the Barroso cabinet because the President of the Commission feared to lose power himself by giving more competences to Olli Rehn (Interview 11).

The EP's approval depended on whether there would be a favourable deal for the major political groups (Interview 16). Thus, if the super-commissioner had been made accountable to the parliament, for instance, it would have been in favour. Accordingly, the EP's official statements were directly linked to its own role and the issue of accountability, as for instance in its resolution on the "Four Presidents Report": "the independent role of the European Commissioner for Economic and Monetary Affairs needs to be reinforced, accompanied by strong accountability mechanisms to both Parliament and the Council" (EP 2012). However, an involvement of the EP was never been part of Schäuble's proposal.

Thus, the ECB was Germany's only ally among the supranational institutions. Already one year before Schäuble's proposal, then ECB President Jean-Claude Trichet had suggested the more far-reaching idea of a European Finance Minister (Bohne 2012). Although the ECB did not adopt an official position since this would go beyond its mandate, almost all interviewees answered that the ECB was in favour of a super-commissioner. First, steps towards more fiscal integration are in the interest of the ECB because they provide more financial stability, enhance the efficacy of the ECB's monetary policy, and consolidate the eurozone and thus the ECB's raison d'être. For the same reason, the ECB is generally in favour of fiscal discipline in the member states and a rule-based approach to supervision. Given that a super-commissioner was seen by the ECB as an appropriate tool to enforce fiscal rules and, due to its discretion in the *College*, to provide more automaticity, the central bank was strongly in favour of the proposal (Interviews 18, 19, 21–24). After Schäuble had announced his plans in October 2012, ECB President Mario Draghi himself stated that he "completely supported" the idea (*Telegraph* 2012).

In sum, most actors preferred to have no super-commissioner. Only the ECB together with three of the "creditor states" (Netherlands, Austria, Estonia) supported the German initiative. With regard to a leader's impact on the outcomes, this is expected to be a rather unfavourable situation: if preferences converge on an outcome different from that preferred by the leader, we expect *ceteris paribus* a weak or no impact (H4, see Sects. 3.3 and 3.4). Thus, the value of the independent variable (unfavourable preference distribution) and the outcome (no institutional or policy change) are congruent.

The last variable accounting for a leader's impact is the institutional constraint. The Commission was clear on this point: "Within the

Commission, any steps designed to reinforce even further than today the position of the Vice President for Economic and Monetary Affairs and the euro, would require adaptations to the collegiality principle and, hence treaty changes" (European Commission 2012: 38). Thus, the realisation of a super-commissioner would not only require an amendment of the Commission's rules of procedure, but also an amendment of Article 250 TFEU (Interviews 1, 2, 13, 15, 25, 27). Given that EU treaty changes require unanimity, this is the highest institutional constraint possible apart from the interdiction of making a certain decision (Sect. 3.4). As Germany was not able to realise its goal, there is congruence between the value of the independent variable (high institutional constraint) and the outcome (no institutional or policy change).

Hence, following the propositions of the book's leadership model, Germany failed to establish a super-commissioner because most followers preferred a different outcome (H4) and the installation of such a commissioner would require treaty change (H5). We can increase our confidence in this explanation by searching for evidence for the underlying causal mechanism. If a leader faces diverging preferences under conditions of high institutional constraints (unanimity), she has basically two options: she can either compensate those who have other preferences or propose a solution from which everyone profits (Sect. 3.3).[22] Thus, if the preference distribution really prevented Germany from reaching its goal, we need to find evidence that Germany was either not willing or not able to compensate the others or to find a win-win solution. In other words, if we find that Germany could not or did not want to compensate the others or find a win-win solution, this necessarily implies that (1) the others did not want the super-commissioner as a solution (cause) and (2) Germany had no chance to reach its goal (effect). The same is true with regard to the theoretical proposition on institutional constraint. A high institutional constraint makes it more difficult to obtain the critical mass of followers (Sect. 3.3). Thus, if the institutional constraint really prevented Germany from realizing its proposal, we need to find evidence that Germany was either not willing or not able to compensate enough of the reluctant followers or, alternatively, to find a win-win solution.

[22]Coercion or blackmailing are no viable options for a leader as they contradict the defining criterion of a common goal (Sect. 2.1).

The available evidence indicates that Germany was not willing to compensate the reluctant member states, which indeed asked for a counter-price to be paid for the super-commissioner. However, there was "no real discussion" (Interview 10) on possible compensating measures Germany could offer. The most concrete counter-demand raised by the other member states was the introduction of Eurobonds (Interviews 25, 27). However, only a few months earlier, Merkel had unmistakeably declared that there would be no joint liability like Eurobonds "as long as I live"[23] (Spiegel 2012a). When the topic came up again in connection with Schäuble's super-commissioner proposal, his spokesman clearly reiterated that "Germany's opposition to euro bonds remains clear and has not changed" (Euractiv 2012b). Hence, Germany's unwillingness to offer a compensation, which due to the unfavourable preference distribution and the high institutional constraint would be as costly as Eurobonds, further confirms the theoretical model. When a leading official in the German Ministry of Finance was asked in spring 2015 why the idea of a super-commissioner had never been realised, he answered that, among other things, the counter-claim for Eurobonds was simply to high (Interview 27). Furthermore, two German government officials stated that the required Treaty change was the major obstacle to the super-commissioner proposal. In sum, the model passes the empirical plausibility test.

Results

The first step of the theoretical model can plausibly explain the emergence of Germany as a leader in the case of the super commissioner proposal. Both theoretical propositions (leader's surplus and status quo costs) pass the congruence test. Germany's benefits of leading—primarily the institutionalization of fiscal discipline and thus the allocation of adjustment costs at the national level—clearly outweighed the costs, which, due to Germany's limited commitment, were virtually inexistent. Also with regard to the second theoretical proposition we find congruence. Although the peak of the crisis was already overcome, the actors still perceived a high pressure for action. Thus, a demand for leadership action that would go beyond the measures already taken by the ECB

[23]Translated by the author from the original: "solange ich lebe".

was still present. Given that there was both a demand for leadership and a supply of it, the model can predict the actual outcome, namely the emergence of leadership. The confidence in this explanation is further strengthened by evidence which corroborates the underlying causal mechanism.

With regard to the second analytical step accounting for a leader's impact, we find perfect congruence for two of the three theoretical propositions: the unfavourable distribution of preferences and the high institutional constraint provide a plausible explanation as to why Germany could not achieve the desired institutional change of establishing a European super-commissioner. Although there is no perfect congruence in the case of the first proposition regarding a leader's power resources (if considered isolated), the model provides an explanation as to why Germany's leadership was unsuccessful. As Germany's power resources are relatively high, but not overwhelming as compared to those of the other actors, we would expect a strong impact only if the preference distribution and the institutional constraint are favourable from the leader's point of view. However, this was not the case with the super-commissioner: Germany was not willing to invest its resources in such a way as to overcome the high institutional constraint and the followers' resistance. As a result, the super-commissioner initiative failed.

The case study bears implications for a theory of political leadership. It shows that the emergence of leadership should be conceptualized as a continuum rather than a binary variable. A leader can decide how many resources she employs, and thus to what extent leading convenes. In the case of the super-commissioner, Germany provided only a "light version" of leadership and confined itself to the provision of common knowledge (instead of employing more expensive negotiation strategies). Pushing the issue further would have implied much bigger costs and, given that the German Finance Minister could easily anticipate these costs, the German government abandoned its leadership ambitions very quickly in this case.

4.3 Successful Leadership: The Fiscal Compact

In shaping the Fiscal Compact, Germany emerged as a leader and successfully influenced the outcomes. Given that there was a high demand for leadership at the time, based on unprecedented spreads in government bonds and the looming collapse of the eurozone, the German government's benefits of sending an effective signal to the financial markets and its voters outweighed the costs of leading. As regards the impact of leadership, the strategic preferences of the other actors facilitated the efforts of the German government, which managed to overcome the high institutional constraint (treaty change) by translating its power resources into classic leadership strategies. While the first section of this chapter is devoted to the description of the case and its relevant actors and preferences, the second section assesses the value of both *explananda*, which are a leader's emergence and her impact (successful leadership). After that, the respective explanatory factors and causal mechanisms are examined. The last section, finally, summarizes the results of this case study and draws conclusions on Germany's role in EMU.

Case Description: Shaping the Fiscal Compact

The Fiscal Compact (formally: "Treaty on Stability, Coordination and Governance in the Economic and Monetary Union") is an international treaty which was agreed upon at the European Council of 8/9 December, finalised and endorsed at the informal European Council of 30 January 2012, and formally signed on 2 March 2012 by all EU member states except the United Kingdom (UK) and the Czech Republic. Judged by EU standards, this is a case of extremely quick decision-making (Tsebelis and Hahm 2014: 1388) and thus well suited for the analysis of political leadership. The Fiscal Compact entered into force on 1 January 2013 and has been ratified by all 25 contracting parties since 1 April 2014.

The signatories commit themselves to a balanced budget. In order to reach that goal they agreed on an automatic correction mechanism anchored in their national law at a constitutional or equivalent level, which shall be triggered if a signatory breaches the agreed benchmark figures. While the principles of this correction mechanism shall be proposed by the Commission, independent national institutions monitor the compliance with the rules. If a signatory fails to implement the treaty provisions into national law, any other contracting party may bring the case to the European Court of Justice, which can impose financial sanctions. Moreover, if a member state is in breach of the agreed deficit criterion, the Commission can issue recommendations which are compulsory unless a majority against them can be mobilized in the Council ("Reversed Qualified Majority Voting"). Those contracting parties already subject to an excessive deficit procedure shall put in place a "budgetary and economic partnership programme" including structural reforms, which are to be endorsed and monitored by the Council and the Commission. Generally, signatories shall report their borrowing plans to Council and Commission. Finally, the granting of financial assistance by the ESM has been made conditional on the ratification of the Fiscal Compact, which within five years after its entry into force should be incorporated into EU law (Eurozone 2012).[24]

As compared to the already existing rules of the reformed SGP, the novelty of the Fiscal Compact consisted not so much in its substance as in the increase of "national ownership" of the rules: the treaty requires member states to transpose the provisions into national legislation and to monitor compliance through independent national institutions (Interviews 6, 10; Buti and Carnot 2012: 907f.). As regards the genesis of the Fiscal Compact, the interview data is contradictory concerning the question whether the idea originated with the ECB or the German Finance Ministry. However, there is a consensus that ECB President Mario Draghi publically coined the term "Fiscal Compact" by presenting the concept in an EP plenary speech, while Germany, and in particular the Chancellery, put the issue on the political agenda and pushed it through in the decision-making phase (Interviews 6, 8, 14, 19, 21, 27).

The central actors in shaping the agreement were the member states. Nevertheless, also the supranational institutions played a role as providers of expertise (ECB, Commission) and participants in the negotiations (Commission, EP). In particular the EP, which was represented by three of its members, did not stick to its formal role as an observer, but participated actively in the negotiations.[25] The actors involved had diverging preferences over outcomes. While Germany, the ECB, and

[24] On 6 December 2017, the European Commission presented a legislative proposal on how to integrate the Fiscal Compact into EU law.

[25] As a result, the EP obtained the so-called "repatriation clause", according to which the Treaty should be incorporated into EU law five years after its entry into force (Art. 16), the right to organize a conference on budgetary issues with national parliaments (Art. 13), and the right for non-Eurozone countries to participate in Euro Summits under certain circumstances (Art. 12.3) (Interviews 1, 6).

a few other member states preferred a Treaty change or a stand-alone treaty outside EU law, the Commission and EP preferred to integrate the Fiscal Compact in EU secondary law. A few member states, among them France and Italy, initially rejected the Fiscal Compact as such. However, once the issue had been put on the agenda (and linked to the ESM agreement), the strategic preferences did not diverge anymore with regard to the Fiscal Compact as such, but only with regard to single details of the treaty (Kreilinger 2012; see below).

Successful Leadership

As outlined in Sect. 3.4, leadership can be assessed by means of three indicators: (1) an actor in a positon of power, who guides a group towards (2) a common goal by (3) making appropriate use of its power resources. All these features apply to Germany's role in shaping the Fiscal Compact. As for instance Peter Ludlow put it with regard to role of the German chancellor in the treaty negotiations:

> The most striking feature of the discussions which preceded the January European Council was undoubtedly [...] the role played by the German Chancellor. This was her Council and Berlin became a focus of attention and activity on a scale which if not unprecedented was certainly unusual. (Ludlow 2012b: 7)

As regards the first feature of leadership, Germany's position of power in EMU has been assessed in detail above: Although not almighty, Germany is the most powerful member state in the eurozone and therefore the ideal candidate if it comes to the provision of leadership (Sect. 4.2).

With respect to the common goal, the Fiscal Compact was supposed to contribute to overcoming the crisis and preserving the common currency. More precisely, it was considered a way to "anchor market expectations regarding the sustainability of public finances in Europe (and narrow the [...] abnormally high government bond spreads)" (Drudi et al. 2012: 894). Thus, although the Fiscal Compact was not the measure preferred by all signatories, it was regarded as a contribution to a common goal that "was paramount to the different preferences of highly solvent and highly indebted member states" (Schimmelfennig 2014: 329). This is reflected in a statement by Herman Van Rompuy, then

European Council President, during the negotiations of the European Council in December 2011: "26 leaders are in favour of joining this effort. They recognise the euro is a *common good*" (President of the European Council 2011b: 1, own emphasis).

Regarding the third indicator for leadership, the employment of resources, Germany translated its resources into a multitude of classical negotiation strategies to realize the treaty. Most prominently, Germany managed to link financial assistance from the ESM to the signing of the Fiscal Compact (issue-linking) and it shifted the decision-making process to the level of the European Council and thus away from the more protracted and less salient community method (arena-shifting). Moreover, Germany engaged in pre-negotiations with France and other member states during both the agenda-setting and the decision-making phase. Alongside such classical bargaining strategies, Germany framed the Fiscal Compact as an indispensable counter-weight to the mutualisation of risk at the European level. Thereby, it used its economic weight and significance for the survival of the eurozone as a bargaining chip to worsen the other actors' no-agreement alternatives ("rule of anticipated reaction") (see below for details).

While the model's first analytical step focuses on the emergence of leadership, the second step deals with its impact. The criteria for assessing a leader's impact are (1) the presence of change, measured by the difference between the ex-ante and the ex-post situation, (2) its desirability, benchmarked against the leader's most preferred outcome, and (3) its initiation by the leader. In the case of the Fiscal Compact, the relevant change is given by the treaty itself. Second, as regards the desirability of this change, the Fiscal Compact largely represents German preferences (Ludlow 2012c: 6). In particular, "the key provisions on fiscal discipline always fulfilled the demands of Germany" (Kreilinger 2012: 6). The only significant deviations from German preferences concern a weaker involvement of the ECJ[26] and the Commission[27] in the case of non compliance with the rules (Interview 27).

[26]According to the final agreement, member states can bring each other before the court for not transposing the Fiscal Compact provisions into their national laws, but not for non-compliance with the rules, as was envisaged by Germany (Interview 27).

[27]While Germany wanted a strong role of the Commission, enabling it to bring member states before the ECJ in case of non-compliance with the rules, France succeeded in downgrading this to a reporting role (Kreilinger 2012: 4; Interview 27).

As far as the third criterion is concerned, the shaping of the Fiscal Compact was clearly a German initiative. Already in May 2010 it became public that the German Finance Ministry was developing and promoting plans for a European debt brake to be implemented in national legislation, as this already existed at the time in the German constitution (Schäfer and Hall 2010). By August 2011, the German government had convinced France to write a joint letter to President Van Rompuy, in which the two governments define excessive public debt and a lack of competitiveness as the principal causes of the crisis, and propose a debt brake and regular Euro summits as solution to it (Bundesregierung 2011b). The Euro summit statement of October 26, 2011, whereby the Eurozone leaders formalized their meetings and committed themselves for the first time to the idea of a debt brake, is based on this initiative (European Council 2011a; Beach 2013: 117).[28] In the following months, Germany strongly promoted the idea and pushed for a quick realization of the treaty (Rinke 2011; see below for further details). In sum, as a French government official in the Permanent Representation put it, "Germany was leading the project of this Fiscal Compact and I would say this was mostly a German demand" (Interview 5).

Hence, the observable outcome is successful leadership: Germany not only emerged as a leader, but also influenced the outcomes in the desired way by bringing about institutional change.

Explaining Germany's Leadership Emergence: Leadership Surplus and Status Quo Costs

The model's first variable accounting for the emergence of leadership is the expected surplus of a leadership candidate, which consists of the expected costs and benefits of leading. Table 4.5 gives an overview of Germany's costs and benefits of taking the lead in shaping the Fiscal Compact as reported by the interviewees. Those respondents who were particularly strongly involved in the shaping of the Fiscal Compact are printed in bold. Those representing the German government are italicised. At the first glance, three observations are striking. Firstly, all of the relevant interviewees said that the Fiscal Compact was a means for

[28] Even the structure of the final treaty, which in large part consists of one section providing the rules for the debt brake (Title III) and another codifying Euro summits (Title IV), still mirrors the original proposal.

Table 4.5 Germany's costs and benefits of leading according to interviewees (Fiscal Compact)

Interview	*Benefits*	*Costs*
	SIGNAL TO...	
	Financial markets	
1	"Sending messages to financial markets that we are doing something"	
6	**Signal that fiscal discipline is implemented**	
8	Regain credibility	
13	Visibility (*vis-à-vis* markets)	
15	**Maintaining the credibility of the SGP**	
24	"Element of seeking to reassure the markets"	
25	*Credible commitment to fiscal consolidation*	
26	*Signalling as secondary purpose*	
27	***Signal to financial markets***	
	German voters	
4	Compensation of German voters for ESM approval	
6	**German government protects taxpayer money from moral hazard in Eurozone**	
8	Public opinion in favour	
13	Visibility (*vis-à-vis* voters)	
15	**"something has to be given in return"**	
25	*Primarily a signal to voters and parliament*	*None: No political resistance by debtor states*
26	*Signalling as secondary purpose*	
27	***Secondarily also a signal to voters***	
	INCREASE OF NATIONAL OWNERSHIP	
6	**Commitment of other member states through their *own* legislation, thereby reducing competitive disadvantage for Germany**	
8	Extension of own regulation on other member states	None: German debt brake already implemented; ESM already de facto decided
26	*Primary purpose: effective enhancement of rules due to substantial institutional change*	
27	***Enhancement of institutional framework and implementation of rules***	

Source Own compilation

the German government to send out a signal in its favour, either to the financial markets or to its own voters. Most interviewees mentioned both targets together. Secondly, none of the interviewees was able to name any costs of leading. Two respondents even gave explicit reasons as to why there were no such costs. Thirdly, only 4 out of 10 relevant interviewees mentioned the achievement of substantial change through the Fiscal Compact as a benefit expected by the German government.

By sending a signal to the financial markets, the German government aimed to reduce the fragmentation risk in the eurozone, which at the time was extraordinarily high (see below) and carried unpredictable consequences for Germany. Among other things, the German government feared that a breakdown of the eurozone would result in "a steep appreciation of its currency, a concurrent slump in exports, and deep and long-lasting recession" (Schimmelfennig 2015: 181). In order to avoid such a scenario, the credibility of the SGP should be regained by issuing a credible commitment to fiscal discipline in the eurozone. This credible commitment consisted in the incorporation of fiscal discipline into national constitutional law, which is considered to weigh more than community law because it is easier to enforce and less likely to be breached (Interviews 6, 27). Hence, as centrepiece of the Fiscal Compact, the debt brake was supposed to generate credibility in the financial markets, reduce uncertainty and diminish government bond spreads (Drudi et al. 2012: 894). As the German Chancellor put it at the time, the Fiscal Compact was part of "a step-by-step process that will re-establish confidence in our common currency" (Euractiv 2011a). While the debt brake with its automatic correction mechanism was not only a credible, but also a costly commitment for the highly indebted member states in the South of the eurozone, it did not bring about any costs for Germany, which already had a debt brake in its constitutional law and a government deficit of only 1.0% in 2011.[29] Therefore, sending a credible signal to the financial markets in order to reduce the fragmentation risk in the eurozone was a "net benefit" for Germany when it came to shaping the Fiscal Compact.

Moreover, the Fiscal Compact allowed the German government to send a signal to its voters at home. After it had become clear that

[29] http://ec.europa.eu/eurostat/tgm/table.do?tab=table&init=1&language=en&pcode=teina200&plugin=1, rev. 2018-02-22.

German participation in a permanent rescue fund (ESM) would be inevitable if a collapse of the eurozone was to be avoided, the German government needed to assure its increasingly sceptical voters that taxpayers' money would be protected from moral hazard in the eurozone (Interview 6; Beach 2013: 116). In other words, the German government felt that "something has to be given in return" (Interview 15) for the financial assistance granted by the rescue funds. Hence, the German Chancellor established a visible link between German participation in the ESM and the adoption of a Fiscal Compact. The first time she presented the idea of treaty amendments to the public, for instance, was just two days after the German Constitutional Court rendered a positive verdict regarding Germany's participation in the eurozone rescue funds (Bundesverfassungsgericht 2011). Thus, as soon as it was clear that the German government was legally authorized to participate in the ESM, the Chancellor suggested treaty amendments to create more "reliability" in the Eurozone.

Moreover, the German government insisted on linking the ESM and the Fiscal Compact institutionally by granting financial assistance only to those member states that subscribed to the Fiscal Compact. Chancellor Merkel even suggested to put the Fiscal Compact and the ESM treaty into one single document (Miller 2012: 9). To keep the linkage between the two treaties visible, the ESM treaty was finally put on the agenda of the same European Council at which the Fiscal Compact was adopted (30 January 2012), although the ESM negotiations had already been completed at the time (Ludlow 2012c: 6). Finally, taking the lead in shaping the Fiscal Compact was particularly beneficial for the German government at a time when there was a rising domestic demand for further decisive steps towards more integration, which was put forward not only by the domestic opposition, but also by public persons such as former Chancellors Kohl and Schröder (Rinke 2011).

While all interviewees mentioned the signal effect of the Fiscal Compact as a benefit of leading for Germany, only 4 referred also to changes in substance the treaty could bring about. According to these interviewees, the Fiscal Compact served to increase the national ownership of the rules which were supposed to ensure fiscal discipline and thus to prevent moral hazard in the eurozone. Before the Fiscal Compact, member states were committed only through EU law, which was perceived to weigh less, to be less enforceable, and thus more likely to be breached. The new treaty would commit them through their own national legislation, an automatic correction mechanism enshrined in national constitutions, and independent national institutions. Germany's benefits of an increase in national ownership would be twofold. First, as explained in Sect. 4.2, the increase of national ownership would allow Germany to shift the adjustment costs of the crisis to the national level. Thus, instead of mutualizing these costs at the European level, the institutionalization of fiscal restraint in national constitutions would make the "debtor states" pay the biggest share (see Frieden and Walter 2017: 379–83; Matthijs 2016b: 145; Schimmelfennig 2015). Second, by committing all other eurozone members to incorporate a debt brake into their constitutional law, Germany would extend its own national regulation on the entire eurozone and thus get rid of a competitive disadvantage. The German debt brake, which had already been decided upon in 2009 by changing the federal constitution, entered into force as of 2011. Thus, whereas Germany had unilaterally committed itself to austerity through constitutional law, the other member states were committed only by the weaker SGP.[30] With regard to moral hazard in the eurozone, this tied Germany's hands, whereby the incentives to "fiscal free-riding" even increased for other member states. But also with regard economic recovery from the crisis (countercyclical deficit spending), the German debt brake constituted a competitive disadvantage.

However, it remains questionable whether the German government really expected an enhancement of fiscal discipline through the adoption of the Fiscal Compact, as was the case with the supercommissioner (Sect. 4.2). First of all, the Fiscal Compact lacks a clear and workable definition for the key concept of "structural budget" as well as a single method for adjusting fiscal balances (Gros and Alcidi 2014: 2). Moreover, the treaty creates ambiguity by introducing targets that conflict with the revised SGP. Would the German government have accepted these vague and ambiguous rules if it had not only wanted to send an effective signal, but also bring about substantial policy change? Indeed, as a Commission administrator confirmed, the treaty was signed under great pressure, time-constraints, and uncertainty regarding its actual contents and significance. Consequently, the Commission was extensively consulted when it came to the transposition of the provisions into national law (Interview 4). The fact that the German government

[30] Some member states already had a debt brake in their national law, but not at a constitutional (or equivalent) level (Interview 4).

insisted on treaty change although the contents did not differ significantly from existing community law corroborate the interpretation that sending a signal to the financial markets and German voters—instead of real policy change—were the primary benefits of leading in the case of the Fiscal Compact. As a research paper for the UK's House of Commons reported:

> Guy Verhofstadt had suggested to the Council Legal Service that everything in the proposed treaty could be introduced by secondary legislation using Articles 136 and 333-334 TFEU, and Protocol 12. The Council conceded that this was correct but said *the treaty was necessary for political and symbolic reasons.* (Miller 2012: 51, own emphasis)

As regards Germany's costs of leading, in contrast, the interviewees agreed that there were no relevant costs involved. The debt brake provided for by the treaty had already been implemented in Germany and the ESM had already been decided upon. Therefore, no significant concessions were needed to realize the Fiscal Compact, which was largely perceived as the legitimate counter-price for Germany participating in the ESM. As a German government official put it quite bluntly: "The debtor states showed their gratitude"[31] (Interview 25). Another reason for the lack of resistance by other eurozone members might have been the perceived pressure for action caused by the financial markets: "there was certainly no resistance against the principle because that is what you want to sell to the markets" (Interview 8). Therefore, the only costs of leading may have consisted in Germany's transaction costs. The German government invested considerable human and time resources to promote the Fiscal Compact in the other member states: German ambassadors approached the respective governments, bilateral meetings took place at the level of heads of unit and between state secretaries, all possible fora were used to promote the idea of a debt brake, including even the IMF and the G7, and the Chancellor herself met her colleagues to promote the Fiscal Compact (Interviews 15, 26; Rinke 2011).

However, putting these transactional costs aside because they can never amount to the costs of a eurozone collapse (signal to financial markets), a lost electoral campaign (signal to voters), or the adjustment

[31] Translated by the author from the original: "Die Nehmerländer zeigten sich erkenntlich."

costs of the eurozone crisis (increase of national ownership), there were no costs of leading in shaping the Fiscal Compact. Thus, a cost-benefit analysis is simple: if the costs are insignificant, the benefits necessarily prevail. Hence, Germany's benefits of leading clearly outweighed the costs, which made for a leadership surplus. According to the first theoretical proposition of the leadership model (H1), we therefore expect that Germany did offer leadership.

The second variable accounting for a leader's emergence are the aggregate status quo costs. As opposed to the costs of leading, they do not appear in the case of action, but are already present or imminent in the case of status quo. The assessment of these costs relies mainly on the interviewees' perceptions and expressions regarding the "perceived pressure for action". As a less subjective proxy, government bond spreads are taken into consideration since they reflect the effective fragmentation risk of the eurozone and thus the gravity of the crisis (Sect. 3.4). Of 19 interviewees who answered the question of when the perceived pressure for action was highest during the crisis, 7 referred to autumn and winter 2011, which is the time when Germany put the Fiscal Compact on the agenda. Another 3 interviewees assessed the pressure for action as very high at the time. A major reason for this assessment is that actors perceived a high risk of having big member states like Italy or Spain entering the sovereign debt crisis at the time, which would have been a potential cause of a eurozone breakdown.

The assessment of the interviewees is corroborated by the development of government bond spreads in the eurozone. As can be seen from Fig. 4.3, the eurozone crisis had reached a temporary peak by the end of 2011 when the Fiscal Compact was shaped—and no one knew how the situation would develop further. Therefore, all actors involved felt that an urgent reaction was needed to calm the financial markets (Interviews 1, 6, 8). It was especially alarming that not only the interests on Spanish government bonds were constantly rising, but also Italian bonds had reached an unprecedented peak of 7.06% in November 2011. It was not clear how big economies like Italy or Spain should be rescued were they to lose their refinancing ability. Moreover, following the G20 summit at Cannes in November 2011, the markets began to put pressure even on supposedly solid member states like France and Austria. Thus, given that the status quo costs were extremely high in autumn and winter 2011, we expect that there was a high demand for leadership and that Germany, being the most powerful leadership candidate (see below), emerged as a leader (H2).

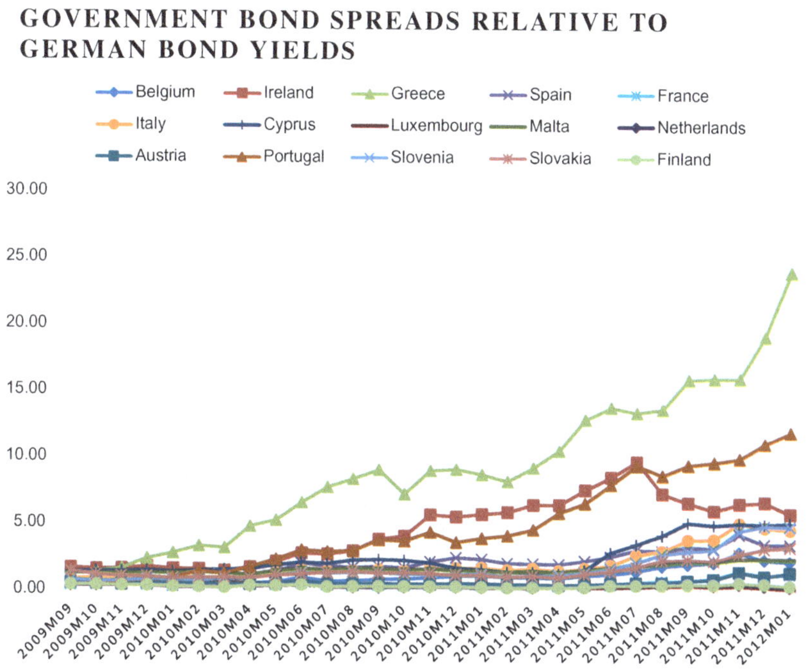

Fig. 4.3 Government bond spreads relative to German bond yields, September 2009–January 2012 (*Source* Eurostat [own illustration])

Confidence in this explanation can be increased by tracing the presumed causal mechanism. With regard to the supply of leadership, we would expect to find evidence that Germany proposed the Fiscal Compact as a measure to reduce the eurozone's status quo costs and to contribute to the common goal of preserving the common currency and overcoming the crisis. With regard to the other member states and the institutional actors, there should be evidence that they took notice of Germany's leadership proposal and that at least some of them objected to it.[32] While the finding of such evidence strengthens the confidence in the model, it does not exclude alternative explanations. If we do not find

[32]As explained in Sect. 3.2, if all actor agree on a solution ex ante, there is no need for a leadership.

this evidence, however, the presumed causal mechanism would be disproved (see Collier 2011).

Germany's leadership offer is most explicitly expressed by two public letters sent to the then President of the European Council Van Rompuy. Although these letters were written together with France, they primarily served to promote the German initiative of a debt brake. Already the earlier letter of August 2011 identifies the alleged causes of the crisis, namely "principally excessive public debt and a lack of competitiveness" (Bundesregierung 2011b: 1), and proposes the codification of Euro summits and the introduction of a balanced budget rule as solutions. The claim to leadership and the alleged contribution to the common goal is most prominently stated in the first paragraph of the letter: "Germany and France consider it their historic mission and stand united to protect and strengthen the economic and monetary union and thus the stability of the single currency" (Bundesregierung 2011b: 1).

One day before the decisive European Council of 8–9 December 2011, Germany and France circulated a second public letter, which later became the template for the first draft of the treaty text (Schoeller et al. 2017: 1217). Also this second letter starts out with general remarks emphasizing the common goal:

> To overcome the current crisis, all necessary measures to stabilize the euro are as a whole will have to be taken. […] We consider this as a matter of necessity, credibility and confidence in the future of Economic and Monetary Union. (Bundesregierung 2011a: 1)

In particular, the German proposal of a common debt brake is presented as a measure to the advantage of all member states:

> *It is undoubtedly in the interest of all* members of the Stability and Growth Union to detect and correct departures from sound economic and fiscal policies long before they become a threat to the stability of the Euro area as a whole. (Bundesregierung 2011a: 2, own emphasis)

As regards the demand-side, it is not only evident that the other member states and the EU institutions took notice of the German proposal, but also that at least some of them objected to it or expressed doubts about its feasibility (Wittrock 2011). Nevertheless, with the exception of the UK, all EU member states expressed their interest in joining the German initiative (Euractiv 2011a). As President Van Rompuy reported to the EP after the decisive December summit:

> An intergovernmental treaty [as proposed by Germany] was not my first preference, nor that of most Member States. However, it will make the Fiscal Compact binding. [...] In fact, 26 leaders indicated their interest in this effort. The recognise the euro is a common good. (President of the European Council 2011a: 3)

The fact that the Fiscal Compact was perceived as a contribution to preserving the common currency—and thus as a (controversial) leadership offer—is also shown by a quotation of the Irish Finance Minister regarding a possible referendum about the treaty ratification: "It really comes down on this occasion to a very simple issue: do you want to continue in the euro or not?" (Euractiv 2011a).

Next to the causal mechanism linking leadership supply and demand, the theoretical model also predicts that in the case of a competition for leadership, the most powerful candidate emerges as a leader (Sect. 3.2). Thus, two further questions must be answered: Was there another leadership candidate besides Germany? If yes, was Germany the most powerful candidate when it came to shaping the Fiscal Compact? In December 2011, President Van Rompuy made an attempt to assume a leading role in shaping the course of action. Within his mandate to prepare a report as basis for discussion on treaty amendments, received from the Euro Summit on 26 October 2011 (European Council 2011a), Van Rompuy presented a proposal which included Eurobonds, a banking license for the ESM, and an alternative legal path instead of Treaty amendments. Yet, the power resources of the European Council President are very limited. Rather than a leader, Van Rompuy could emerge as a "political manager, [...] responsible for identifying the bases of consensus, fostering the latter and articulating it in the Conclusions" (Ludlow 2012a: 31). He lacks important powers such as a right of initiative, possibilities of coalition building, or material resources for side-payments. As a result, his attempt to take over leadership was not only harshly rejected by the German government, but also substituted by the Franco-German proposal which was circulated only one day after Van Rompuy's report (Euractiv 2011b; Ludlow 2012a: 9–11; Wittrock 2011). Hence, by striking a deal with France, Germany managed to side-line the European Council President and thereby impose itself as a leader.

Explaining Germany's Leadership Success: Resources, Preferences and Institutional Constraint

As demonstrated above, Germany not only emerged as a leader, but also brought about an institutional change by shaping the Fiscal Compact. The model's first variable that accounts for a leader's impact are her power resources. Germany's power resources were assessed in Sect. 4.2. Regarding its economic resources, Germany is extremely powerful. Only the ECB has more material capacities, but often lacks the institutional resources to employ them. Germany, by contrast, enjoys a de facto veto, but no formal institutional powers to shape policy or institutional change that would significantly exceed those of the other actors. Finally, Germany's ideational resources exceed those of the other member states, but are smaller than those of the EU's institutional actors. In sum, Germany's power resources exceed those of the other actors, but they are not overwhelming. With regard to the analytical model, this high, but relatively undistinguished value should have the effect that Germany's impact on the outcomes is principally likely (H3), but that the other two variables' impact is more decisive. In other words, given that Germany's power resources are not so high that strategic and institutional obstacles could easily be wiped away, we expect that the distribution of preferences among the actors and/or the institutional constraint on the leader make a substantial difference with regard to the outcome.

The second variable that accounts for a leader's impact is the distribution of preferences among the actors involved.[33] In the case of the Fiscal Compact, the dominant conflict of interest was once again that between "creditor states" and "debtor states":

> Relative economic positions as 'Euro-winners' (Germany) and 'Euro-losers' (France, Italy, Spain) push countries to take certain positions, with Euro-winners supporting strengthened discipline, whereas Euro-losers support reforms that create mechanisms to assist them in their domestic restructuring. (Beach 2013: 116f.)

[33] The values of this variable can range from a strong convergence on the leader's preferred outcome to a strong convergence on an outcome different from the one preferred by the leader. The unit of interest are the actors' strategic preferences at the beginning of the case study (see Sect. 3.4).

Yet, against the background of strong market pressures in autumn 2011 "there was a collective recognition" that the Fiscal Compact was needed as a signal to calm the markets and stabilize the eurozone despite the diverging interests of creditor and debtor states (Interview 15; also 1, 5, 7, 8, 10, 25, 27). Therefore, except for the UK, there was no resistance against the Fiscal Compact per se. If there were concerns, these were mainly raised against the institutional set-up or related to specific details (see below; Interviews 7, 10, 25, 27). As President Van Rompuy confirmed in a speech to the EP after the crucial December summit: "As I said, there was a broad agreement on the substance. As regards the form, everybody agreed that these new commitments should be made binding, but they there were different views as to how this could be done" (President of the European Council 2011a: 2).

This preference constellation represents a so-called "battle of the sexes". Both creditor and debtor states prefer a Fiscal Compact to no agreement at all. Their preferences differ only with regard to the concrete design of the agreement. This is precisely where the function of a leader comes in: a leader serves as a focal point on the Pareto frontier or, in less technical terms, she guides a group with diverging preferences towards a common goal by deciding for one possible outcome among many. This meant that in principle the "Fiscal Compact was supported by 26 of the 27 EU Member States – all the Eurozone States and all the non-Eurozone States except the UK" (Miller 2012: 1; also Ludlow 2012a: 23). However, their level of support differed according to their national situation and depended on questions of how to deal with their debt level, how to set up the independent national institutions for monitoring, and how to reach a majority for ratification in the national parliaments (Interview 10). Therefore, the debates and negotiations turned on the form of the agreement (EU secondary law vs. intergovernmental treaty) and technical details such as the concrete role of the ECJ and the Commission as well the legal status of the "debt brake" (constitutional vs. non constitutional law), but not on the substance of the treaty itself (Interviews 7, 27). Accordingly, there were only minor changes from the first draft to the final version of the treaty (Kreilinger 2012; Beach 2013: 119–23). The reported concerns of some non-Eurozone countries (Denmark, the Czech Republic, Hungary, and Sweden) regarded rather their parliamentary approval than the content of the treaty (Miller 2012: 8; Ludlow 2012a: 23).

Initially, France was the most sceptical state. The government's main concern regarded the restriction of national budgetary competences. Only after Germany offered to include Euro-summits in the treaty, which met the French demand for a more discretionary and intergovernmental economic governance in the euro area, did France give up its resistance (Interviews 5, 8; Beach 2013: 117, 126). During the negotiations, France pushed for a weaker role for the Commission: the right to bring non-compliance to the ECJ, as suggested by Germany, was downgraded to a mere reporting role as regards the transposition of the agreement into national legislation (Interviews 5, 27; Kreilinger 2012: 4). Besides France, Italy was also sceptical in the beginning and succeeded during the negotiations in restricting the scope of the reversed qualified majority voting (RQMV) to the issue of national deficits, thereby excluding national debts (Kreilinger 2012: 3).

However, the only member state that from the outset was unwilling to subscribe to the German initiative was the UK. The UK's reluctance was due to domestic reasons and concerned primarily the integrity of the City of London as a financial centre. Instead of announcing a veto already early in the process, however, the British government engaged in bilateral meetings with the German government and presented a list of demands for concessions, which proved unacceptable to the other member states. Given that these bilateral pre-negotiations did not bring about any operational outcome, both the German and British governments came to the conclusion that a final agreement including the UK would not be feasible. Consequently, when the British Prime Minister David Cameron presented his demands at the summit, the German Chancellor was very quick to suggest going on without the UK (Ludlow 2012a: 11–5, 21–3, 32; Miller 2012: 4–14).

As regards the supranational institutions, the Commission was in favour of the treaty contents as proposed by Germany, but clearly preferred a solution within community law (Interviews 8, 10, 12). Thus, apart from minor details, the Commission's objections were not directed against the principle of the Fiscal Compact as such, but against its institutional set-up: "The Commission as an institution is a strong believer in the Community method and less of a believer in intergovernmental conference methods. […] We prefer to work in the Community way and not in a voluntary between-states way. That's why we have the EU" (Interview 12). The Commission found a natural ally in the EP, which also pursued the goal to integrate the Fiscal Compact into EU law or to shape it as similar as possible to existing community law (= revised SGP), so that it could be integrated at a later point in time. Both institutions were invited to the negotiations although they had no formal right to participate in the shaping of an intergovernmental agreement. In the negotiations, the EP actually succeeded in introducing the so-called "repatriation clause" into the treaty, according to which the Fiscal Compact shall be incorporated into the legal framework of the EU within 5 years after its entry into force (Interviews 16, 28, 30, 33; Miller 2012: 49–53).

The ECB, finally, was Germany's strongest supporter (Interviews 6–8, 12, 14, 15, 18–20, 23–27). Not only is ECB President Mario Draghi reported to have coined the name "Fiscal Compact" in a plenary speech at the EP earlier in 2011 (Interviews 6, 7, 19, 21), the ECB was also strongly involved in the shaping of the treaty through background discussions, workshops, studies and research papers, and even trips of their officials to EU capitals for exchanges of views on the topic (Interviews 6, 8, 14, 18, 19, 21, 24, 27). The reason for the ECB's preferences is its understanding of the Fiscal Compact as a "supporting tool for the effectiveness of its monetary policy" (Interview 21). From the ECB's point of view, the Fiscal Compact was a means to cover a future programme of government bonds purchases from highly indebted Eurozone member states. Thus, the ECB found itself in a position very similar to that of Germany: if it should assume the role of a "lender of last resort", it needed the security that this would not result in a permanent mutualisation of common debt (Interview 6).

In sum, in the case of the Fiscal Compact, none of the actors objected the treaty, except for the UK. To be sure, France and Italy especially were sceptical at the beginning. However, against the background of strong market pressures, there was a general agreement that such a signal was needed to calm the markets and stabilize the Eurozone. Although the Commission and EP would have preferred a solution within EU law, they had no major objections against the contents of the Fiscal Compact as such. The ECB was once again Germany's strongest supporter. Hence, the actors' strategic preferences weakly converged on the outcome preferred by Germany. The value of the independent variable and the outcome are congruent.

The last variable that accounts for a leader's impact is the institutional constraint. It ranges from complete discretion by the leader (= no institutional constraint) to the interdiction of making certain decisions

(= maximal institutional constraint). In the case of the Fiscal Compact, which was originally supposed to be realized through treaty change and therefore required de jure unanimity, the institutional constraint was too high despite converging preferences, as a veto by the UK would have sufficed to frustrate the German plans. This, however, was anticipated by the German government, which slightly lowered the institutional constraint by switching to an intergovernmental agreement outside EU law, thereby excluding the UK. Nevertheless, in order to achieve the desired outcome of sending an effective signal to the markets, the support from almost all of the 17 eurozone countries was necessary, which corresponds to de facto unanimity (Tsebelis and Hahm 2014: 1389). Hence, the institutional constraint in the case of the Fiscal Compact corresponds to decision-making by participation under de facto unanimity (Sect. 3.4). This represents the highest institutional constraint possible apart from the legal interdiction against making a certain decision.

Thus, with regard to the second step of the model explaining the impact of leadership, only one hypothesis (preference distribution) passes the congruence test directly. Given that Germany's power resources alone do not suffice to explain its impact in shaping the Fiscal Compact and the high institutional constraint makes it even less likely, we need to find evidence that Germany made extensive use of its power resources to overcome the institutional constraint. Only if Germany obtained the approval of almost all followers through the translation of its resources into leadership strategies under the condition of a favourable ex-ante distribution of preferences, can the model explain Germany's impact. In Sect. 3.3, two different causal mechanisms connecting resources and outcomes are suggested: (1) the translation of power resources into strategies, and (2) the "rule of anticipated reaction".

In shaping the Fiscal Compact, Germany used a multitude of leadership strategies.[34] Most notably, the shaping of the Fiscal Compact was an instance of arena-shifting by the German Chancellor. First, Angela Merkel shifted the issue, which in large part could have been realized through secondary legislation (Miller 2012: 3f.), to the highest level of the heads of state and government. In this way, the Commission and EP could not participate in decision-making under their formal rights of the Ordinary Legislative Procedure. Moreover, the signal effect of the legal

[34] See Sect. 3.3 for an overview of the single strategies.

provisions was considerably strengthened: "Merkel's primary objective was to send a political signal from the top, not to engage in turf war with the Commission or with any other institution" (Ludlow 2012b: 3). Second, when it turned out that the UK would veto a Treaty change, Merkel pushed for another arena-shift, namely the endorsement of an international treaty outside EU law (see below).

A second subset of strategies used by the German government is agenda-managing, understood as the placement of certain issues, their linkage, or their exclusion from the agenda. Germany made extensive use of these strategies. Most prominently, by making the financial assistance of the ESM conditional on the ratification of the Fiscal Compact, Germany ensured the signature of peripheral countries that otherwise might have been reluctant regarding the implementation of further budgetary restrictions (Interview 10; Miller 2012: 55). This purposeful linkage of the two treaties, which represent austerity (Fiscal Compact) and solidarity (ESM) respectively, was made visible by putting both of them on the agenda of the European Council of 30 January 2012 despite the fact that the ESM negotiations had already been concluded at the time (Ludlow 2012c: 6). Another instance of issue-linkage regarded France, which initially rejected the idea of a constitutional debt brake. However, for supporting the idea of a balanced budget rule, it obtained the inclusion of Euro summits in the treaty, which met its wish for a discretionary and intergovernmental economic governance in the euro area (Beach 2013: 117, 126). Finally, at the crucial December Council, Germany also engaged in agenda-exclusion by vetoing two further proposals related to the Fiscal Compact: "one to allow the ESM and European Financial Stability Facility (EFSF) to exist together after 2012 with a joint lending power of €940bn; and another to allow the ECB to print money to underwrite ESM and EFSF debt" (Miller 2012: 9).

A third important subset of strategies regards coalition building. Most importantly this concerns the exclusion of the UK. The German government never really tried to include the UK's demands. When it became clear that the UK would not depart from its demands either, the Chancellor and her diplomats tried to convince the other member states of a new treaty without the UK (Beach 2013: 118f.). Already one week before the decisive European Council in December 2011, Merkel clearly signalled that she would prefer an agreement among the 17 euro area members to a treaty change by all 27 EU members if the latter meant making concessions to the UK (Crossland 2011; Hawley 2011).

This became most obvious when she interrupted Prime Minister David Cameron who was presenting the UK's demands in the European Council negotiations, saying that she would have preferred a treaty change with all 27 states, but that she wanted a decision the same night. Van Rompuy drew the immediate conclusion that the member states could not go ahead at 27. Strictly speaking, the UK did thus not exercise a veto, but was excluded by the other member states under the lead of Germany (Ludlow 2012a: 23; 2012b: 30, Footnote 21). Hence, by excluding the UK through an intergovernmental treaty outside EU law, coalition-building was combined with arena-shifting.

Another way of combining coalition-building with arena-shifting are pre-negotiations. Throughout crisis management, Germany regularly practiced the strategy of striking a deal with one or a few crucial actors ahead of the multilateral negotiations by joining forces with France (Schild 2013). When it came to the Fiscal Compact, already the first step (problem-definition and agenda-setting) was made together by publishing a joint letter to Van Rompuy, which later became the template for the Euro summit statement of October 26, 2011 (see above). Before the decisive December summit, the German Chancellor adopted the same strategy again. Three days before the summit, on 5 December 2011, she met the French President in Paris (Crossland 2011). This time the aim was different, however.

Firstly, it became evident at the time that the UK would not accept any kind of treaty amendment. Thus, Germany needed French support to bring about a new treaty without the UK. Secondly, the President of the European Council, Herman Van Rompuy, was working on own plans on how to achieve a final agreement in parallel (see above). Thus, Germany also needed to secure French support against Van Rompuy's charge. When the President of the European Council finally presented his proposal only two days ahead of the summit, Germany and France replied within only one day by releasing a joint letter rejecting Van Rompuy's ideas and outlining their own common position (Bundesregierung 2011a). This letter anticipated the crucial elements, partly even word for word, of the ensuing Euro Area Statement (European Council 2011c) and the first negotiation draft of the Fiscal Compact (European Council 2011b) (see Table 3 in Schoeller et al. 2017: 1217). The proposals of Van Rompuy, instead, did not appear anymore in these two documents. Thus, the Franco-German letter replaced the Van Rompuy proposal as an informal negotiation agenda.[35] As regards preference attainment, all proposals of the joint letter except for the codification of Euro summits reflected originally German preferences. While the details of the treaty content were negotiated in a working group building on the structures of the Eurogroup Working Group throughout the month of January, the German Chancellor and French President met several times to discuss the concrete content in parallel to the negotiations. However, Merkel not only met Sarkozy in this time, but also her Italian, Austrian, Portuguese, Swedish, Belgian, and Spanish colleagues for the same purpose (Ludlow 2012b: 7f.).

Finally, a fourth set of leadership strategies is the provision of common knowledge, understood as the definition of problems and the presentation and promotion of solutions to them. Most evidently this happened through the joint letter with France in August 2011 (see above). When it eventually came to the promotion of these ideas, Germany made use of all its diplomatic weight. German ambassadors approached the respective governments in the MS, bilateral meetings took place at all levels from the heads of units in the ministries up to the ministers themselves, all possible fora were used to promote the idea, including IMF and G7 summits, and the Chancellor arranged bi- and trilateral meetings with her colleagues: "on her agenda was always the Fiscal Compact at that time" (Interview 15). Thus, in the words of Rinke (2011), the German government functioned like a clandestine EU Presidency for that purpose.

The alternative causal mechanism describing the translation of power resources into leadership impact is subtler: followers anticipate that if they do not have special regard to the leader's preferences, her reaction can be harmful to them. This is what Carl Friedrich named the "rule of anticipated reaction(s)" (1963: 199–215). Although this second causal mechanism is more difficult to observe, several interviewees stated that many member state governments agreed on the Fiscal Compact because they feared that Germany would otherwise abandon its support for risk-sharing measures in the Eurozone, such as the rescue funds (Interviews 5, 10, 15, 25). As a closely involved EU official put it:

[35] Formally, the negotiation agenda was provided by the Council Legal Service.

> If you want an ESM, a permanent firewall, a certain firepower of the ESM, it needs to go hand in hand with commitments on the fiscal side. It was always clear to everybody negotiating the ESM treaty that this is subject to progress on the Fiscal Compact side. Things were always somehow linked. (Interview 10)

However, the Fiscal Compact was not just signed in the concrete context of the ESM agreement, but also in the shadow of further steps to be taken in the future because "everybody knew: if the Germans are not on board, the whole thing collapses" (Interview 15).

Results

The book's model can plausibly explain Germany's successful leadership in the case of the Fiscal Compact. With regard to Germany's emergence as a leader, both theoretical propositions passed the empirical test. First, an effective signal to the financial markets and domestic voters in conjunction with further institutionalization of fiscal discipline in the eurozone outweighed the low costs of leading for Germany (H1). These costs were particularly low because except for the UK there was no noteworthy resistance from other member states, and Germany had already implemented a debt brake in its own constitution. Thus, Germany expected a leader's surplus and offered to take the lead by shaping the Fiscal Compact. Second, the status quo costs, which consisted in a looming collapse of the eurozone in case Spanish and Italian bonds would have risen further, were extremely high at the time and created a strong demand for leadership (H2). Hence, as expected by the theoretical model, Germany emerged as a leader because rising sovereign bond yields created a high demand for leadership and Germany's expected benefits of leading clearly outweighed the costs. Moreover, the competition for leadership between the German government and the President of the European Council corroborates the model's assumption that in case of a struggle for leadership, it is the most powerful candidate that emerges as leader.

As regards the impact of leadership, ample evidence for Germany's extensive use of strategies corroborates the second step of the theoretical model: given that most of the strategic preferences already converged on the outcome preferred by Germany, the German government managed to overcome the high institutional constraint (unanimity) by translating its power resources into leadership strategies (linkage to ESM; exclusion of veto player [UK] through arena-shifting). This shows that the model's propositions are to be understood *ceteris paribus*. A leader's impact cannot be explained by just focusing on one explanatory factor alone, but only by taking into account its interplay with the other independent variables provided for by the model.

Germany's (Non-)Leadership in EMU

The three case studies allow us to draw conclusions on Germany's role as a potential leader in EMU (see Bulmer and Paterson 2018: Chapter 6). Given that Germany greatly profits from the euro in economic and political terms, it has generally been committed to the preservation of the single currency.[36] This explains why the German government eventually agreed on "solidarity measures" like state bailouts or common rescue funds when they seemed inevitable for the survival of the currency union. However, when there was leeway in shaping a common response to the crisis, Germany sought to shift the adjustment costs to the national level by enforcing austerity instead of mutualising these costs at the European level and thereby assuming a major part itself (see Frieden and Walter 2017: 379–83; Matthijs 2016b: 145; Schimmelfennig 2015: 179–83). Thus, Germany has been "reluctant" (Bulmer and Paterson 2013; Newman 2015) only when it came to "*solidarity*" measures like the financial assistance to Greece (Sect. 4.1), but it provided leadership if the proposed solutions regarded the institutionalization of fiscal discipline ("*austerity*"), as was the case with the super-commissioner or the Fiscal Compact (Sects. 4.2 and 4.3). However, due to its limited shaping power, it did so with varying success (super-commissioner vs. Fiscal Compact).

While it is true that Germany is a de facto veto player in EMU as its economic resources exceed those of all other member states, its shaping power has clear limits. In particular, Germany's institutional resources do not stand out in the euro area (Sect. 4.2). Hence, it is much easier for the German government to maintain the status quo in EMU than to bring about policy or institutional change (even if the latter is in its

[36] Germany's export-driven economic performance, extremely low interests on sovereign debt ("flight to safety"), and its relatively powerful position at the European ("hegemony") and global level are but a few benefits from the euro.

own interest). In other words, Germany does not get whatever it wants in EMU, but it can block whatever it does not want. This is one reason as to why crisis management has been characterized by "muddling through" rather than bold innovation.

Next to the lack of shaping power, there is also an unfavourable incentive structure for German leadership. First, there are almost no "pull-factors". Given that the potential for austerity in the euro area is virtually exhausted as long as it is not accompanied by appropriate risk-sharing mechanisms, every effort going beyond the minimum necessary to preserve the single currency is hardly beneficial for Germany. Moreover, taking the lead is costly: not only would Germany risk becoming the eurozone's "lender of last resort", there would also be considerable domestic costs to consider (see Bulmer 2014: 1256–9). Second, there is a lack of "push-factors" as for the time being, Germany profits in multiple ways from the status quo in the euro area (see Jacoby 2015: 198–201). Thus, in the light of these adverse circumstances, the emergence of German leadership in EMU is currently rather unlikely.

References

Ardagna, Silvia, and Francesco Caselli. 2014. The Political Economy of the Greek Debt Crisis: A Tale of Two Bailouts. *American Economic Journal: Macroeconomics* 6 (4): 291–323.

BBC. 2012. EU Summit: Merkel Agenda for Euro Reform Riles France. BBC NEWS, October 18. Available online at http://www.bbc.com/news/world-europe-19986603, rev. 2018–02–14.

Beach, Derek. 2013. The Fiscal Compact, Euro-Reforms and the Challenge for the Euro-Outs. In *Danish Foreign Policy Yearbook 2013*, ed. Nanna Hvidt and Hans Mouritzen, 113–133. Copenhagen: Danish Institute for International Studies (DIIS).

Bénassy-Quéré, Agnès et al. 2018. Reconciling Risk Sharing with Market Discipline: A Constructive Approach to Euro Area Reform. CEPR Policy Insight 91, London.

Bohne, Martin. 2012. Weder neu noch konsensfähig. tagesschau.de, October 16. Available online at http://www.tagesschau.de/wirtschaft/schaeuble-eu104.html, rev. 2015–05–23.

Böll, Sven. 2012. Zukunft der Währungsunion: Schäuble präsentiert Masterplan für den Euro. SPIEGEL ONLINE, October 16. Available online at http://www.spiegel.de/wirtschaft/soziales/euro-krise-schaeuble-praesentiert-masterplan-a-861475.html, rev. 2015–05–26.

Bonatti, Luigi, and Andrea Fracasso. 2013. The German Model and the European Crisis. *Journal of Common Market Studies* 51 (6): 1023–1039.

Bulmer, Simon. 2014. Germany and the Eurozone Crisis: Between Hegemony and Domestic Politics. *West European Politics* 37 (6): 1244–1263.

Bulmer, Simon, and William E. Paterson. 2013. Germany as the EU's Reluctant Hegemon? Of Economic Strength and Political Constraints. *Journal of European Public Policy* 20 (10): 1387–1405.

Bulmer, Simon, and William E. Paterson. 2018. *Germany and the European Union: Europe's Reluctant Hegemon?* London: Red Globe Press.

Bundesregierung. 2011a. Joint Letter by Germany and France to the President of the European Council, December 7. Available online at https://www.bundesregierung.de/ContentArchiv/DE/Archiv17/_Anlagen/2011/12/2011-12-07-englischer-brief.pdf?__blob=publicationFile&v=2, rev. 2016–05–17.

Bundesregierung. 2011b. Letter to President Van Rompuy, August 17. Available online at http://archiv.bundesregierung.de/ContentArchiv/DE/Archiv17/_Anlagen/2011/08/2011-08-17-dt-franz-brief-eng.pdf?__blob=publicationFile&v=4, rev. 2015–07–16.

Bundesverfassungsgericht. 2011. Verfassungsbeschwerden gegen Maßnahmen zur Griechenland-Hilfe und zum Euro-Rettungsschirm erfolglos - Keine Verletzung der Haushaltsautonomie des Bundestages, September 7. Available online at https://www.bundesverfassungsgericht.de/SharedDocs/Pressemitteilungen/DE/2011/bvg11-055.html, rev. 2015–11–03.

Buti, Marco, and Nicolas Carnot. 2012. EMU Debt Crisis: Early Lessons and Reforms. *Journal of Common Market Studies* 50 (6): 899–911.

Collier, David. 2011. Understanding Process Tracing. *Political Science and Politics* 44 (4): 823–830.

Crossland, David. 2011. Germany and France Agree: Merkozy to Seek New EU Treaty to Tackle Crisis. SPIEGEL ONLINE, December 5. Available online at http://www.spiegel.de/international/europe/germany-and-france-agree-merkozy-to-seek-new-eu-treaty-to-tackle-crisis-a-801858.html, rev. 2013–12–02.

De Grauwe, Paul. 2013. Design Failures in the Eurozone: Can They Be Fixed? LEQS Paper 57, London.

Dor, Eric. 2015. The Exposure of European Countries to Greece. IESEG Working Paper EQM 01, Lille.

Drudi, Francesco, Alain Durré, and Francesco P. Mongelli. 2012. The Interplay of Economic Reforms and Monetary Policy: The Case of the Eurozone. *Journal of Common Market Studies* 50 (6): 881–898.

EFSF (European Financial Stability Facility). 2011. Newsletter 3, November. Available online at http://www.efsf.europa.eu/attachments/201111-efsf-newsletter-n03.pdf, rev. 2015–11–03.

EFSF (European Financial Stability Facility). 2015. Lending operations, February 27. Available online at http://www.efsf.europa.eu/about/operations/index.htm, rev. 2015–11–03.

EP (European Parliament). 2012. Towards a Genuine Economic and Monetary Union. European Parliament Resolution of 20 November 2012 with Recommendations to the Commission on the Report of the Presidents of the European Council, the European Commission, the European Central Bank, and the Eurogroup 'Towards a Genuine Economic and Monetary Union' (2012/2151(INI)), P7_TA(2012)0430, Brussels.

ESM (European Stability Mechanism). 2012. Vertrag zur Einrichtung des Europäischen Stabilitätsmechanismus', February 2. Available online at http://www.bundesfinanzministerium.de/Content/DE/Standardartikel/Themen/Europa/Stabilisierung_des_Euro/Finanzhilfemechanismen/2012-01-27-esm-anl.pdf?__blob=publicationFile&, rev. 2015–11–03.

Euractiv. 2010a. EU Leaders Withhold Details of Greece Rescue Plan, February 11. Available online at http://www.euractiv.com/section/euro-finance/news/eu-leaders-withhold-details-of-greece-rescue-plan/, rev. 2016–05–03.

Euractiv. 2010b. EU Ministers Give Greece Timetable for Recovery, February 17. Available online at http://www.euractiv.com/section/euro-finance/news/eu-ministers-give-greece-timetable-for-recovery/, rev. 2016–05–03.

Euractiv. 2010c. EU to Launch First Eurozone Rescue Operation in Greece, February 10. Available online at http://www.euractiv.com/section/euro-finance/news/eu-to-launch-first-eurozone-rescue-operation-in-greece/, rev. 2016–02–26.

Euractiv. 2010d. Germany Puts New Conditions on Aid to Greece, April 26. Available online at http://www.euractiv.com/section/euro-finance/news/germany-puts-new-conditions-on-aid-to-greece/, rev. 2016–02–29.

Euractiv. 2010e. Greece's Austerity Plan Paves Way for Bailout, March 4. Available online at http://www.euractiv.com/section/development-policy/news/greece-s-austerity-plan-paves-way-for-bailout/, rev. 2016–02–29.

Euractiv. 2011a. Europe's New Treaty: Towards a Multi-speed Union, December 15. Available online at http://www.euractiv.com/future-eu/europes-new-treaty-multi-speed-u-linksdossier-509753#group_positions, rev. 2015–11–06.

Euractiv. 2011b. Franco-German 'Stability Pact': A Coalition of the Willing to Save the Euro? December 8. Available online at http://www.euractiv.com/section/euro-finance/news/franco-german-stability-pact-a-coalition-of-the-willing-to-save-the-euro/, rev. 2016–05–17.

Euractiv. 2011c. Van Rompuy Tables Blueprint for Eurozone 'Fiscal Pact', December 7. Available online at http://www.euractiv.com/section/euro-finance/news/van-rompuy-tables-blueprint-for-eurozone-fiscal-pact/, rev. 2016–05–17.

Euractiv. 2012a. Crisi: Monti, no aiuti, grazie; Rajoy, no per ora forse, October 29. Available online at http://www.euractiv.it/it/news/economia-finanza/6159-crisi-monti-no-aiuti-grazie-rajoy-no-per-ora-forse.html, rev. 2015–05–26.

Euractiv. 2012b. Schäuble Urges Big Leap Forward on 'Fiscal Union', October 16. Available online at http://www.euractiv.com/section/future-eu/news/schauble-urges-big-leap-forward-on-fiscal-union/, rev. 2016–02–26.

Euractiv. 2012c. EU Summit Deal Aims for Full 'Banking Union' in 2014, October 19. Available online at http://www.euractiv.com/euro-finance/summit-advances-eu-plan-banking-news-515515, rev. 2015–05–26.

Eurogroup. 2010. Statement on the Support to Greece by Euro Area Members States, April 11. Available online at http://www.consilium.europa.eu/uedocs/cms_data/docs/pressdata/en/ec/113686.pdf, rev. 2018–02–08.

European Commission. 2012. A Blueprint for a Deep and Genuine Economic and Monetary Union: Launching a European Debate, COM(2012) 777 final/2, November 30, Brussels.

European Commission. 2015. The EU as a Borrower, April 24. Available online at http://ec.europa.eu/economy_finance/eu_borrower/index_en.htm, rev. 2016–02–26.

European Council. 2010. Statement by the Heads of State or Government of the European Union, February 11. Available online at http://www.consilium.europa.eu/uedocs/cms_data/docs/pressdata/en/ec/112856.pdf, rev. 2018–02–08.

European Council. 2011a. Euro Summit Statement, Brussels, October 26. Available online at http://www.consilium.europa.eu/uedocs/cms_data/docs/pressdata/en/ec/125644.pdf, rev. 2016–05–17.

European Council. 2011b. Draft—International Agreement on a Reinforced Economic Union, December 16. Available online at https://de.scribd.com/doc/75872473/Draft-International-Agreement-on-a-Reinforced-Economic-Union?in_collection=3302201, rev. 2016–03–30.

European Council. 2011c. Statement by the Euro Area Heads of State or Government, December 9. Available online at http://www.consilium.europa.eu/uedocs/cms_data/docs/pressdata/en/ec/126658.pdf, rev. 2016–03–30.

Euro Summit. 2010. Statement by the Heads of State and Government of the Euro Area, March 25. Available online at http://www.consilium.europa.eu/uedocs/cms_data/docs/pressdata/en/ec/113563.pdf, rev. 2018–02–22.

Eurozone. 2012. Treaty on Stability, Coordination and Governance in the Economic and Monetary Union. Brussels, March 2. Available online at http://www.eurozone.europa.eu/euro-area/topics/treaty-on-stability,-coordination-and-governance-%28tscg%29/, rev. 2015–11–06.

Featherstone, Kevin. 2011. The Greek Sovereign Debt Crisis and EMU: A Failing State in a Skewed Regime. *Journal of Common Markets Studies* 49 (2): 193–217.

Financial Times. 2012. The Dilemma of German Leadership: Berlin Should Make More Explicit Offers and Demands, January 30. Available online at http://www.ft.com/intl/cms/s/0/636b1c86-4b60-11e1-a325-00144feabdc0.html, rev. 2018–02–07.

Frieden, Jeffry, and Stefanie Walter. 2017. Understanding the Political Economy of the Eurozone Crisis. *Annual Review of Political Science* 20 (1): 371–390.
Friedrich, Carl J. 1963. *Man and His Government*. New York: McGraw-Hill.
Gros, Daniel, and Cinzia Alcidi. 2014. The Case of the Disappearing Fiscal Compact. CEPS Commentary, May 11, Brussels.
Hawley, Charles. 2011. 'No Immediate Solution': Merkel Pledges New Fiscal Unity for Europe. SPIEGEL ONLINE, December 5. Available online at http://www.spiegel.de/international/europe/no-immediate-solution-merkel-pledges-new-fiscal-unity-for-europe-a-801338.html, rev. 2013–12–02.
Heipertz, Martin, and Amy Verdun. 2010. *Ruling Europe: The Politics of the Stability and Growth Pact*. Cambridge: Cambridge University Press.
Jacoby, Wade. 2015. Europe's New German Problem: The Timing of Politics and the Politics of Timing. In *The Future of the Euro*, ed. Matthias Matthijs and Mark Blyth, 187–209. Oxford: Oxford University Press.
Janning, Josef. 2013. State Power Within European Integration: On the Limits and Context of Germany's Power in the Union, DGAPanalyse kompakt 1/2013, Berlin.
Jones, Erik. 2010. Merkel's Folly. *Survival* 52 (3): 21–38.
Karagiannis, Yannis, and Mattia Guidi. 2014. Institutional Change and Continuity in the European Union: The Super-Commissioner Saga. *Acta Politica* 49 (2): 174–195.
Kreilinger, Valentin. 2012. The Making of a New Treaty: Six Rounds of Political Bargaining, Policy Brief Notre Europe 32, Paris.
Krotz, Ulrich, and Joachim Schild. 2013. *Shaping Europe: France, Germany, and Embedded Bilateralism from the Elysée Treaty to Twenty-First Century Politics*. Oxford: Oxford University Press.
Lamers, Karl, and Wolfgang Schäuble. 2014. More Integration Is Still the Right Goal for Europe. *Financial Times*, August 31. Available online at http://www.ft.com/intl/cms/s/0/5565f134-2d48-11e4-8105-00144feabdc0.html, rev. 2018–02–14.
Ludlow, Peter. 2010a. *Brussels and Copenhagen: The European Council and the New Global Disorder*. Briefing Note: Eurocomment.
Ludlow, Peter. 2010b. *In the Last Resort: The European Council and the Euro Crisis, Spring 2010*. Briefing Note: Eurocomment.
Ludlow, Peter. 2010c. Van Rompuy Uses Greek Crisis to Assert His Leadership. Euractiv, March 3. Available online at http://www.euractiv.com/section/eu-priorities-2020/opinion/van-rompuy-uses-greek-crisis-to-assert-his-leadership/, rev. 2016–02–29.
Ludlow, Peter. 2012a. *The European Council of 8, 9 December 2011*. Preliminary Evaluation: Eurocomment.
Ludlow, Peter. 2012b. *The European Council of 30 January 2012: Between German Hegemony and 'More Europe'*. Preliminary Evaluation: Eurocomment.

Ludlow, Peter. 2012c. The Informal European Council of 30 January 2012: The Agenda, Eurocomment.

Matthijs, Matthias. 2016a. Powerful Rules Governing the Euro: The Perverse Logic of German Ideas. *Journal of European Public Policy* 23 (3): 375–391.

Matthijs, Matthias. 2016b. The Three Faces of German Leadership. *Survival* 58 (2): 135–154.

Matthijs, Matthias, and Mark Blyth. 2011. Why Only Germany Can Fix the Euro: Reading Kindleberger in Berlin. Foreign Affairs Snapshot, November 17. Available online at https://www.foreignaffairs.com/articles/germany/2011-11-17/why-only-germany-can-fix-euro, rev. 2018–02–07.

Matthijs, Matthias, Miguel Otero-Iglesias, and Hubert Zimmermann. 2016. A New German Hegemony: Does It Exist? Would It Be Dangerous. In *Key Controversies in European Integration*, 2nd ed., ed. Hubert Zimmermann and Andreas Dür, 234–250. London: Palgrave.

Mayhew, Alan, Kai Oppermann, and Dan Hough. 2011. German Foreign Policy and Leadership of the EU—'You Can't Always Get What You Want … But You Sometimes Get What You Need'. SEI Working Papers 119, Brighton.

Merkel, Angela. 2009. Pressekonferenz der Bundeskanzlerin nach dem Europäischen Rat, December 11. Available online at http://www.bundeskanzlerin.de/ContentArchiv/DE/Archiv17/Mitschrift/Pressekonferenzen/2009/12/2009-12-12-pk-bk-bruessel.html, rev. 2018–02–08.

Miller, Vaughne. 2012. The Treaty on Stability, Coordination and Governance in the Economic and Monetary Union: Political Issues. Research paper 12/14, March 27, House of Commons Library, London.

Morisse-Schilbach, Melanie. 2011. 'Ach Deutschland!': Greece, the Euro Crisis, and the Costs and Benefits of Being a Benign Hegemon. *International Politics and Society* 1: 26–41.

Newman, Abraham. 2015. The Reluctant Leader: Germany's Euro Experience and the Long Shadow of Reunification. In *The Future of the Euro*, ed. Matthias Matthijs and Mark Blyth, 117–135. Oxford: Oxford University Press.

Otero-Iglesias, Miguel. 2017. Still Waiting for Paris: Germany's Reluctant Hegemony in Pursuing Political Union in the Euro Area. *Journal of European Integration* 39 (3): 349–364.

Paterson, William E. 2011. The Reluctant Hegemon? Germany Moves Centre Stage in the European Union. *Journal of Common Market Studies* 49 (s1): 57–75.

President of the European Council. 2011a. Remarks by President of the European Council Herman Van Rompuy at the European Parliament, December 13. Available online at www.consilium.europa.eu/en/press/press-releases/2011/12/pdf/remarks-by-president-herman-van-rompuy-at-the-european-parliament/, rev. 2015–11–06.

President of the European Council. 2011b. Remarks of Herman Van Rompuy, President of the European Council, following the meeting of the European

Council, December 9. Available online at http://www.consilium.europa.eu/en/press/press-releases/2011/12/pdf/remarks-president-van-rompuy,-following-the-meeting-of-the-european-council/, rev. 2016–05–12.

Riegert, Bernd. 2012. EU Puts Off Talk of Schäuble Proposals. Deutsche Welle, October 17. Available online at http://www.dw.de/eu-puts-off-talk-of-sch%C3%A4uble-proposals/a-16312796, rev. 2015–05–23.

Rinke, Andreas. 2011. Stunde der Entscheidung: Wie 'Merkozy' die Grundlagen eines neuen Europas schufen, *International Politik – Die Zeitschrift*. Available online at https://zeitschrift-ip.dgap.org/de/ip-die-zeitschrift/themen/europaeische-union/stunde-der-entscheidung, rev. 2015–11–03.

Schäfer, Daniel, and Ben Hall. 2010. Berlin Calls for Eurozone Budget Laws. *Financial Times*, May 16. Available online at http://www.ft.com/intl/cms/s/0/5ff35db4-6117-11df-9bf0-00144feab49a.html#axzz46Cvvypd9, rev. 2016–05–12.

Schäuble, Wolfgang. 2014. Strategy for European Recovery. Keynote speech given at the Fifth Bruges European Business Conference, March 27. Available online at https://www.coleurope.eu/system/files_force/speech-files/schaeuble-collegeofeurope2014.pdf?download=1, rev. 2016–05–04.

Schelkle, Waltraud. 2012. European Fiscal Union: From Monetary Back Door to Parliamentary Main Entrance. *CESifo Forum* 13 (1): 28–34.

Schild, Joachim. 2013. Leadership in Hard Times: Germany, France, and the Management of the Eurozone Crisis. *German Politics and Society* 31 (1): 24–47.

Schimmelfennig, Frank. 2014. European Integration in the Euro Crisis: The Limits of Postfunctionalism. *Journal of European Integration* 36 (3): 321–337.

Schimmelfennig, Frank. 2015. Liberal Intergovernmentalism and the Euro Area Crisis. *Journal of European Public Policy* 22 (2): 177–195.

Schoeller, Magnus, Mattia Guidi, and Yannis Karagiannis. 2017. Explaining Informal Policy-Making Patterns in the Eurozone Crisis: Decentralized Bargaining and the Theory of EU Institutions. *International Journal of Public Administration* 40 (14): 1211–1222.

Sikorski, Radoslaw. 2011. I Fear Germany's Power Less Than Her Inactivity. *Financial Times*, November 28. Available online at http://www.ft.com/intl/cms/s/0/b753cb42-19b3-11e1-ba5d-00144feabdc0.html#axzz1ksboHuSM, rev. 2018–02–07.

Spiegel. 2012a. Merkel zur Schuldenpolitik: 'Keine Eurobonds, solange ich lebe'. SPIEGEL ONLINE, June 26. Available online at http://www.spiegel.de/politik/ausland/kanzlerin-merkel-schliesst-euro-bonds-aus-a-841115.html, rev. 2016–01–25.

Spiegel. 2012b. Reform der Währungsunion: Brüssel reagiert verhalten auf Schäubles Plan. SPIEGEL ONLINE, October 16. Available online at http://www.spiegel.de/politik/deutschland/bruessel-reagiert-verhalten-auf-schaeuble-plan-a-861579.html, rev. 2015–05–26.

Spiegel, and Wolfgang Schäuble. 2011. Der Spiegel im Gespräch mit Finanzminister Wolfgang Schäuble – Wir wollen nicht herrschen, October 31. Available online at http://www.bundesfinanzministerium.de/Content/DE/Interviews/2011/2011-10-31-spiegelgespraech.html, rev. 2015–05–21.

Spiegel, Peter. 2014. If the Euro Falls, Europe Falls. *Financial Times*, May 15. Available online at http://www.ft.com/intl/cms/s/0/b4e2e140-d9c3-11e3-920f-00144feabdc0.html, rev. 2015–05–15.

Steinmeier, Frank-Walter, and Peer Steinbrück. 2010. Germany Must Lead Fightback. *Financial Times*, December 14. Available online at http://www.ft.com/intl/cms/s/0/effa001c-07ba-11e0-a568-00144feabdc0.html, rev. 2018–02–07.

Tagesschau. 2010. Regierung bleibt skeptisch. tagesschau.de, March 21. Available online at https://www.tagesschau.de/wirtschaft/regierung106.html, rev. 2016–05–03.

Tagesschau. 2012. Schäuble will die EU umbauen. tagesschau.de, October 16. Available online at http://www.tagesschau.de/ausland/schaeuble582.html, rev. 2016–05–04.

Techau, Jan. 2014. The Right Kind of German Leadership for Europe. Judy Dempsey's Strategic Europe Blog, October 28. Available online at http://carnegieeurope.eu/strategiceurope/?fa=57046, rev. 2018–02–07.

Telegraph. 2012. Mario Draghi Backs Wolfgang Schaeuble's 'Super Commissioner' Plan. *The Telegraph*, October 28. Available online at http://www.telegraph.co.uk/finance/financialcrisis//Mario-Draghi-backs-Wolfgang-Schaeubles-super-commissioner-plan.html, rev. 2015–05–26.

The Economist. 2013. The Reluctant Hegemon, June 15. Available online at http://www.economist.com/news/leaders/21579456-if-europes-economies-are-recover-germany-must-start-lead-reluctant-hegemon, rev. 2017–03–07.

Thompson, Helen. 2013. The Crisis of the Euro: The Problem of German Power Revisited. Sheffield Political Economy Research Institute (SPERI) Paper 8, Sheffield.

Tsebelis, George, and Hyeonho Hahm. 2014. Suspending Vetoes: How the Euro Countries Achieved Unanimity in the Fiscal Compact. *Journal of European Public Policy* 21 (10): 1388–1411.

Verdun, Amy. 2015. A Historical Institutionalist Explanation of the EU's Responses to the Euro Area Financial Crisis. *Journal of European Public Policy* 22 (2): 219–237.

Véron, Nicolas. 2011. Europe Must Change Course on Banks. VOX Column, December 22. Available online at https://voxeu.org/article/europe-must-change-course-banks, rev. 2018–02–07.

Wittrock, Philipp. 2011. Taking on the Doubters: Chancellor Merkel's Difficult Battle in Brussels. SPIEGEL ONLINE, December 8. Available online at http://www.spiegel.de/international/europe/taking-on-the-doubters-Chancellor-merkel-s-difficult-battle-in-brussels-a-802444.html, rev. 2013–11–30.

Interviews

Interview 1. 2014. Council of the European Union, senior official/administrator. Brussels, Belgium, November 6.

Interview 2. 2014. European Commission, senior official. Brussels, Belgium, November 7.

Interview 3. 2014. European Commission, DG ECFIN, official. Brussels, Belgium, November 12.

Interview 4. 2014. European Commission, DG ECFIN, administrator. Brussels, Belgium, November 13.

Interview 5. 2014. Permanent Representation of France. Brussels, Belgium, November 13.

Interview 6. 2014. European Commission, DG ECFIN, senior official. Brussels, Belgium, November 14.

Interview 7. 2014. European Council, senior official/assistant. Brussels, Belgium, November 17.

Interview 8. 2014. Council of the European Union, official. Brussels, Belgium, November 18.

Interview 9. 2014. European Commission, DG ECFIN, administrator/administrator. Brussels, Belgium, November 20.

Interview 10. 2014. Senior EU official. Brussels, Belgium, November 20.

Interview 11. 2014. Permanent Representation of the Netherlands. Brussels, Belgium, November 24.

Interview 12. 2014. European Commission, DG ECFIN, official. Brussels, Belgium, November 25.

Interview 13. 2014. Council of the European Union, senior official. Brussels, Belgium, November 25.

Interview 14. 2014. ECB official. Brussels, Belgium, November 26.

Interview 15. 2014. Council of the European Union, senior official. Brussels, Belgium, November 27.

Interview 16. 2014. European Parliament, official. Brussels, Belgium, November 27.

Interview 17. 2014. European Commission, DG ECFIN, official. Brussels, Belgium, November 28.

Interview 18. 2015. European Central Bank, official. Frankfurt, Germany, March 9.

Interview 19. 2015. European Central Bank, senior official. Frankfurt, Germany, March 10.

Interview 20. 2015. European Central Bank, senior official. Frankfurt, Germany, March 11.
Interview 21. 2015. European Central Bank, official/official/administrator. Frankfurt, Germany, March 12.
Interview 22. 2015. European Central Bank, senior official. Frankfurt, Germany, March 12.
Interview 23. 2015. European Central Bank, senior official. Frankfurt, Germany, March 12.
Interview 24. 2015. European Central Bank, senior official. Frankfurt, Germany, March 13.
Interview 25. 2015. Federal Ministry of Finance, government official. Berlin, Germany, March 17.
Interview 26. 2015. Federal Ministry of Finance, government official. Berlin, Germany, March 19.
Interview 27. 2015. Federal Ministry of Finance, senior official. Berlin, Germany, March 23.
Interview 28. 2015. European Parliament, senior official. Brussels, Belgium, February 2.
Interview 29. 2015. European Parliament, Member of the European Parliament. Brussels, Belgium, February 4.
Interview 30. 2015: European Parliament, official. Brussels, Belgium, February 6.
Interview 31. 2015. Council of the European Union, administrator. Brussels, Belgium, February 9.
Interview 32. 2015. European Parliament, official. Brussels, Belgium, February 10.
Interview 33. 2015. European Commission, DG ECFIN, official/official. Brussels, Belgium, February 11.
Interview 34. 2015. Council of the European Union, official. Brussels, Belgium, February 11.
Interview 35. 2015. European Parliament, senior official. Brussels, Belgium, February 12.

CHAPTER 5

Analysing Leadership II: The EU Institutions in the Eurozone Crisis

This chapter provides three case studies analysing the role of the EU institutions in eurozone crisis management. The first case study examines how and why the European Commission did not emerge as a leader in handling the controversial issue of Eurobonds (Sect. 5.1). The second case study sheds light on the role of the European Parliament (EP) by analysing how it emerged, but ultimately failed as a leader in the case of Eurobonds (Sect. 5.2). The third case study, finally, focuses on the European Central Bank's (ECB) successful leadership in announcing its Outright Monetary Transactions (OMT), better known as the famous declaration of "whatever it takes" (Sect. 5.3).

5.1 No Leadership: The European Commission and Eurobonds

The issue of Eurobonds is not only interesting from a leadership perspective, but also enlightening with regard to eurozone politics in general, and EU inter-institutional relations in particular. While the Commission did not take the lead on Eurobonds, the EP did so, but failed (Sect. 5.2). The status quo costs were the same in both cases. Therefore, this chapter argues that the difference between Parliament and Commission was the respective "leader's surplus". Although the Commission is in possession of considerably more resources to provide leadership, Sect. 5.1 reveals that it expected more harm from taking the lead on Eurobonds than it could have benefitted from it.

M. G. Schoeller, *Leadership in the Eurozone*, Palgrave Studies in European Union Politics, https://doi.org/10.1007/978-3-030-12704-6_5

The section starts out by describing the case of Eurobonds and introducing the relevant actors and their preferences. After the case description, the value of the dependent variable (emergence of leadership) is determined and the explanatory factors (leadership surplus, status quo costs) are assessed. Finally, the section summarizes the results of this case study.

Case Description: Debating Eurobonds

The Commission's standing in economic governance is debated. While many academics agree that the eurozone crisis has weakened the Commission's role as an agenda-setter, much of the literature also suggests that the Commission has been strengthened as guardian of the EU's rules; for some authors it is even the "unexpected winner of the crisis" (Bauer and Becker 2014: 213; see Dehousse 2016; Nugent and Rhinard 2016: 1208f.; Savage and Verdun 2016: 102f.). While this case study does not seek to answer the question concerning the Commission's general evolution and influence in EMU, it does unveil new insights regarding the Commission's role as a policy-initiator by asking why the Commission did not emerge as a leader in the issue of Eurobonds. After all, Eurobonds are a pro-integrationist proposal that should not only be in the interest of the Commission, but also contribute to the common good of the eurozone as a whole (see below).

There are manifold proposals of how the issuance of common eurozone debt could be designed. The Commission's Green Paper on Eurobonds (European Commission 2011) distinguished three broad approaches: (1) the full substitution of Eurobonds for national bonds, (2) the partial substitution of Eurobonds for national bonds, with joint and several guarantees; and (3) the partial substitution of Eurobonds for national bonds, with several (but not joint) guarantees.[1] Moreover, the proposed options of how to contain the related risk of moral hazard vary significantly as well. Without going into these technical details, this book uses the term "Eurobonds" to denote all types of common debt issuance under joint guarantees at the European level. This includes also "Eurobills" (short-term bonds) and the so-called "Redemption

[1] Eurobonds with several (but not joint) guarantees could simply be issued alongside national debt or they could be granted seniority over national bonds and collaterals (such as cash, gold, a special tax, part of the VAT or any other income stream) (Interview 24; European Commission 2011: 9).

Fund" proposal (German Council of Economic Experts 2012; European Commission 2014).[2]

The idea of Eurobonds (or "EU bonds") is older than the eurozone crisis. Commission Presidents Delors and Prodi suggested the issuance of common debt in order to finance the EU budget long before the eruption of the crisis. In November 2008, Jean-Claude Juncker, at the time Eurogroup chairman and Prime Minister of Luxembourg, proposed the idea as a measure against the EU's economic crisis in an interview with the German tabloid *Bild* (Bild 2008). In December 2010, Juncker proposed Eurobonds again in a *Financial Times* article co-authored with the Italian Economy and Finance Minister, Giulio Tremonti (Juncker and Tremonti 2010).

Still, the first time the issue entered the agenda of eurozone crisis management was in January 2011, when Member of the European Parliament Sylvie Goulard tabled a draft report for the negotiations of the so-called "Sixpack" legislation, in which she demanded the introduction of Eurobonds (European Parliament 2011a: 22f.). The EP kept the issue on the political agenda at least until summer 2012 when the launch of the OMT suspended the crisis (Sect. 5.3). In November 2011, the Commission issued a Green Paper on the feasibility of Eurobonds as a result of a package deal with the EP in the context of the "Sixpack" negotiations. At the same time, however, it made clear that it would not go on with a legislative proposal in the near future (Euractiv 2011a). In 2013, the Commission set up an expert group investigating on a redemption fund and eurobills, which was a condition imposed by the EP for its agreement on the so-called "Twopack" legislation. The last time Eurobonds received public attention in the context of crisis management was in December 2012, when they were mentioned in the Commission's "Blueprint for a Deep and Genuine Economic and Monetary Union" (European Commission 2012) and in the so-called "Four-Presidents-Report" (President of the European Council 2012).

[2] Debt issuance *without* joint guarantees is excluded from this analysis, as it would not contribute to a common goal. In the simple version, Eurobonds without joint guarantees would not obtain an AAA rating, but at best the weighted average of the member state ratings and at worst that of the lowest-rated member state. In both cases they would not contribute to a common goal. In the enhanced version, Eurobonds without joint guarantees could be granted seniority over national bonds and collateral to obtain an AAA rating. However, given that this would allow only for a partial issuance alongside national bonds, it would have detrimental effects on the credit quality of "weaker" member states' government bonds. Thus, also in this latter case, Eurobonds without joint guarantees could at best be a short-term solution and would thus not contribute to a common goal.

The central actors concerning any decision on Eurobonds are, once again, the member states as the issuance of common debt under joint guarantees would require treaty change. However, also the Commission and the ECB play a crucial role as these are the institutions with the necessary expertise to make concrete proposals regarding the technical design of Eurobonds. Moreover, both institutions could become the issuing authority of common eurozone debt. Finally, the EP plays an important role, too, since the introduction of Eurobonds would ultimately require its consent.[3] These actors' preferences diverged significantly, however. While a group of southern member states, together with France and the EP, were clearly in favour of Eurobonds, another group of northern countries around Germany rejected the proposal. Although the Commission might internally be in favour of Eurobonds, its strategic preferences were neutral, if not unfavourable (see below). The ECB, finally, favoured the introduction of Eurobonds in the long run, but for the time being remained against them as they would not be backed by a real fiscal union with a proper system of conditionality.

No Leadership by the Commission

A leader has emerged if there is (1) an actor in a positon of power, who guides a group towards (2) a common goal by (3) making appropriate use of its power resources (Sect. 3.4). While two of these indicators, namely the position of power and the common goal, are given in the case of the Commission's role in the Eurobonds saga, the third one is missing. As the Commission did not use its resources in such a way as to guide the Eurozone towards the introduction of common bonds, it did not emerge as a leader in this case.

Already in 1970, David Coombes described the function of the Commission as twofold:

> […] in some aspects the Commission is expected to act as a bureaucracy and to have the essential characteristics of an implementative, 'goal-seeking' organization, while in others it must behave as if it

[3] Eurobonds could either be set up intergovernmentally through the simplified revision procedure (Art. 48.6 TFEU) or under EU law using the ordinary treaty change procedure in conjunction with the so-called "flexibility clause" (Art. 352 TFEU). Both the simplified revision procedure and the use of the flexibility clause require the EP's consent.

> constituted the *political leadership of the Community, acting as an initiating, 'goal-setting' body.* (234, own emphasis)

However, Coombes also pointed out that there is an inherent tension, if not incompatibility, between the Commission's political and bureaucratic function (1970: 240). Indeed, the above-mentioned debate about the Commission's role in eurozone crisis management is characterized by the implicit differentiation between the two functions and the question which of the two has actually been fulfilled by the Commission.

While it can be debated whether the Commission has exercised a leading role in crisis management (Chang and Monar 2013), it is less controversial that the Commission has the resources to do so (Nugent 1995; Nugent and Rhinard 2016). In general, it is the Commission's institutional resources—and in particular its formal right of initiative—which put it in a position of authority. In the particular issue of Eurobonds, however, the Commission's non-material resources (expertise and legitimacy) play an even bigger role since the Commission would have to act as an informal agenda-setter and provider of common knowledge. At any rate, as Neill Nugent has pointed out:

> leadership capacity is not the same as leadership exercised. Acting within a framework of varying constraints and rapidly changing circumstances the Commission must, if it is to operationalize its leadership capacity effectively, mobilize the resources at its disposal and take advantage of the opportunities presented within its operating contexts. (1995: 621)

Thus, next to a position of power, the Commission needs to employ its resources in an appropriate way. Before it is shown that in the issue of Eurobonds this has not been the case, it needs to be clarified whether Eurobonds would actually contribute to the common goal of preserving the common currency and overcoming the crisis.

Although Eurobonds would at least in the short run be to the disadvantage of single member states like Germany,[4] they are generally regarded as a Pareto-improving solution to the crisis as they would provide

[4]Common debt based on joint and several liability would not only imply risk-sharing in the sense that fiscally solid countries would guarantee for the debt of "fiscal sinners". It would also redistribute the interest burden since those with supposedly sound budgets would lose their low interest rates in favour of those paying high interests.

stability to the eurozone and correct some of its inbuilt design failures (De Grauwe 2013: 28; Schelkle 2012: 31–3; European Commission 2011: 4–7). As outlined at the beginning of Chapter 4, a non-optimal currency area not only needs institutions to prevent moral hazard (austerity), but also ways of organizing the inevitable mutualisation of risk (solidarity). Eurobonds are such a way. To qualify as a contribution to a common goal, however, Eurobonds would need to fulfil some requirements to prevent moral hazard and uneven risk sharing in the Eurozone. They would need to be partial and to be accompanied by adequate mechanisms providing compensation to fiscally more solid countries as well as an effective control over national budgets. Furthermore, Eurobonds would require rules prescribing how the financial means raised at the markets are to be distributed and employed in the eurozone.

Equipped with such provisions, Eurobonds would fulfil a number of functions for the eurozone. To begin, they would prevent future sovereign debt crises by lowering the funding costs for highly indebted member states. Second, they would reinforce financial stability in the eurozone by providing a source of robust collateral for the eurozone banking system. They would, furthermore, facilitate the transmission of ECB monetary policy into the real economy and improve the efficiency of the eurozone's financial markets by providing low benchmark yields based on high liquidity and credit quality. Finally, Eurobonds would enhance the role of the euro as an international reserve currency due to larger issuance volumes and higher liquidity as compared to national bond markets (see European Commission 2011: 4–7).

Hence, Eurobonds would contribute to the common goal of preserving the single currency and would thus make the eurozone as a whole better off. However, similar to the case with the Fiscal Compact (Sect. 4.3), this does not mean that Eurobonds were the solution preferred by all actors involved. While all actors shared the goal of overcoming the crisis and preserving the euro, their preferences over the ways to reach that goal diverged. This applies also to the case of Eurobonds, which is but one possible solution.

Thus, while two indicators for the emergence of leadership are given—namely an actor in possession of power resources (Commission) and a common goal (stabilizing the eurozone)—there is no evidence for the third indicator, as the Commission did not employ its resources to guide the other actors towards the introduction of Eurobonds. Instead of making use of leadership strategies, the Commission rather defended the status quo (Hodson 2013: 305, 310). It even tried to avoid using the term "Eurobonds" or making public statements on the topic (Interview 29). Apart from its "Blueprint for a Deep and Genuine Economic and Monetary Union", where Eurobonds are mentioned as a possible long-term measure, the Commission only issued a "Green Paper on the feasibility of introducing Stability Bonds" (European Commission 2011). This, however, was not the Commission's own initiative, but the consequence of a deal with the EP on the adoption of the Sixpack legislation: the Commission offered to present a report on the feasibility of Eurobonds if the EP in return would give up its resistance in the trialogue negotiations (Interviews 13, 16; Euractiv 2011b). Although most of the accounts converge on the fact that the Commission was principally—that is, unofficially and regardless of the situational circumstances—in favour of Eurobonds, they unanimously agree that the Commission has not pushed the issue at all (Interviews 1–3, 6, 10, 13, 16, 25).

In sum, despite the fact that the Commission is in the position to provide leadership in the EU and Eurobonds would contribute to a common goal in the eurozone, the Commission did not employ its resources in such a way as to guide other actors towards the realization of common bond issuance. With regard to the value of the dependent variable, this means that the Commission did not emerge as a leader in the case of Eurobonds.

Explaining the Commission's Lack of Leadership: Leadership Surplus and Status Quo Costs

According to this book's leadership model (Chapter 3), the first explanatory factor accounting for a leader's emergence is her surplus, which results from the expected costs and benefits of leading. Table 5.1 summarizes those interview answers that concern the Commission's leadership surplus in the case of Eurobonds. Answers from interviewees who were directly involved in the issue of Eurobonds are printed in bold. Those representing the Commission are italicised. As can be seen at first glance, the Commission's expected costs of leading by far exceeded its benefits. All but one respondent immediately referred to the high costs the Commission would have had to bear in case of leading. These costs derive from the low chances of success. The main reason for this assessment is the fierce resistance of Germany and, to a lesser extent, of other "creditor states". According to a closely involved senior official of the

Table 5.1 The commission's costs and benefits of leading according to interviewees (Eurobonds)

Interview	*Benefits*	*Costs*
		CREDIBILITY
2		***"Pursuing this controversial debate without prospects of reaching a satisfactory agreement would put even more at risk the fragile confidence that the EU was building up a response to the crisis"***
9	***None, no chance of success***	***Loss of reputation***
13	**None, no chance of success**	**Loss of reputation**
17		*Loss of neutrality as agenda-setter and deal-maker*
25		Association with 'loser topic'[a]
		LEGITIMACY
2		***Telling Dutch and German citizens to share reputational risk (ratings)***
3		*Commission is not measured against the promotion of good or bad ideas, but against what it can realize*
9	***See above***	***Loss of reputation***
13	**See above**	**Loss of reputation**
17		*Loss of neutrality as agenda-setter and deal-maker*
		"KILLING THE IDEA"
9	***See above***	***"There is no point to initiate if you know that [...] [the issue] will be killed right away"***
15		pushing more strongly for Eurobonds would have killed the entire idea
		BUREAUCRATIC RESOURCES
1		Other priorities: 6 + 2pack, Banking Union
		BARGAINING POSITION
3		*Worsening of Commission's bargaining position in more important issues*
	INSTITUTIONAL POWER?	
6	***Possible increase of institutional power***	
9	***Possible increase of institutional power (but unrealisable)***	

Source Own illustration
[a]Translated by the author from the original: "Negativthema"

Commission, taking the lead on Eurobonds "would end up in a big disappointment" as "you cannot embark in such an operation with just a few number of member states committed. The strength of the tool is meaningless if you [...] don't have the main players involved in it" (Interview 2).

The Commission's costs of leading in the case of Eurobonds would consist primarily in its loss of credibility and legitimacy. The Commission feared that taking the lead on Eurobonds would result in a considerable loss of credibility because it would either not be able to achieve Eurobonds at all, or only by making painful concessions. On the one hand, this regarded the credibility of the Commission as a competent agenda-setter and honest broker. If the Commission had lost the battle on Eurobonds, it would have been accused of "bad judgement" (Interview 13) and it would have lost the trust of member states in its qualities as "neutral" negotiation manager. On the other hand, the expected defeat in a battle on Eurobonds would have damaged the credibility of the eurozone and its crisis-management *vis-à-vis* the financial markets: "pursuing this controversial debate without prospects of reaching a satisfactory agreement would put even more at risk the fragile confidence that the EU was building up a response to the crisis" (Interview 2). In sum, the Commission feared a loss of confidence in the eurozone's capability of fighting the crisis in general, and in its own capabilities as agenda-setter, honest broker, and crisis-manager in particular.

Moreover, the Commission was concerned with its (output) legitimacy. On the one hand, taking the lead on Eurobonds would have resulted in a loss of perceived legitimacy among the citizens in financially more solid member states such as Germany and the Netherlands because of its negative distributional consequences for these countries. On the other hand, the Commission feared a general loss of legitimacy as regards its function as the EU's executive. As one interviewee put it, unlike the EP, the Commission is not measured against the promotion of good or bad ideas, but against what it manages to realize (Interview 3).

A further type of expected costs was not so much related to the damage the Commission would suffer, but rather to the project itself.[5] The Commission feared that by pushing for Eurobonds without any realistic

[5] Of course, any damage to the project of Eurobonds would indirectly also be to the disadvantage of the Commission.

chance of success, the idea and any chance of a later realisation would have been eliminated once and for all. Therefore, the Commission, which in principle would be in favour of Eurobonds, opted not to address the topic directly, but to postpone it to a more favourable moment in the future (Interview 15). As a Commission official working on the issue of Eurobonds explained: "There is no point to initiate if you know that there will be even no discussion, that it will be killed right away. […] You need to be realistic of what you are pushing for or not" (Interview 9).

Finally, two further types of costs regarded the Commission's bureaucratic resources and its bargaining position *vis-à-vis* Germany. First, it was expected that by taking the lead on Eurobonds, the Commission would have to invest valuable bureaucratic resources (in terms of time and staff) which could be used for other projects with a higher chance of success, such as the Six- and Twopack legislation and the Banking Union (Interview 1; also Hodson 2013: 309f.). Indeed, at the time the interviews for this case study were conducted (November 2014), the Commission's staff, who had worked on the Green Paper on Eurobonds and in the Expert Group on the Redemption Fund, already dealt with other issues such as Capital Markets Union. Second, any concession the Commission could have obtained from Germany in relation to Eurobonds would have weakened its position on other issues that were considered more important in the short term.

Contrary to all the perceived costs of leading, there were no benefits expected by the Commission as Eurobonds did not have any chance of success. To be sure, the Commission was well aware that if it had become the common issuance agency of Eurobonds, this would have enhanced its institutional power. However, given that Eurobonds were regarded as unrealistic anyways, this was not even considered a potential benefit of taking the lead on the issue (Interviews 1, 6, 9, 13).

As outlined in Sect. 3.4, a cost-benefits analysis can be conducted if (1) there is a "common currency" to balance cost and benefits against each other, (2) either costs or benefits are insignificant or non-existent, or (3) they consist in the actor's institutional death or survival, respectively. In the case of Eurobonds, the second option applies: given that from the Commission's point of view there were no benefits of taking the lead, the costs clearly prevailed. Even a potential increase in institutional power through the introduction of Eurobonds would be counterbalanced by the loss of other power resources, such as the Commission's credibility, its legitimacy, and its bureaucratic resources.[6] According to the first theoretical proposition of this book's leadership model (H1), we therefore expect no supply of leadership by the Commission and thus no emergence of leadership.

The second variable accounting for a leader's emergence are the group's perceived status quo costs. As pointed out in Chapter 4, these costs were high throughout the entire crisis. Not surprisingly, the (re-) emergence of the Eurobonds proposal coincided with the onset of eurozone crisis management. At the European Council summit of 9 and 10 May 2010, where the temporary bailout fund ESFS was established, the Commission explicitly argued in support of Eurobonds (Interview 25). As pointed out by a majority of interviewees (68.4%), this was one of the most critical moments in crisis when the perceived pressure for action was highest. Still, after promoting the issue at this single occasion, the Commission refrained from further pursuing the idea. At this point, the EP stepped into keep the topic in the discourse. Among other instances, the EP introduced the issue to the negotiations on the so-called Sixpack (January–September 2011) and Twopack legislation (February 2012–March 2013), and to the debate evolving around the Commission's blueprint and the Four Presidents' roadmap towards a genuine EMU (November–December 2012) (Sect. 5.2).

Hence, Eurobonds were present throughout the entire period of crisis management covered by this book. Given that status quo costs during the crisis were constantly high, we expect a generally high demand for leadership to solve the (re-)financing problem in the eurozone. If there had been also supply of leadership by the Commission—for example by actively promoting Eurobonds—the theoretical model would predict the emergence of the Commission as a leader in the issue (H2). However, since the Commission did not offer any leadership in this case, this expectation does not apply to the issue of Eurobonds.

Results

The book's first theoretical expectation predicts that if the expected benefits of leading exceed the perceived costs of it, leadership is offered

[6] Yet, while the loss in power would occur with or without the eventual introduction of Eurobonds, the gain would only materialize in the unlikely case of leadership success. Hence, from an ex-ante perspective, the costs would in any case exceed the benefits of leading.

and—under the condition that there is also a demand—emerges. With regard to the Commission's role in debating and (non) promoting the issue of Eurobonds, this expectation has proved plausible: given that the Commission's expected costs of leading clearly exceeded its benefits, the Commission did *not* offer leadership and did therefore not emerge as a leader in the case of Eurobonds.

To be sure, the interview material points to at least one instance in which Commission representatives pronounced themselves in favour of Eurobonds (European Council summit of 9 and 10 May 2010). However, neither did the Commission employ its resources to convince the opponents of Eurobonds, thereby assuming leadership, nor did it ever declare itself in favour of Eurobonds in public. The same is true with regard to the Commission's "Blueprint for a Deep and Genuine Economic and Monetary Union". While short-term Eurobills and a Redemption Fund are described as possible medium-term steps, Eurobonds are mentioned in not more than two sentences as a very last step of EMU integration; they are not described—let alone advocated—in any way (European Commission 2012: 12f., 28–30).

In contrast, the interview material converges on the fact that although the Commission would principally be in favour of common debt, it consistently avoided pushing the issue or taking an official stand on it. This becomes especially evident with regard to the Commission's way of handling the expert group on a redemption fund. Although this would have been the chance for the Commission to promote the issue of common debt without formally taking the initiative on it, the working group "was kept very low-key" (Interview 10) and presented a relatively reserved and neutral position in its final report. Thus, the Commission not only refrained from pushing the issue of Eurobonds, but even actively avoided giving it any public salience. As a closely involved Member of Parliament put it: "He [Olli Rehn] was himself convinced but Barroso and the rest of the Commission, under the pressure of some member states, were doing everything at this time for not even tackling the issue or pronouncing the word" (Interview 29). In accordance with this book's conceptualization of leadership (Chapter 2), such behaviour equals a refusal to lead.

In sum, the book's theoretical model appears plausible as it can deliver an explanation as to why the Commission did not emerge as a leader in the case of Eurobonds. In the light of the low chance of success, the Commission had to expect more harm from taking the lead than it could have profited. Thus, this case shows once again that leadership is not an altruistic sacrifice of particular actors, but inextricably linked with those actors' individual benefits. From a normative point of view, one might argue that the Commission should push for the common good of the entire eurozone even if its realization is highly unlikely or the eventual lack of success might entail more costs than benefits for the EU's executive. As this case study shows, however, no such normative considerations, but rather a rational cost-benefit analysis determined the Commission's behaviour when it came to the question of leadership (see Hodson 2013; Warren et al. 2017).

5.2 Failed Leadership: The European Parliament and Eurobonds

Despite being a relatively weak actor in terms of resources, the EP emerged as a leader in the case of Eurobonds. This was possible because there was a leadership vacuum with regard to a solution for the refinancing problems of single eurozone members. In contrast to the Commission, the Parliament expected to benefit from taking the lead by stimulating a public debate and thus increasing its perceived legitimacy. Yet, the Parliament failed to change the status quo because of its scarce power resources, the heterogeneity of preferences among member states, and the high institutional constraint, which consisted in treaty change.

The case of Eurobonds, here broadly understood as the issuance of common debt, has been presented in the preceding Sect. 5.1, which focuses on the European Commission. This chapter, by contrast, analyses the role of the EP.[7] The issue of Eurobonds highlights the EP's capability to influence the public debate and thereby to set the political agenda. In doing so, the EP not only ensures the input legitimacy of EU economic governance, but it also attempts to enhance its output legitimacy. In the concrete case of Eurobonds, the EP thus goes beyond its competences as co-legislator in the field of multilateral surveillance. It even goes beyond a parliament's traditional role of holding the executive accountable. Instead, the EP enters the stage of problem-definition

[7] For the purpose of the analysis, the EP is treated as a unitary institutional actor, which is able to adopt a coherent external position despite internal divides and disagreements (see O'Keeffe et al. 2016).

and agenda-setting, where it holds only few institutional competences. Hence, next to analysing the EP as a potential leader (see Judge and Earnshaw 2008; Shackleton 2017), this chapter speaks to a broad strand of literature dealing with the EP's (self-)empowerment in EU policy-making and institutional reform (e.g. Héritier et al. 2019, forthcoming; Hix and Høyland 2013; Rittberger 2003). Moreover, the chapter adds to the ongoing analysis of the EP's crisis and post-crisis role in EU econonomic governance (Bressanelli and Chelotti 2018; Crum 2018; Fromage 2018; Warren 2018).

As the case of Eurobonds has already been described above (Sect. 5.1), this chapter starts out by directly assessing the values of the two dependent variables, namely the emergence and impact of leadership. The subsequent sub-sections then shift the focus to the assessment of the independent variables and the causal mechanisms accounting for the two outcomes. Finally, the chapter draws the conclusions of this case study.

Failed Leadership

The dependent variable of the first analytical step is the emergence of leadership, which is given if there is (1) a common goal and (2) an actor in a position of power that (3) uses its resources to guide a group towards the achievement of that common goal ("strategies").

As to the first criterion (common goal), the value-added of Eurobonds for overcoming the crisis and preserving the single currency is explicated in Sect. 5.1. Regarding the second criterion (position of power), the EP has to rely on its legitimacy as the EU's only directly elected institution. Given that its economic resources are virtually insignificant as compared to other relevant actors such as member states or the ECB, and its institutional power does not reach that of the Commission or member states either, the EP needs to build on its non-material resources. Still, although it is not an ideal leadership candidate in EMU, the EP can fill a leadership vacuum by employing non-material resources through the instrumental use of public discourse, and by extending its restricted institutional resources through the skilful employment of informal bargaining strategies (Héritier et al. 2019, forthcoming).

Indeed, as regards the third indicator for the emergence of leadership (strategies), the EP promoted Eurobonds through the stimulation of a public debate and the use of bargaining strategies *vis-à-vis* the

Commission and member states. Under the lead of Sixpack rapporteur Sylvie Goulard, the EP (re-)introduced the idea of Eurobonds through the trialogue negotiations at the beginning of 2011. While Goulard's draft report demanded the actual establishment of Eurobonds, the final report asked the Commission "to present a report, [...] accompanied, where appropriate, by legislative proposals and, if necessary, a Treaty change to set up a system of common issuance of European sovereign bonds (eurosecurities) under joint and several liability" (European Parliament 2011c: Art. 8a.5; see 2011a: 13, 22f.). Since then, the EP kept on promoting Eurobonds and pushing the issue in negotiations.

In a resolution adopted in July 2011, the EP proposed Eurobonds as a possible measure to overcome the crisis and "calls on the Commission to carry out an investigation into a future system of Eurobonds" (European Parliament 2011b: 4). By linking this demand to the approval of the Sixpack legislation, where the EP had a veto right under the Ordinary Legislative Procedure, the EP obtained the Commission's promise to present a report on Eurobonds (Euractiv 2011b). Following up the Commission's Green Paper on Eurobonds, issued in November 2011, the EP launched an own-initiative procedure on the feasibility of introducing stability bonds, which even contained a roadmap leading from the immediate establishment of a "Redemption Fund", via the issuance of Eurobills and partial Eurobonds, through to the introduction of genuine European debt (European Parliament 2012c, 2013).

Moreover, the EP promoted Eurobonds in several resolutions. For instance, in a resolution February 2012, the EP called "for the establishment of project bonds [and] a roadmap for stability bonds" (European Parliament 2012a: 2). Furthermore, in a "topical subject" resolution on the feasibility of introducing stability bonds, which was adopted in the same month, the EP stated that "stability bonds could be an additional means of incentivising compliance with the stability and growth pact" and that "further work needs to be undertaken as regards the options presented in the Green Paper" (European Parliament 2012b: 2). Additionally, in its legislative initiative resolution "Towards a genuine Economic and Monetary Union", the EP considered Eurobonds as "a possible way to supplement EMU" in the longer run (European Parliament 2012e). Moreover, EP President Martin Schulz promoted Eurobonds in the exchange of views with the heads of state and government taking place at the beginning of European Council meetings (Ludlow 2012: 22). Finally, when negotiating the so-called Twopack regulations, the EP delayed a final agreement until it obtained the establishment of a Commission expert group investigating on Eurobills and a Redemption Fund (Interview 33).

Because of these actions, the EP was generally perceived as a promoter of Eurobonds, although a considerable number of Members of the EP (MEPs) were against the issuance of common debt (Interviews 2, 31). The proponents of Eurobonds within the EP can be divided into federalists, who considered Eurobonds an unavoidable step towards a genuine EMU and an instrument to lower average interests for sovereign bonds in the long term, and socialists, who regarded Eurobonds as a tool to lower interest rates in the so-called "debtor states" in the short term. Of these two groups, only the former insisted on combining Eurobonds with strong conditionality. Nevertheless, during the seventh legislative term 2009–2014, the two political camps were able to build an influential block in favour of Eurobonds. The short-term strategic target of this block, and especially of the federalists, was not the immediate introduction of Eurobonds, but the evocation of a public debate on common debt. This was clearly against the preferences of the Commission and the Council, which both tried to avoid any public engagement with the topic (Sect. 5.1; Interviews 29, 32, 33).

The battle over how to reach this goal started *within* the EP during the Sixpack negotiations. In order to obtain a majority for this legislation, the European People's Party (EPP) needed the Alliance of Liberals and Democrats for Europe (ALDE), which gave its vote only in exchange for the inclusion of Eurobonds into the legislative package. Although the original amendment[8] of the draft report, which would have provided for the actual introduction of Eurobonds, was deleted during the trialogue negotiations, a small but operative review clause, which commits the Commission to "present a report [...] on the possibility of introducing euro-securities" (European Parliament/Council 2011: Art. 13.4) remained. From the EP's point of view, this—and the fact that the Commissioner for Economic and Monetary Affairs Olli Rehn had to declare in front of the Plenary to present not only a report but, if appropriate, even a legislative proposal—is considered a victory in the battle for Eurobonds (Interview 29).

[8] European Parliament (2011a: Amendment 37).

Given that there is a strong faction in the EP against Eurobonds, some practitioners and observers refrain from describing the EP as a promotor of Eurobonds. However, not only has the EP been perceived as a promoter of Eurobonds by the Commission and member states (Interviews 1, 2, 33); in its report and resolutions, it actually asked for feasibility studies and a roadmap towards the common issuance of public debt or the establishment of Eurobonds (e.g. European Parliament 2011a, 2012d, e). Even looking into the EP's internal divisions of the seventh legislative term, one finds a broad cross-factional and cross-ideological basis in support of Eurobonds. A survey, which was conducted with 100 MEPs[9] between 16 October and 11 December 2012, shows that approximately 58% of MEPs supported Eurobonds. This majority included 54% of EPP members, 80% of S&D members, and 87% of ALDE members (ComRes 2013). Moreover, as O'Keeffe and colleagues (2016) have shown, the EP's internal divisions in the field of EU economic governance during the crisis had no significant influence on its external behaviour as a unitary actor in the negotiations with the Commission and Council.

Hence, relying on its legitimacy as the EU's only directly elected institution and its co-decision rights in multilateral surveillance, the EP promoted Eurobonds as a tool to reach the common goal of preserving the common currency and overcoming the crisis. In other words, the EP emerged as a leader in the case of Eurobonds.

As regards the second analytical step (impact), the EP's leadership turned out to be unsuccessful, though. This does not mean that the EP had no achievements to celebrate. Not only did it make the reluctant Commission publish a Green Paper on Eurobonds, it also managed to get a public declaration on Eurobonds by then Economic and Monetary Commissioner Olli Rehn. His promise to even table a legislative proposal if appropriate was considered immensely important with regard to the creation of a public debate. Given that the Commission had to that point avoided any public engagement with the topic, the proponents of Eurobonds regarded this a real victory. Nevertheless, Eurobonds have not materialized and no other policy or institutional change implying the issuance of common debt has been achieved by the EP. Moreover,

[9] The data are weighted by party group and region to be representative of the entire EP (ComRes 2013: 8).

Eurobonds have never made it to the agenda of any formal meeting of the Eurogroup, ECOFIN Council, or any of its preparatory bodies. From the other institutions' point of view, the furthest that could have been achieved were the provisions in the Six- and Twopack legislation that obliged the Commission to come up with a Green Paper and to set up an expert group on a Redemption Fund and Eurobills (Interviews 8, 33). Hence, the value of the second step's dependent variable is the absence of policy or institutional change—and thus leadership failure.

Explaining the European Parliament's Leadership Emergence: Leadership Surplus and Status Quo Costs

The first theoretical proposition accounting for the emergence of leadership concerns the expected costs and benefits of the potential leader ("leader's surplus"). Like the Commission, the EP must have been aware of the resistance of some member states and could thus not hope for the actual introduction of Eurobonds. Therefore, if the conjecture is correct, there must have been benefits of leading for the EP which are not linked to the eventual realization of Eurobonds. Table 5.2 summarizes the interviewees' answers regarding the EP's leadership surplus.

Strictly speaking, the creation of a public debate on Eurobonds and a more federal Union is not a benefit for the EP as such, but rather for those MEPs driving the case for Eurobonds (namely the federalist members of ALDE) who thereby keep their own political agenda in the public

Table 5.2 The Parliament's costs and benefits of leading according to interviewees (Eurobonds)

Interview	*Benefits*	*Costs*
16, 29, 32	Creating a **public debate**	
3, 15	Increasing the EP's **legitimacy** as promoter of the EU's common good	
25	Increasing the EP's **institutional power** (as EP could obtain quasi-budgetary competences)	
3, 15, 17		**None** (as EP is not held responsible for realization)

Source Own illustration

sphere. However, given that in the case of Eurobonds the EP represented the goals of ALDE (see above), this distinction does not make any difference as regards the explanation of the EP's external behaviour. What matters is that by taking the lead on Eurobonds, the EP could reach the goal of causing the desired public debate even if there was no chance to actually realize the issuance of common debt. Therefore, this is indeed a benefit of leading for the EP.

Moreover, by advocating Eurobonds as a solution to the eurozone crisis, the EP presented itself as promoter of the EU's common good and thereby increased its perceived legitimacy without being held responsible for the implementation of the idea. Especially for the EP, as the EU's only directly elected institution, legitimacy is a crucial power resource on which it has regularly based its demands for an expansion of its legislative powers (Rittberger 2014: 1175f.). However, whereas the Commission refrained from taking the lead because of its low chances of success, the EP could benefit precisely *because* the actual introduction of Eurobonds was unrealistic. Were Eurobonds to become a realistic option, the EP might not even be able to mobilize a majority for them, given the negative distributional consequences for financially more solid member states. However, as long as Eurobonds were only an idea, which in theory contributes to the common good of overcoming the crisis, but in practice is not implementable, the EP could only profit by "selling a nice idea to the public" (Interview 15) without being responsible for its realization. This strategy is similar to what has been called "blame-shifting" in the literature. The EP not only presents itself as the eurozone's actual promoter of the common good, it can even accuse member states of being those exacerbating the crisis due to their national egoisms. In this way, the blame for the crisis (or its poor management) is shifted from the European level and its institutions to the national level.

Finally, the EP's potential gains in institutional power constitute a further benefit of leading. In the case of an eventual introduction of Eurobonds, the EP could become the institution scrutinizing the issuance and appropriation of common debt, and thus gain new accountability powers.

With regard to the costs of leading, all interviewees agreed that there were no significant costs to be feared by the EP: being the EU's legislative body, the EP is assessed according to whether its initiatives can contribute to the common good, but not whether it manages to realize them (which is primarily the task of the executive). In other words, the EP can push for an issue "without having the consequences in mind" (Interview 17). This is especially true as long as the issue is not on the negotiation table. If this were the case, the EP would also need to invest its resources into costlier negotiation strategies such as agenda-managing, coalition-building, or unilateral action.

Hence, given that there were no significant costs of leading for the EP, the benefits necessarily prevailed. Thus, the EP's leadership surplus consisted primarily in the creation of a public debate on a more federal EU and an increase of its perceived legitimacy. According to the first theoretical proposition of this book's leadership model (H1), we therefore expect that the EP offered leadership in the case of Eurobonds and—under the condition that there was also a demand for leadership—emerged as a leader on the issue. The model's second theoretical proposition posits that if the aggregate status quo costs are high, there will be a strong demand for leadership (H2). As elaborated above, status quo costs were constantly high throughout the crisis and the issue of Eurobonds was permanently present in the discourse on how to preserve the common currency. Thus, also according to this second part of the explanation, we expect that the EP emerged as a leader in the case of Eurobonds given that there was a high demand for a solution to the eurozone's persisting (re-)financing problem.

Confidence in the two conjectures can be further strengthened by tracing their underlying causal mechanisms. With regard to the EP's offer of leadership (H1), we should therefore find expressions by which the EP signalled its preferences to change the status quo in such a way as to remove the related costs for the entire group (see Sect. 3.2). More specifically, there should be evidence that the EP framed the proposed Eurobonds as something all parties involved would ultimately profit from, thereby invoking the notion of a common goal. As regards the second conjecture (H2), we expect evidence indicating that potential followers took notice of the EP's leadership offer, and that at least some of them objected to it (see Sect. 3.2). Both the leader's offer and the followers' reaction to it provide so-called "hoop tests" (Collier 2011; Van Evera 1997: 31). In other words, if we do not find the described evidence, or if we find that the EP openly preferred the status quo to the introduction of Eurobonds, this would disconfirm the analytical model.

With regard to the EP's offer of leadership, there is evidence that the EP framed Eurobonds as a common goal all parties would profit from. This happened mainly through its non-binding resolutions and own-initiative reports (European Parliament 2011b, 2012a, b, c, e). In a resolution on anti-crisis measures, for instance, the EP calls on the Commission to determine "the conditions under which such a system [of Eurobonds] would be ***beneficial to all participating Member States and to the eurozone as a whole***" (European Parliament 2011b: 4, own emphasis). Furthermore, the EP pointed out that Eurobonds

> could foster integration of the European sovereign debt market, lower borrowing costs, increase liquidity, budgetary discipline and compliance with the Stability and Growth Pact, promote coordinated structural reforms, and make capital markets more stable, which will foster the idea of the euro as a global 'safe haven'. (European Parliament 2011b: 4f.)

In addition, influential MEPs presented Eurobonds as best solution to the eurozone crisis via press statements (Euractiv 2012c). The same is true for statements by the then President of the EP, which shows that the EP acted indeed as a unitary actor when promoting Eurobonds. Answering the question about how to solve the ongoing crisis, EP President Schulz said: "We need to reduce the interest burden of the affected countries in southern Europe. *The best way* to accomplish that would be with euro bonds" (Spiegel/Schulz 2012, own emphasis). By contrast, no evidence could be found that the EP, or any representative of the EP as a whole, preferred the status quo by rejecting Eurobonds.

With regard to the demand for leadership, we find evidence that the EP's promotion of Eurobonds was considered by the other relevant actors and that at least some of them objected to it. This becomes most evident in Olli Rehn's speech, in which he promised that the Commission would present a report on Eurobonds and, if appropriate, a legislative proposal as demanded by the EP. In this statement, Eurobonds are described as a contribution to the eurozone's common goal making everyone better off:

> You have got a commitment from the Commission to do a study on Eurosecurities [...] These eurosecurities would aim to strengthen fiscal discipline and increase stability in the euro area through markets, as well as, by taking advantage of the increase in liquidity, ensuring that the Member States enjoying the highest credit standards would not suffer from higher interest rates. The report will, if appropriate, be accompanied by legislative proposals. (European Commissioner for Economic and Monetary Affairs 2011: 2f.)

Also the resulting Green Paper is explicit about the EP's initiative and its purpose to overcome the crisis and stabilize the eurozone (European Commission 2011: 2f.). At the same time, Eurobonds were rejected by several member states, among them Germany, Finland, and the Netherlands. The most explicit objection came famously from the German government, with Chancellor Merkel stating that "there won't be Eurobonds as long as I live"[10] (Spiegel 2012; Spiegel/Schulz 2012; Interviews 1, 10, 11).

In sum, the first step of the leadership model can plausibly explain the EP's emergence in the case of Eurobonds. Against the background of relatively high status quo costs emerging from the re-financing problems of fiscally less solid eurozone states and the related economic and political consequences for the entire eurozone (H2), the EP emerged as a leader because its expected benefits—primarily the stimulation of a public debate and the increase of its legitimacy—outweighed the (virtually not existent) costs (H1). Both theoretical propositions passed a congruence test and are corroborated by additional evidence on the underlying causal mechanisms. Still, the emergence of a leader is not sufficient for her impact. The following section will therefore explain the failure of the EP's leadership attempt.

Explaining the EP's Leadership Failure: Resources, Preferences and Institutional Constraint

Once an actor has emerged as a leader, she needs to make use of her power resources in order to bring about the desired institutional or policy change. Thus, the book's first theoretical proposition accounting for a leader's impact posits: If a leader possesses many power resources (in relation to the resources of the followers), she will *ceteris paribus* have a strong impact on the outcomes (H3a). Power resources are disaggregated into material, institutional, and ideational resources (Sect. 3.4).

In the case of non-state actors, material resources are measured by those budgetary capacities which they can deploy to influence the EU economic and fiscal governance. The EP lacks material power resources as it can neither influence eurozone crisis management with own budgetary capacities, nor control the funds provided by member states.

[10] Translated by the author from the original: "Keine Euro-Bonds, solange ich lebe".

The EP's score on this indicator is thus considerably lower than that of the other institutional actors (cf. Sect. 5.1 for the Commission and Sect. 5.3 for the ECB).

The assessment of the EP's institutional resources is more complex, though.[11] Since the entry into force of the Lisbon Treaty in December 2009, the EP's competences in the field of economic governance have primarily been based on Article 121.6 TFEU, which grants the EP co-decision rights for multilateral surveillance. Based on Art. 136, the same applies to provisions relating specifically to members of the eurozone (Fasone 2014: 171).[12] Further legislative powers regard the EP's involvement in the simplified treaty revision procedure, for which it has to give its initial consent (Art. 48.6 TFEU), and the possibility to conclude inter-institutional agreements in areas where no competences are provided for by the Treaties. Finally, the President of the EP can represent its institution in the beginning of European Council meetings and Euro Summits. However, it is unlikely that the President can exert any substantial influence in these meetings going beyond a recital in the Conclusions or a favourable press release (Interview 34).

On the one hand, the EP has been able to informally extend these institutional powers—and especially its co-decision rights in multilateral surveillance—to participate in legislation for which it formally did not have any competences, such as Regulation 1177/2011 in the Sixpack legislation or the shaping of the intergovernmental Fiscal Compact. On the other hand, the EP still remains excluded from all areas which concern the actual use of national budgetary means. This regards most prominently the eurozone's permanent rescue fund (European Stability Mechanism [ESM]).

As regards formal agenda-setting, the EP can adopt legislative initiative resolutions, by which it can ask the Commission to submit a legislative proposal within a set period of time. However, the Commission can refuse to submit the requested proposal. In general, own-initiative reports by the EP seem to be a rather weak tool to influence legislation.

[11]The following elaboration on the EP's institutional resources is largely based on Héritier et al. (2019, forthcoming), Chapter 7.

[12]As regards monetary policy, Art. 284.3 makes the ECB accountable to the EP. First, the ECB must present an annual report on its activities and monetary policy to the EP. Second, the President of the ECB and the other members of the Executive Board may be heard by the competent committees of the EP.

One interviewee observed that in the Council they are not even read due to their non-binding nature (Interview 34).

Finally, the EP has obtained some scrutiny powers to hold Council, Eurogroup, and the other supranational institutions accountable. This regards mainly the so-called "Economic Dialogues" whereby the EP's competent committee can invite the Presidents of the Council, Commission, and, where appropriate, the Presidents of the European Council or the Eurogroup as well as the national Finance Ministers to discuss relevant aspects of the EU's economic governance and the European Semester. However, the Economic Dialogue is a relatively weak tool, too, given that it does not allow for any binding commitments or enforcement powers on the side of the EP. Moreover, participation to the Dialogue takes place on a voluntary basis.

In sum, as far as institutional power resources are concerned, the EP finds itself in a weak position as compared to the Commission and the member states. Most importantly, its co-decision rights apply only to the area of multilateral surveillance. Other aspects of the EU's economic governance are organized intergovernmentally and treated in the Eurogroup, the ECOFIN Council, and the European Council. In the small but important field of multilateral surveillance, where the EP is formally on equal footing with the Council, it can hardly shape the legislation according to its actual preferences, but needs to restrict itself to relatively marginal amendments to the Commission proposal (see Bressanelli and Chelotti 2016, 2018). As an MEP put it in the interviews:

> very often the public [...] does not realize that we do not have a total liberty of redrafting a text. [...] Of course, in theory we can redraft completely, but the Council is also working on the same basis and it will not be always very clever to reorganize everything. (Interview 29)

Therefore, the EP's co-decision power is more of a "negative" decision-making right insofar as it can withhold its final approval of a proposed legislative act, rather than the prerogative of actively shaping legislation. This permits the EP to avoid unpleasant decisions, but as regards policy or institutional innovation, it often enables little more than agreements on the lowest common denominator. Second, the mentioned agenda-setting and scrutiny powers are both very weak due to their non-binding nature: neither can the EP force the Commission or member states to initiate legislation, nor does it have any enforcement powers—let alone sanctions—if it comes to the monitoring of the implementation. Finally, as opposed to the Commission and member states, the EP naturally does not have any executive competences.

Ideational resources, finally, comprise information, expertise, credibility, and legitimacy. Information and expertise are measured by taking the institution's administrative staff specializing in EU economic governance as proxy. As explicated in detail in Sect. 4.2, compared to member states and other EU institutions, the EP has only few staff members whose core task are matters of EU economic governance. Although it has increased its staff in the area of economic governance since the beginning of the crisis—not least by setting up a specialised Economic Governance Support Unit—the EP cannot compete with the EU or member state executives in this regard (Interviews 16, 28).

The EP's credibility, in contrast, is higher than that of member states. Being a supranational institution, the EP is naturally a more credible candidate for the promotion of the EU's common good than single nation states. However, the EP still consists of elected MEPs who arguably want to be re-elected, pursue individual agendas, and are more exposed to national (party) politics than the Commission (let alone the politically independent ECB).

Hence, the biggest power resource of the EP is its legitimacy:

> To compensate for the lack of institutional bargaining resources, the EP takes recourse to non-material bargaining resources by exerting normative pressure, which is most effective, when opponents of more supranational parliamentarism cannot credibly deny the claim that integration undermines the EU's standard of legitimacy. (Rittberger 2014)

Being the EU's only directly elected supranational institution, the EP seems best placed to promote the common interest of its citizens. The venue to deploy this power resource is the public debate which is influenced through press releases and conferences, interviews and public appearances of MEPs, debates in the plenary, non-binding resolutions and own-initiative reports, and the publication of studies and briefings. In this way, the EP attempts to exert peer pressure on Commission and member states and thereby influence their political agenda (Interviews 16, 26).

Nevertheless, as opposed to the other actors in EU economic governance, the EP possesses very few power resources: its material resources are equal to zero, its institutional resources are less than those of member states and Commission, and it has less information and expertise. Hence, according to the book's theoretical propositions, we expect no, or only a very weak influence on the outcomes.

The second theoretical expectation regarding a leader's impact is the distribution of preferences—if preferences converge around the outcome preferred by the leader, she will *ceteris paribus* have a strong impact on the outcomes (H4a). Broadly speaking, the distribution of preferences among the member states reflected once again the cleavage between the typically northern "creditor states" and mainly southern "debtor-states". The firmest opponent of Eurobonds was Germany. Although Germany has not ruled out Eurobonds once for all, but rather considered them the very last step of a fiscal union which would include strong conditionality for debtor states, more supranational control, and effective enforcement of fiscal discipline, it presented itself in public as well as in the committees and preparatory bodies as "most violently against it" (Interview 10; also Interviews 2, 25; Kade et al. 2011). Thus, chancellor Merkel's statement of June 2012 that "there won't be Eurobonds as long as I live"[13] (Spiegel 2012) has become emblematic for Germany's stand in the issue. Germany has been supported by the Netherlands, Finland, Austria, and Estonia (Interviews 1, 10, 11).

On the other side, a group of southern member states, Luxembourg, and France openly advocated Eurobonds. Although France most of the time abstained from strongly pushing the issue due to strategic compromises it had struck with Germany, it never concealed that it was clearly in favour of Eurobonds (Interview 5). Luxembourg's position is exceptional in the sense that despite its low interest rates, it took a pro-integrationist stance in favour of Eurobonds (Interview 1). This might be attributed to the political agenda of its then Prime and Finance Minister Jean-Claude Juncker, who, together with then Italian Minister of Economy and Finance Tremonti, wrote a much-noticed article in the *Financial Times* to promote Eurobonds as a solution to the eurozone crisis (Juncker and Tremonti 2010; Interview 29). Further proponents of Eurobonds were Italy, Spain, Belgium, Greece, Cyprus, and Portugal (Interviews 1, 2, 3, 10; Euractiv 2012b).

[13] Translated by the author from the original: "Keine Euro-Bonds, solange ich lebe".

As regards the other supranational institutions, the Commission avoided taking a clear stance as regards Eurobonds (Sect. 5.1). The ECB's position also appeared ambiguous. On the one hand, the issuance of common debt would considerably facilitate the ECB's monetary policy, since intervention in one single market is easier than intervention in 19 national markets. Moreover, Eurobonds would make the controversial mutualisation of debt at the ECB (e.g. through its OMT programme) less needed. Eurobonds would also stabilize the eurozone as a whole and thus be in the ECB's natural self-interest. On the other hand, the ECB is "relatively sceptical [...], if not against" (Interview 18) Eurobonds because of their potential to create moral hazard and fiscal profligacy. Thus, similar to the German position, the ECB supported Eurobonds only on the condition of a further pooling of fiscal responsibility (Interviews 19–23). Given that this degree of fiscal union was considered unrealistic at the time, the ECB preferred no Eurobonds to the issuance of common debt without a proper system of conditionality behind them. This was reflected by Mario Draghi's answer to MEPs, who interviewed him as candidate for the office of ECB President: "[Eurobonds] would introduce an implicit subsidy from fiscally sound to fiscally less sound member states [...] This might unduly reward unsound policies and impair incentives for fiscal prudence in the future. At the same time, fiscally sound member states would see part of the benefits of their prudence transferred to other states" (Euractiv 2011b).

In sum, the preference constellation was fairly heterogeneous. This is the median value of the variable as operationalized in Sect 3.4. With regard to the analytical model, this relatively undistinguished value changes the weighting of the variables, making the impact of the other two more decisive. In other words, given that the distribution of preferences is neither extraordinarily favourable nor completely detrimental to the EP's success of leading, we expect that the EP's power resources and/or the institutional constraint make the substantial difference with regard to the outcome.

The last variable accounting for a leader's impact is the institutional constraint, which ranges from complete discretion by the leader via decision-making by consent or participation, through to the interdiction of making certain decisions (Sect. 3.4, Table 3.4). If the institutional constraint is low, the leader will *ceteris paribus* have a strong impact, and vice versa. In the case of Eurobonds, which imply the issuance of common debt under joint and several guarantees, a Treaty change would be the only way to avoid a breach of the so-called "no-bailout clause". The legal procedure for the necessary Treaty amendment would depend on whether a purely intergovernmental framework like the ESM would be established, or if the issuance of common debt would be placed under EU law. While in the former case the simplified revision procedure could be used (Art. 48.6 TFEU), an establishment under EU law would require the ordinary procedure together with the use of the so-called "flexibility clause" (Art. 352 TFEU) (European Commission 2011: 11). In both cases, unanimity among member states would be required. This is the highest institutional constraint apart from the complete interdiction of making a decision. Thus, according to the model's fifth theoretical proposition, we expect that due to the high institutional constraint, the EP has only a weak (or even no) influence on the outcomes.

In sum, the model's second analytical can step can provide a plausible explanation for the EP's failure to bring about institutional change in the form of Eurobonds. Against the background of heterogeneous preferences and a strong institutional constraint (unanimity), the EP lacked the power resources to obtain the approval of *all* member states, which would have been the only way to provide successful leadership. In order to increase the confidence in the propositions of this second step, their presumed causal mechanisms can be traced. While there are no observable implications for the first proposition—the EP did *not* have the necessary resources to apply leadership strategies or provoke an anticipated reaction—expressions by Commission and Council officials can indirectly corroborate the model if they indicate that the EP could not employ the necessary strategies, or that its reactions to being ignored were not feared by the other actors ("anticipated reaction"). Indeed, Commission officials explained that "the Parliament stands at the sideline" (Interview 3) and cannot influence legislation and crisis management the same way as Commission or member states due to its weak competences in agenda-setting and decision-making as well as its lack of expertise (Interview 11). A Council official was even more explicit by stating that the EP's strategies fail whenever it cannot build on formal decision-making rights:

> They make huge conferences on economic governance [...] and they give the impression they have a say there. They write own-initiative reports on the European semester – to be honest – which here nobody reads [...] But, let's say, apart from the noise created in the public sphere and in the press, this has no impact on our work whatsoever. (Interview 34)

This makes also clear that the "rule of anticipated reaction", according to which other actors accommodate the leader's preferences because they fear the reaction in case they ignore them, cannot apply to the EP.

With regard to the conjecture on institutional constraint, these interview expressions also illustrate that the EP did not have the resources to compensate the opponents of Eurobonds (or to make them accept the proposal) so as to overcome the strong institutional constraint of unanimity. However, this evidence qualifies only for a 'straw-in-the-wind' test as it is neither sufficient nor necessary to claim causal inference. The interview expressions slightly weaken alternative explanations and affirm the relevance of the hypotheses, but they do not confirm them (Collier 2011: 825f.).

Results

The first analytical step of the book's theoretical model provides a plausible explanation as to why the EP emerged as a leader in the case of Eurobonds. For both theoretical propositions, the values of the independent variables are congruent with the outcome. As regards the first proposition, the EP's benefits of leading—namely the stimulation of a public debate and the increase of its legitimacy—outweighed the (virtually not existent) costs. Thus, we expect that the EP offered leadership, and, provided that there was also a demand for it, emerged as a leader. With regard to the second proposition, high status quo costs resulted in a strong demand for leadership, which was supposed to solve the "debtor" states' (re-)financing problems and thereby the related economic and political consequences for the entire Eurozone. Hence, given that there was both a demand for and a supply of leadership, the model predicts actual outcome, namely the EP's emergence as a leader in the case of Eurobonds.

The model's second analytical step, which accounts for a leader's impact, can provide a plausible explanation for the EP's leadership failure: the EP remained unsuccessful because it lacked sufficient power resources, preferences were heterogeneous, and the introduction of Eurobonds implied treaty change and thus a strong institutional constraint. Hence, two of the three conjectures, namely those on power resources and institutional constraint, directly pass the congruence test. In the case of preference distribution, the value of the independent variable (heterogeneous) is not perfectly congruent with the outcome. However, heterogeneity is the median value of the variable and as such undistinguished: it is neither particularly favourable nor extremely unfavourable to the EP's impact on the outcomes. Thus, while the confidence in this conjecture cannot be increased by means of the congruence method or process tracing, it does not diminish the plausibility of the model either.

The case study entails further interesting results. If the most powerful actors are not willing or capable of providing leadership, less powerful actors might unexpectedly emerge as leaders. In the case of Eurobonds, Germany was not willing to provide leadership for obvious reasons. Moreover, neither the Commission nor other big member states like France, which actually would have been in favour, took the lead. This was the chance for the EP as an even less powerful actor to step in and fill the leadership vacuum. Although the EP lacks the resources to act as a "strong" leader in the EU, it still found itself in a position of authority based on its legitimacy as the EU's only directly elected institution, it translated its primarily non-material resources into strategies, and it tried to guide the behaviour of others (Commission and member states) towards the common goal of stabilizing the Euro and overcoming the crisis. In short, the EP provided leadership. Hence, a leadership vacuum can be the reason as to why we sometimes observe surprisingly weak leaders. However, if the preference distribution and the institutional constraint is not to their advantage, they unsurprisingly fail.

A second interesting result emerges from the comparison of the Commission's and EP's attitude towards Eurobonds. As soon as it became clear that Eurobonds would not have a realistic chance of being introduced, the Commission abandoned the issue and even avoided using the word "Eurobonds". The Commission did so although it was principally in favour of the proposal. At the same time—and under identical circumstances—the EP started to strongly promote the issue although it was aware that Eurobonds could not be realized in the short term. This demonstrates that even if we assume the same basic interests for EP and Commission, namely the increase of their institutional power, they still face different payoff structures: while the Commission could only lose by promoting Eurobonds, the EP could only win by doing so. Hence, the initiatives and behaviour of EU institutional actors not only depend on their resources and preferences, but are considerably constrained by their institutional roles.

5.3 Successful Leadership: The European Central Bank and Outright Monetary Transactions

When announcing OMT ("whatever it takes"), the ECB emerged as a leader by default and guided the eurozone to a decisive policy and institutional change. The ECB did so at a time when the fragmentation of the eurozone seemed to be as close as never before and all realizable measures by the member states appeared largely exhausted. Although the ECB's costs of leading, which consisted in the creation of moral hazard and a loss of legitimacy and independence, were very high, its benefits were even higher: the announcement of OMT safeguarded the ECB's own survival. As regards the impact of leadership, the ECB was able to put a preliminary end to the eurozone crisis due to its paramount power resources, the favourable preference constellation, and the low institutional constraint.

As the ECB is politically independent and can thus make discretionary decisions within its mandate, it does not require an active followership. This raises the questions of how we can recognize leadership by the ECB if we see it, and who are the central bank's followers? As this book deals with leadership in the eurozone, the ECB's potential followers must be the eurozone members. Moreover, in line with the book's definition of leadership, the ECB's action must serve a common goal that benefits all members of the eurozone. In the context of eurozone crisis management, this goal consists in overcoming the crisis and preserving the common currency. Based on the book's theoretical model, we further expect a demand for leadership. This demand may be expressed openly or—as this case study will illustrate—by an abstention from open criticism of the ECB even when member state governments do not approve its measures. Finally, there is no leadership without followership. As this case study will show, the ECB needs the member states' support despite its political independence in order to be credible in the financial markets. Without the member states' (tacit) followership, the ECB could no longer fulfil its mandate of maintaining price stability in the medium term. In the long run, public support for the single currency would crumble, which would directly jeopardize the ECB's *raison d'être*.

This sub-chapter first introduces the relevant events, actors, and preferences in the case of OMT. It then determines the value of both dependent variables, which are the emergence and the impact of leadership. The following sections examine the independent variables and the causal mechanisms of the two steps, respectively. Finally, the chapter draws the conclusions of what constitutes a leadership case *par excellence*.

Case Description: Announcing Outright Monetary Transactions

In July 2012, government bond spreads in the eurozone had reached an unprecedented height. This happened despite the impressive amount of anti-crisis measures decided upon in the preceding months (agreements on ESM, banking supervision, and direct bank recapitalization), and it came along with new speculations about a collapse of the eurozone. In this situation, when the crisis once again escalated and all realistic alternatives seemed to be exhausted, ECB President Mario Draghi announced in a speech at the Global Investment Conference in London on 26 July 2012 that the ECB would prevent a fragmentation of the eurozone at any cost: "Within our mandate, the ECB is ready to do whatever it takes to preserve the euro. And believe me, it will be enough" (President of the European Central Bank 2012). Following this statement, the ECB announced on 2 August 2012 that it "may undertake outright open market operations of a size adequate to reach its objective [...] Over the coming weeks, we will design the appropriate modalities for such policy measures" (European Central Bank 2012a).

As a consequence of these announcements, government bond spreads narrowed (see Fig. 5.2). This not only provided sudden stability to the eurozone, but it actually suspended the crisis by removing its most immediate trigger (Altavilla et al. 2014; De Grauwe and Ji 2015: 747f.). The plan to buy sovereign bonds on secondary markets without predefined limits existed already prior to Draghi's announcement in London. However, apart from maybe a very narrow circle of people around the ECB President, nobody had been informed about his intentions to actually declare the launch of such a programme at that time. While the decision of the ECB's Governing Council, which had not been informed either, confirmed the announcement only a few days later, the technical details of OMT still needed to be elaborated in the following weeks (Interviews 13, 18, 20, 22).

On 6 September 2012, the Governing Council eventually delivered the technical features of the announced "outright transactions in secondary sovereign bond markets that aim at safeguarding an appropriate monetary policy transmission and the singleness of the monetary policy"

(European Central Bank 2012b). There would be no ex-ante quantitative limits, eligible government bonds would have a maturity of one to three years and no seniority, and the purchases would be conditional on the existence of a macroeconomic adjustment programme with the ESM (see Lombardi and Moschella 2016: 859).

Although the ECB is politically independent, it has to take the behaviour of other actors into account when it decides on its monetary policies. This regards mainly eurozone governments, which may indirectly constrain or enable certain ECB decisions through their fiscal and economic policies. Moreover, the ECB ultimately relies on the normative backing of member states since it would lose its legitimacy and credibility without their support. Both are indispensable conditions for its effectiveness. In its concrete monetary policy decisions, however, the ECB decides alone and does not need the consent of member states. While the Commission and the EP are even less important than the member states, they still play a certain role in the ECB's decisions as they can legitimize the ECB's measures in public. This is especially true for the EP, which has the right to hold the ECB accountable on the basis of an annual report to be presented by the ECB President to the EP and through hearings with the Executive Board members by the competent committee. In the case of OMT, these actors' preferences diverged only slightly. Most member states as well as the Commission and EP welcomed the ECB's decision. Only Germany, the Netherlands, and Austria were initially against the programme. However, once it had been announced, they publicly supported the ECB as any other reaction would have left them worse off (see below).

Successful Leadership

The dependent variable of the first analytical step is the emergence of leadership. A leader has emerged if there is (1) an actor in a position of power that guides a group towards a (2) common goal by (3) making appropriate use of its resources ("strategies").

As regards the first indicator, the ECB is an extremely powerful actor in the eurozone. Much of its power is based on its political independence. Moreover, in the context of crisis management it has become clear that also the ECB's paramount material resources as well as its expertise and credibility by far exceed those of the member states (see below). Indeed, with regard to all three types of power resources—material, institutional, non-material—member states turned out to be dependent on the ECB (see Beukers 2013: 1592f.). This position of power was reinforced by the reluctance of member states to establish a fully integrated economic and fiscal union as well as the urgency to come up with quick responses to the crisis under tight institutional constraints (see Hall 2012: 366):

> Amid the rigidity of the pre-crisis EMU rules on the one hand, and the paralysis of the Member States on the other, the ECB was the only actor within EMU that had the capacity to respond quickly and effectively in order to prevent a collapse of the Eurozone. (Krampf 2016: 467)

With regard to the second indicator, a common goal, OMT directly aimed at preserving the common currency and overcoming the crisis by removing the high government bond spreads in the eurozone, which prevented an effective monetary policy and threatened to drive single member states into default (European Central Bank 2012b). In other words, the announcement of OMT contributed to the survival of the eurozone and thus to its common goal. Whereas this was recognized by all actors involved, this does not mean that OMT were also the measure preferred by everyone.

Finally, as the euro's issuing authority and only decision-maker of the eurozone's monetary policy, the ECB could directly translate its unique material and institutional resources into shaping the desired policy and institutional change. The appropriate strategy was that of unilateral action, or, as one ECB official put it, "ad hoc fire-fighting" (Interview 23; see also below). This strategy, combined with the ECB's institutional rights, provided it with the opportunity to exploit a first-mover advantage. By announcing "to do whatever it takes to preserve the euro" without informing member state governments beforehand, the best thing the latter could do was to back the ECB's decision and confirm that it acted within its mandate (Blackstone and Walker 2012). Any other reaction would have compromised the ECB's credibility, (re-)fuelled speculation against single member states, and thus increased the risk that the ECB had to act on its promise and buy government bonds indeed.

In sum, by announcing OMT, the ECB emerged as a leader in the management of the eurozone crisis because it found itself in (1) a position of power and (2) used its resources to guide the other actors towards (3) a common goal.

The criteria for the assessment of the second dependent variable, namely a leader's impact, are (1) the presence of a change, measured by the difference between the ex-ante and the ex-post situation, (2) its desirability, benchmarked against the leader's most preferred outcome, and (3) its initiation by the leader (Sect. 3.4).

The policy and institutional change analysed in this case study consists in the announcement of OMT by the ECB Governing Council on 2 August 2012, which confirmed Mario Draghi's earlier statement of July 26. This announcement represented a policy change because it enlarged the ECB's spectrum of policy instruments (Salines et al. 2012: 668). More precisely, an ECB programme providing for the potentially unlimited purchase of government bonds was unprecedented in the eurozone. At the same time, the announcement constituted a major institutional change as the ECB thereby became the eurozone's de facto lender of last resort (De Grauwe and Ji 2015: 752). According to the institutional practice before the OMT announcement, the ECB could only make limited purchases of government bonds to safeguard the transmission of its monetary policy. However, with "the announcement of the OMT program and given the success of this program, it has become clear [...] that the ECB is the ultimate guarantor of the sovereign debt in the Eurozone" (De Grauwe and Ji 2015: 748). Krampf is therefore right when he attests that the "behaviour of the ECB during the crisis was indeed inconsistent with pre-crisis EMU policy principles" (2016: 467).

The desirability of this change, which is the second criterion for a leader's impact, is proven by its effect. The announcement of OMT led to a decline in government bond spreads and thus to the suspension—if not the end—of the eurozone crisis. As Altavilla and colleagues have shown, for instance, the announcement led to a 2% decrease in Spanish and Italian 2-year bond yields as well as positive effects for growth and credits in the two member states, without any negative effects on interests or growth in Germany and France (2014: 15). De Grauwe and Ji have tested whether the collapse of the spreads and thus the preservation of the common currency was really caused by the ECB's announcements rather than by other economic developments. They found that

> the sharp decline of the spreads since OMT is totally dissociated from changes in fundamentals. The latter play no role at all in explaining this decline in the spreads. This result strongly suggests that the ECB's OMT announcement was quite effective in turning around market sentiments.

These became very positive and corrected for the excessive pessimism that existed before the announcement. (2015: 747f.)

It is important to emphasize that, like in the case of the Fiscal Compact (Sect. 4.3), the primary purpose of OMT was not so much to bring about a change in substance, but rather to send an effective signal. The announcement of the OMT did therefore not automatically imply the accumulation of sovereign debt in the house of the ECB, as feared by critics of the measure, but it signalled to the markets that the eurozone had an inexhaustible backstop. From this point of view, OMT are primarily a "dissuasion weapon" (Interview 2). Given that member state governments can block OMT by denying the concerned member state an ESM program,[14] the mere announcement of OMT does not imply that they will also be used. As Paul Krugman noted: "the ECB's efforts rely to an important extent on a bluff, in the sense that nobody knows what would happen if OMT were actually required" (2014).

The assessment of the last criterion, which regards the question of whether the relevant change was actually initiated by the alleged leader, is straightforward. OMT were invented, announced, and developed solely by the ECB as the only decision-maker in the eurozone's monetary policy.[15]

In sum, the launch of OMT is a leadership case *par excellence*. By committing "to do whatever it takes to preserve the euro" and through the ensuing announcement of OMT, the ECB did precisely what this book defines as successful leadership (Sect. 2.4): the ECB used its power resources in such a way as to guide the other eurozone actors towards a common goal, namely the suspension—if not the end—of the eurozone crisis. The announcement of OMT not only represents a policy change, but also an informal institutional change as regards the ECB's role as a potential 'lender of last resort'.

[14]An consolidation programme under the ESM is a condition for the activation of OMT.

[15]Like all other actors examined by this work, also the ECB is a heterogeneous organization whose decisions at the European level are always the result of prior internal decision-making rounds. In the case of the OMT, this regards the strategic interaction of the national central banks governors and the members of the Executive Board (including the ECB President) in the Governing Council. However, given that this takes place at a different analytical level, the question of who initiated the OMT *within* the ECB is irrelevant for this analysis.

Explaining the ECB's Leadership Emergence: Leadership Surplus and Status Quo Costs

Following the first theoretical proposition of this book, a leader emerges if the expected benefits outweigh the costs of leading. Figure 5.1 gives an overview of the ECB's costs and benefits of leading in the case of OMT as mentioned by the interviewees. As can be seen from Fig. 5.1, there is one benefit of leading, namely the restoration of the ECB's effectiveness in the transmission of its monetary policy and thus the preservation of the eurozone (the ECB's *raison d'être*), which already by the number of mentions outweighs all the costs of leading.

Table 5.3 gives a more detailed overview of the ECB's expected benefits of leading according to the individual interviewees. Answers by interviewees who were particularly strongly involved in the events surrounding the announcement of the OMT are printed in bold. Answers by ECB officials are italicised.

The most frequently mentioned benefit of leading is the signal that could be sent to the financial markets in order to stop over-reactions (self-fulfilling expectations) or even purposeful speculating against certain member states. By sending this signal, the ECB could not only restore the effectiveness of its monetary policy, but also prevent the eurozone from falling apart. In this way, it ultimately ensured its own institutional survival.

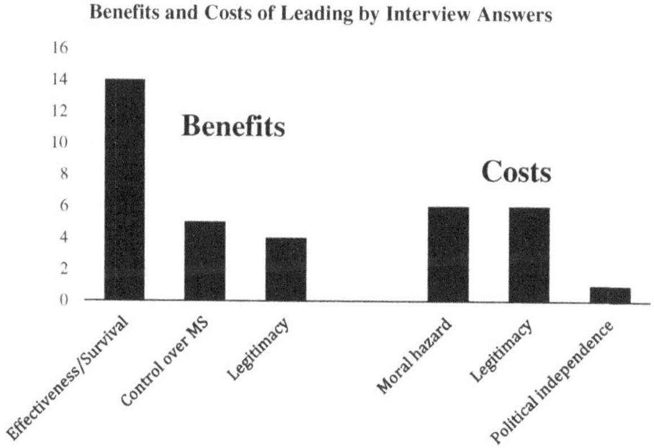

Fig. 5.1 Costs and benefits of leading by interview answers (*Source* Own illustration)

Table 5.3 The ECB's benefits of leading according to interviewees (OMT)

Interview	*Benefits*
	EFFECTIVENESS => SURVIVAL
2	**Effective signal not to speculate against the euro ⇨ preserving the euro = preserving the ECB**
5	Ensuring effectiveness of own monetary policy and existence of eurozone
11	ECB's *raison d'être* is to provide effective monetary policy for eurozone
13	**Saving the euro as "lender of last resort"**
14	*Saving the Euro; restoring own credibility vis-à-vis financial markets due to (a) conditionality (grip over member states' fiscal policy) (b) unlimited capacity of OMT*
15	**Own survival (euro was facing collapse)**
18	***Effective transmission of monetary policy***
19	***Restoration of the ECB's ability to fulfil its mandate of price-stability***
20	***Signal not to speculate against euro in order to maintain price-stability***
21	***Signal against over-reaction in markets; preventing contagion; containing redenomination risk***
22	***Stopping speculation against euro in the context of rising interests for Italian and Spanish bonds => avoidance of eurozone disintegration***
23	*Avoidance of systemic risk and self-fulfilling equilibria*
24	***Ensuring stability and avoiding redenomination risk***
27	**ECB found itself endangered in its existence**
	CONTROL OVER MS
3	Control over concerned member states' fiscal policy through conditionality
11	Getting grip on member states' fiscal policy through conditionality
13	**Gaining influence over politicians through conditionality**
14	*Solution to problem of preceding SMP programme ("We had no control"): getting leverage on member states*
19	***Enforceable conditionality against background of failed SMP***
	LEGITIMACY
2	**Increase of reputation**
11	Increase of reputation in the EP
13	**Increase of reputation**
14	*Improving standing with EP*

Source Own illustration

The first aspect is, at first glance, of rather technical nature. Given that the high interest rates for certain government bonds were based on over-reactions of the financial markets and thus not "justified" by the real economy and actual credit risk, the ECB's monetary policy was rendered ineffective. As long as state bonds were higher than economically justified, the ECB's lowering of the base rate was not passed on by the banks in the form of lower interests for their loans. This meant that the ECB's monetary policy did no longer affect the real economy and price stability. By announcing OMT, however, the ECB signalled to markets to better stop speculating against the euro because it would buy as many government bonds as necessary to lower the interest rates and—as opposed to the markets—its resources to do so are unlimited. Thus, in case of an attrition war between the ECB and markets about interest rates, the ECB would win it for sure, whereas the actors in the markets would risk to lose a lot of money. Hence, by announcing OMT, the ECB could, first of all, restore the effectiveness of its monetary policy.

The restoration of its effectiveness is obviously related to the ECB's *raison d'être* because only by having the possibility of effectively intervening on the markets, the ECB can fulfil its mandate (and primary objective) of ensuring price stability in the euro area (Art. 127.1 TFEU). Thus, in the words of an ECB official who was involved in drafting the original idea of OMT, their main benefit was "restoring order in the monetary policy transmission" (Interview 18). However, at the time the ECB's institutional survival was jeopardized in a much more concrete way, which consisted in the rise of mainly Italian and Spanish bond yields. This directly jeopardized the integrity of the eurozone as bailing out Italy or Spain not only represents an economic problem, namely the lack of resources, but also a political problem consisting in the lack of political feasibility or willingness (Interview 22). Therefore, calming the markets and stopping the speculation against the euro corresponded to the avoidance of monetary disintegration and thus to the preservation of the ECB's reason to exist.

The ECB's unilateral action to preserve the eurozone and thereby its own existence bears normative implications. The mutualisation of risk, for instance through the accumulation of sovereign debt at the ECB in case OMT were activated, is a political decision, which therefore should have been made by the finance ministers or heads of state and government. It was arguably the inactivity of member states which forced the ECB to make such a move if it wanted to avoid a collapse of the eurozone (see below). As a senior ECB official put it:

> There were only two alternatives: either the ECB appearing as lender of last resort to governments or Germany moving on towards Eurobonds or Redemption Fund, or something to stop the crisis. [...] the action of Draghi provided a huge amount of relief to Merkel and Schäuble and

> enabled them again to put pressure in economic governance on the others without the German government being obliged to do something. (Interview 22)

This assessment has been unwittingly confirmed by a high-ranking official in the German Finance Ministry, who stated that the ECB found itself endangered in its existence and therefore made a unilateral decision, which actually should have been made in the ECOFIN Council (Interview 27). It goes without saying that a decision with such enormous distributional consequences bears implications for the ECB's perceived legitimacy (see below).

A further benefit of leading, which was mentioned less often, however, is the control the ECB could gain over member states' fiscal policies by linking OMT to an ESM consolidation programme ("memorandum of understanding"), which was supervised by the Troika and thus partly by the ECB itself. The lack of influence over national budgetary policies has been considered a major flaw of the "Securities Markets Programme" (SMP) which preceded OMT. Firstly, the ECB needed to trust that member states, whose bonds it had purchased, would pursue a sustainable and disciplined fiscal policy. Given that the ECB did not have any leverage on these member states, however, it not only created moral hazard, but even risked violating its mandate since an eventual sovereign default would result in prohibited monetary financing by the ECB. Secondly, the SMP did not function as a credible signal to the markets as member states did not change their behaviour. A case in point is the confidential letter, signed by the outgoing ECB President Trichet and his designated successor Draghi, sent on 5 August 2011 to the Italian government asking it to implement tough austerity cuts. The leaking of this letter was politically charged not only because the ECB had denied any link between its bond purchases and government behaviour, but also because it provided a checklist to the markets of what austerity measures the Italian government must implement to consider its bonds safe (Dinmore and Atkins 2011). As regards the ECB's credibility as well as the effect on Italian bonds in case the government would fail to implement the measures demanded by the ECB, this situation constituted a disaster for the ECB. In the words of an ECB official, under the SMP "we had no control" (Interview 14).

Thus, thanks to OMT the ECB could not only rely on a consolidation programme to be negotiated with member states *before* purchasing their bonds, but also control the compliance with that programme through its participation in the Troika. Through the link to the ESM, credible conditionality was created as non-compliant member states would also lose the next disbursement tranche from the ESM. Hence, OMT empowered the ECB as an institution (Interview 11).

However, the ECB's actual benefits of this conditionality are controversial. To be sure, on the one hand the link to the ESM would entail more control for the ECB and increase the effectiveness of its measures if OMT really came into operation. On the other hand, however, it made the ECB dependent on the approval of member states and led to further politicization not least through its involvement in the Troika (Interviews 18, 22–24, 27). As for instance the German Finance Minister Wolfgang Schäuble noted with regard to an activation of OMT, the ECB "cannot make these decisions because it has bound them to conditions that are beyond its control [...] ESM decisions are subject to a unanimous vote and we will not approve of such a programme as announced by the ECB" (CESifo 2014).

Finally, the third and least frequently mentioned benefit of leading for the ECB is an increase in legitimacy. While two of the four interviewees who mentioned this benefit referred to the ECB's reputation in public, where it could have expected to be acknowledged as the actor that saved the eurozone (Interviews 2, 13), the other two referred to the ECB's standing with the EP, which was predominantly in favour of OMT (Interviews 11, 14).

While the effectiveness of the ECB's monetary policy, and ultimately its institutional survival, is clearly the most frequently mentioned benefit among all respondents (61%), it is almost the only answer among strongly involved ECB officials (86%). Only one of these six interviewees mentioned as a second benefit also the ECB's gain of control over member states (see above). An expected increase of legitimacy, by contrast, was not mentioned by any of the ECB officials directly involved in announcing or shaping OMT. This increases our confidence that the preservation of its effectiveness and survival was the primary benefit of leading for the ECB when it announced OMT.

The ECB's expected costs of leading, by contrast, are listed in Table 5.4. Answers by interviewees who were particularly strongly involved in the events surrounding the announcement of OMT are printed in bold. Answers by ECB officials are italicised. Basically two types of costs were mentioned: the creation of moral hazard and the loss

Table 5.4 The ECB's costs of leading according to interviewees (OMT)

Interview	*Costs*
	MORAL HAZARD
4	Moral hazard: OMT calmed the markets, thereby buying time for debtor states and strengthening their position in programme negotiations
15	**Creation of moral hazard (although considerably reduced by link to ESM)**
18	***Incentives for moral hazard (although mitigated by link to conditionality)***
21	***Moral hazard (although mitigated by link to ESM programmes)***
22	***Endangering stability by sending wrong signals to debtor states***
23	*No pressure for reform in member states*
	LEGITIMACY
3	Public opinion in Germany and, to a minor extent, in Finland and the Netherlands
8	Decrease of legitimacy in German public
14	*Court cases and public opinion in Germany*
20	***Perceived legitimacy in public (however, no significant cost)***
22	***In case of failure: result of defaults would result in prohibited monetary financing and loss of credibility***
24	***Legal issues and loss of trust in ECB***
	POLITICAL INDEPENDENCE
24	***OMT make ECB's actions dependent on member states' policy decisions***

Source Own illustration

of legitimacy. Only one interviewee mentioned also the ECB's loss of political independence as a cost of introducing OMT.

As regards moral hazard, the ECB feared that by acting as a de facto "lender of last resort", member states would lose the incentives for fiscal discipline because they would count on the ECB to eventually bail them out. Although many interviewees acknowledged that this risk was considerably reduced by linking OMT to the ESM consolidation programmes, thereby introducing conditionality, the problem could not be completely eradicated since there is no certainty that member states, once a programme has been signed and the ECB has purchased their bonds, would actually comply and implement the agreed austerity measures and structural reforms.

More importantly, however, by announcing OMT, the ECB took away the market pressure on "debtor states", as it restored their ability to refinance themselves. This strengthened their position *vis-à-vis* the "creditor states", which could result in more lenient programmes, subsequent revisions in favour of the "debtor states", or less compliance in the implementation. In other words, through the OMT announcement "debtor states" got the chance to free-ride on the lower interest rates provided by their membership in the eurozone. This is impressively shown by an account of a Commission official who was a member of the Troika delegation that negotiated a revision of the original consolidation programme to the advantage of Portugal[16] in late summer 2012: when the ECB announced the launch of OMT on 6 September, the negotiations were "suddenly blocked" because Portugal's access to the financial markets was restored; thus, the announcement of OMT strengthened the bargaining power of the Portuguese government *vis-à-vis* the Institutions (Interview 4). Hence, a major cost of leading consisted in the creation of moral hazard despite the linked conditionality. This entails the additional risk that in case a member state defaults, the bonds purchased by the ECB lose their value, which would result in prohibited monetary financing.

The second major cost was the feared loss of legitimacy. In particular possible legal actions against OMT—which indeed were brought to the German Constitutional Court after the announcement of OMT—were considered a source of loss of trust in the ECB. This raises the question as to why the ECB, as a politically independent institution, would worry at all about its legitimacy. The answer lies in the expectation that a loss of the ECB's legitimacy, as perceived by the public, would lead to decreasing support or acceptance by member state governments. As a direct consequence, also the support for the euro as a common currency would decline. While in the short run this would damage the ECB's credibility in the financial markets and thus its effectiveness, it would threaten its entire *raison d'être* in the long term. However, interviewees also emphasized that the expected legitimacy costs were either not significant for the ECB's decision (Interviews 20, 21, 23), regarded only Germany and a few other member states like Finland or the Netherlands (Interviews 3, 8, 14), or would play a role only in case of an eventual failure of OMT, namely member state default (Interview 22).

A final cost of leading is strongly related to such a loss of legitimacy. As elaborated above, the ECB linked OMT to the ESM consolidation programmes and thus made its monetary decisions dependent on the consent of member states. Although mentioned by only one interviewee,

[16] More precisely, a more lenient fiscal adjustment path was agreed.

this nexus implies a loss of political independence for the ECB, and could thus ultimately damage its legitimacy and credibility (Interview 24).

As pointed out in Sect. 3.4, a cost-benefit analysis can be conducted if (1) there are no significant costs or benefits, (2) one of the two elements directly implies the institutional survival or death of the potential leader, or (3) we find a "common currency" to directly balance costs against benefits. Whereas options (1) and (3) do not apply in this case as the ECB's expected increase of effectiveness, for instance, can hardly be weighed against its feared loss of legitimacy, option (2) allows for a cost-benefit analysis. As explicated above, OMT ensured the ECB's institutional survival, which in line with the book's theoretical assumptions outweighs all possible costs of leading. Indeed, there is strong evidence that the ECB realistically feared that the *status quo* would inevitably result in a fragmentation of the eurozone and thus in the end of its institutional *raison d'être*. Therefore, the ECB's benefits of leading consisted in its institutional survival. Moreover, the exaggeratedly high interests on Spanish and Italian bonds prevented an effective monetary policy transmission. As long as these interest rates were so high, the ECB's reduction of the base rate to guarantee price stability had no effect. Hence, the ECB secured its own right to exist by taking the lead. This assessment is corroborated by the distribution of answers regarding the ECB's costs and benefits of leading: the preservation of its own effectiveness and ultimate survival clearly outweighed all the other mentioned costs and benefits (Fig. 5.1).

According to our first theoretical proposition, which predicts that leadership emerges if its expected benefits exceed the related costs (H1), we thus expect that the ECB offered leadership. Under the condition that there was also a demand for leadership and no other candidate being more powerful, we further expect that the ECB also emerged as a leader.

The second proposition accounting for a leader's emergence regards the aggregate *status quo* costs (H2). The conjecture predicts that these costs create a demand for leadership which, if met by a leadership offer, leads to the actual emergence of leadership.[17] *Status quo* costs were high

[17] In the case of OMT, one may object that no demand is needed for the ECB's emergence as a leader as it could have announced and even launched OMT without any other actor perceiving a need for it. In practice, however, it is not only highly improbable that the ECB would do so; there would also be strong objections by the negatively affected member states which would most probably bring actions against the ECB in front of the European Court of Justice and—most importantly—the ECB could not rely on its mandate to secure price stability in the eurozone and would thus lack the legal basis for its measures.

throughout the crisis. However, according to most interviewees, the perceived pressure for action was never as high as in the beginning of the crisis (spring 2010) and in summer 2012 when OMT were announced.[18] The perceived costs, feared to become manifest in case of *status quo*, consisted in the default of Italy and/or Spain and the ensuing fragmentation of the eurozone. This assessment is reflected and corroborated by the development of government spreads at the time. For reasons of better distinctiveness, Fig. 5.2 shows the spreads without Greek bond yields.

What can be clearly seen from these figures is that, alongside a second peak by the end of 2011, the spreads in the eurozone—and thus its fragmentation risk—were never as high as in July 2012 when Mario Draghi publicly committed to doing "whatever it takes". Especially Spanish bond yields were as high as never before during the crisis, and Italian bonds had almost reached the level they had during the government crisis in November 2011 when Prime Minister Silvio Berlusconi eventually stepped down.

According to the second theoretical proposition (H2), we therefore expect an extraordinary high demand for leadership; not least because, as opposed to former critical moments in the crisis, this time the politically feasible instruments (such as a permanent bailout fund) on the part of the member states seemed exhausted. In sum, given that there was both a demand for leadership due to high *status quo* costs and a supply of it by the ECB, whose benefits of leading exceeded the related costs, the first analytical model can plausibly explain the ECB's emergence as a leader.

Confidence in this explanation can be further strengthened by evidence for the presumed causal mechanisms underlying the theoretical propositions. With regard to the emergence of leadership, we expect that the ECB presented the launch of OMT as a way to reduce the group's *status quo* costs and thus as a contribution to a common goal. Moreover, there should be evidence that the other actors took notice of this leadership offer and that at least some of them objected to it. The search for such evidence constitutes a "hoop test": while finding evidence increases the confidence in the conjecture, it does not exclude alternative explanations. If we do not find respective pieces of evidence, however, the

[18]Of the 18 interviewees who comprehensively answered the question concerning the most critical moment during the crisis, 10 named summer 2012. Even 14 out of 18 respondents (77.8%) stated that in summer 2012, the perceived pressure for action was very high (10) or rather high (4) as compared to other periods of crisis management.

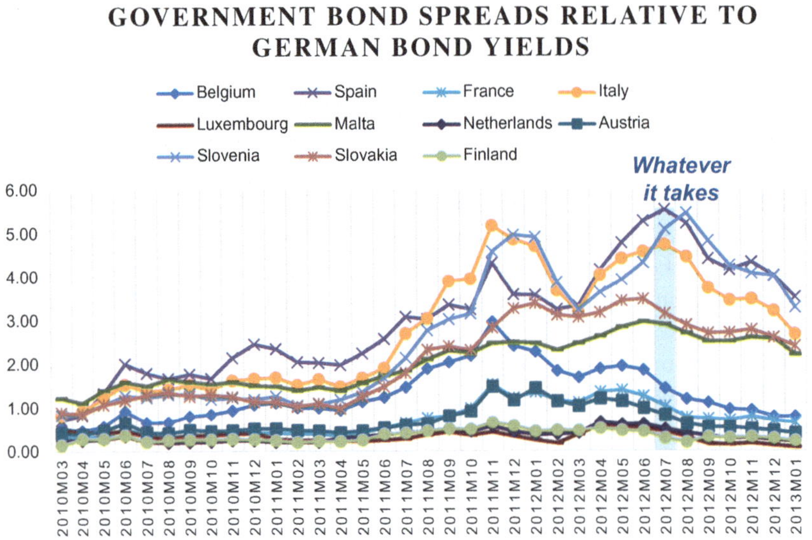

Fig. 5.2 Government bond spreads relative to German bond yields, March 2010–January 2013 (excl. Greece) (*Source* Eurostat [own illustration])

presumed causal mechanism would be disproved (Collier 2011; Van Evera 1997: 31).

As regards the supply of leadership, the ECB indeed presented OMT as a contribution to the common goal of preserving the euro and overcoming the crisis. When the ECB presented the technical details of the OMT programme, for instance, President Mario Draghi explained that it "is now time [...] for the ECB to graduate from the narrowly inflation-focused priority rooted in the German model and assume greater responsibility for the functioning, or even *the survival, of the system*" (Euractiv 2012a, own emphasis). Also the ECB's official press release stated that OMT "aim at safeguarding [...] the singleness of the monetary policy" (European Central Bank 2012b). In any case, the original statement "to do whatever it takes to preserve the euro" (President of the European Central Bank 2012) already defines any ensuing action as a contribution to the eurozone's common goal.

As regards the demand for leadership, the other actors perceived the ECB's announcement as a leadership offer, although some member states objected behind closed doors (Interviews 1, 2, 10, 11, 13, 14, 16, 17, 25–27).

In order to safeguard the ECB's political independence, most actors refrained from publicly commenting on the ECB's decision. However, Germany and France publicly welcomed the launch of OMT as an obligation of the European institutions to protect the integrity of the euro area (Waterfield 2012). This statement shows that the two member states indeed perceived the ECB's announcement as an attempt to lead by guiding the eurogroup towards a common goal (see Spiegel et al. 2012). The same is true for the Commission and the EP. Most telling in this regard is the reaction of then EP President Martin Schulz: "This courageous decision is a major step towards resolving the sovereign debt crisis and restoring the stability of the euro zone" (Euractiv 2012a). This does not mean, however, that there were no objections against the ECB's measures. As outlined below, the German government especially urged the ECB not to activate OMT.

Explaining the ECB's Leadership Success: Resources, Preferences and Institutional Constraint

The model's first variable accounting for a leader's impact concerns the leader's power resources, which can be disaggregated into material, institutional, and ideational resources. In the case of non-state actors, material resources are measured by their financial capacities to influence EMU governance. According to this measure, the ECB's material resources exceed those of all other actors, and are theoretically even unlimited, since the central bank is the only actor that can actually create money in the euro area. On the one hand, this capability regards the provision of liquidity to banks, which are crucial for economic stability and the refinancing of member states. On the other hand, this concerns member state finances directly as the ECB can influence their refinancing options by buying or selling their bonds. Of course, the ECB's firepower is limited by its mandate, which prohibits monetary financing. However, firstly also the member states are limited in the appropriation of their financial capacities by the "no-bailout clause" (Art. 125 TFEU). Secondly, even within its mandate, the ECB's material capacities still exceed those of the member states by far. One example of these paramount material resources was the ECB's support to the Irish banking sector which before 2010, when the EU/IMF programme was agreed upon, amounted to 140bn euro (including ELA), or 85% of the Irish GDP at the time.[19] As one ECB official put it, the single member states' contributions to the financial assistance for Ireland (eurozone total: 67.5bn) were "peanuts" in comparison (Interview 14).

In order to assess the ECB's institutional resources, one needs to distinguish between monetary policy and economic (including fiscal and financial) policy. As regards the former, the ECB possesses all relevant resources because within its mandate, laid down by primary law, it is the only authorised actor. Thus, it holds all the rights ranging from agenda-setting via decision-making through to the implementation of its decisions. As regards economic policy, in contrast, the ECB's institutional resources do not include any formal right of decision-making. However, the ECB does have formal and informal participation, consultation, and monitoring powers.

First, the ECB participates in all relevant fora of agenda-setting or decision-making in the eurozone.[20] Its President is to be invited to all Council meetings relevant for the European System of Central Banks.[21] More importantly, however, the ECB President is also a de facto full member of the eurogroup which is the venue where s/he conveys the ECB's policy recommendations to member states. As regards both Council and Eurogroup, the ECB not only participates through its President in the official summits, but also—and with regard to substance maybe even more importantly—by having staff members in all preparatory bodies and committees.[22] Since the outbreak of the eurozone crisis, the ECB President also participates in the meetings of the euro area's heads of state and government ("Euro Summits"). Furthermore, the ECB is part of the so-called "Macroeconomic Dialogue", which takes place twice a year between representatives of ECB, Commission, Council, and social partners. The ECB President may also be invited to the regular meetings between the Presidents of the European Council, the Eurogroup, and the Commission. Finally, as regards the eurozone's rescue funds, the ECB can appoint observers and its President can participate as observer in the ESM's Board of Governors, where the crucial

[19] http://www.ecb.europa.eu/press/html/irish-letters.en.html, rev. 2016-01-29.

[20] The outline of the ECB's *institutional* resources is largely based on Beukers (2013).

[21] The European System of Central Banks is composed of the ECB and the national central banks of all EU member states.

[22] These are the Economic and Financial Committee (EFC), the Economic Policy Committee (EPC), and the Eurogroup Working Group (EWG).

decision about financial assistance and consolidation programmes are made (Beukers 2013: 1583–6).

Second, the Treaties grant the ECB a right of consultation as regards primary and secondary legislation at the European *and* national level in its field of competence (Art. 127.4 TFEU). In the context of crisis management, the ECB thus gave its opinion on the drafts of the Fiscal Compact (Kreilinger 2012: 3f.) and on the proposal of the Sixpack- and Twopack legislation, for instance. Moreover, as regards implementation, the ECB has monitoring rights through its role in the Troika. In the context of the revised Stability and Growth Pact, the ECB can be invited by the Commission to join it on its surveillance missions in eurozone states. These missions may also include the renegotiation of the consolidation programmes, in which the ECB assumes a formal negotiator role (Beukers 2013: 1588–90).

To be sure, the ECB's participation and consultation rights are weak powers given that they are not binding. However, while it is true that the ECB has no formal means to commit the member states to follow its policy recommendations, the functional links between monetary policy and economic governance provide the ECB with a strong informal power base to give more weight to its opinions. As for instance Beukers points out:

> Member States need liquid banks and the ECB can provide this liquidity. Because of these close links between banks and Member States, the ECB can influence Member States by making central bank liquidity provision to credit institutions 'conditional' upon a specific course of action. (2013: 1592)

In other words, due to its superior material resources and its exclusive institutional rights in monetary policy, the ECB's voice cannot be ignored by member states.

Ideational resources, finally, can be differentiated into information (expertise), credibility, and legitimacy. The ECB's expertise clearly exceeds those of member states and the EP, and arguably also that of the Commission. As a proxy for expertise, the number of administrative staff who specialize in EMU matters has been used. The ECB employs 523 staff members, followed by the Commission (391), Germany (117), and the EP with only 40 permanent staff. The numbers are corroborated by the subjective assessments of the interviewees. Due to its high number of experts as well as its access to country-specific data through national central banks (whose staff is not even considered in the figure reported above), the ECB is highly appreciated as a technical advisor in economic governance. This expertise constitutes a power resource to influence member states' policy decisions, including the suggestion of concrete amendments to legislative proposals (Interviews 14, 21, 22, 24).

Being a supranational institution, the ECB enjoys more credibility to serve the EU's common good than single member states. Moreover, the ECB's credibility exceeds that of the EP and the Commission because it is political independent and thus free of political influences or constraints that could prevent it from exclusively pursuing the eurozone's common interest (which actually coincides with its institutional self-interest). This high degree of credibility is further underpinned by the ECB's large material and exclusive institutional resources in the eurozone's monetary policy.

With regard to its legitimacy, finally, the ECB's record is mixed. Assessed by democratic standards, the ECB has no input legitimacy by definition as it is politically independent. Thus, apart from the legal bases laid down by the Treaties, the ECB's can only rely on its output legitimacy which is defined by its mandate to maintain price stability (Art. 127.1 TFEU). As long as the ECB achieves this goal without causing significant redistributive consequences, its legitimacy should be considered relatively high. However, as soon as the ECB's actions imply clear winners and losers, and are not unambiguously backed by its mandate, it will lose legitimacy. Still, being a supranational institution, the ECB is more legitimated to act as a leader in the eurozone than a single member states. Compared to the EP and the Commission, however, the ECB lacks input legitimacy and thus appears less appropriate as a leadership candidate.

In sum, the ECB possesses most material resources of all relevant actors. Also as regards its ideational resources, specifically expertise and credibility, the ECB is more powerful than the other actors (not so regarding its legitimacy). Its institutional resources are most difficult to compare. Formally, the ECB is very powerful in the area of monetary policy because it is the sole decision-maker, but it is relatively weak in economic governance because it has no formal rights of decision-making. Informally, however, the ECB's powers in economic governance are not to be underestimated given the functional links between monetary and economic policy. In any case, the analysis shows that the ECB is an extremely powerful actor in the euro area. Furthermore, like in the case of Germany, we can observe that power resources are interrelated. The ECB's capability to provide (theoretically unlimited) liquidity as well as its outstanding expertise, for instance, provide for its high credibility and its informal institutional power.

According to the book's third theoretical proposition (H3), which predicts that the impact of leaders increases with the amount of power resources at their disposal, we therefore expect that the ECB was successful in bringing about policy or institutional change to the benefit of the eurozone.

The next theoretical proposition of the model (H4) specifies the second condition accounting for a leader's impact: If preferences converge around the outcome preferred by the leader, she will *ceteris paribus* have a strong impact on the outcomes—and vice versa. According to the respondents interviewed for this case study, only three member states, namely Germany, and to a minor extent Austria and the Netherlands, were initially against the announcement of OMT. However, the surprising statement of Mario Draghi and the ensuing effect on the markets changed their strategic preferences. If they had openly opposed OMT even after their announcement, they would have damaged the credibility of the ECB and thus the OMT's welcome effect. In this case, they would not only suffer the same *status quo* costs as before, but they would also have reinforced the doubts in the markets whether the eurozone would actually be able or willing to preserve the common currency and avoid sovereign default. In short, by opposing OMT, the sceptical member states would even have exacerbated their situation. Thus, they assumed a neutral position, or, in the words of one interviewee, "those who were sceptical decided not to be vocal" (Interview 2).

The most sceptical member states was certainly Germany. Its strategic preferences were "mixed" (Interview 27), however. While it welcomed the signal effect of the announcement, not least because it would remove pressure on Germany to take the lead itself by agreeing on further forms of risk mutualisation, it strongly fought the activation of OMT or any design that would allow the ECB to launch them without the member states' approval. As one interviewee stated, after the Governing Council's decision of 2 August, the German government clearly conveyed in all fora that an activation of OMT "would not be welcome and that the ECB would be well advised not to go ahead" (Interview 10). In public, however, also the German government backed the ECB's decisions for the above-mentioned reasons (Blackstone and Walker 2012: 4f.;

Henning 2016: 189). Germany's resistance behind closed doors was directly opposed by France and Italy, which strongly pushed for an activation of OMT. Among the supranational institutions, not only the Commission, but also the EP clearly welcomed the ECB's decision on OMT (Interviews 10, 11, 13, 14, 16, 17, 22, 25–27).

In sum, most actors[23] welcomed the ECB's unconventional measures. Therefore, preferences strongly converged on the outcome preferred by the ECB. According to the operationalization of this variable, this is the most favourable value with regard to a leader's success (Sect. 3.4). Based on the model's fourth theoretical proposition (H4), and under the condition that the values of the other two variables (power resources and institutional constraint) are not to the disadvantage of the ECB, we expect a strong impact, and thus successful leadership, in the case of the OMT announcement.

The last proposition accounting for a leader's impact concerns the institutional constraint, which determines the leader's latitude in decision-making: If the institutional constraint is low, the leader will *ceteris paribus* have a strong impact on the outcomes, and vice versa (H5). According to the Treaties, the ECB is "independent in the exercise of its powers [...]. Union institutions, bodies, offices and agencies and the governments of the Member States shall respect that independence" (Art. 282.3 TFEU). In line with the operationalization of this variable, this means that as long as the ECB acts within its mandate, it faces the lowest possible degree of institutional constraint: namely full discretion in decision-making (Sect. 3.4, Table 3.4). However, is the ECB also de facto independent, or does its political independence exist only on paper?

All interviewees of this book, who have dealt with the ECB during the crisis or are responsible for its relations with other institutions, agreed that the ECB is not only formally, but also de facto independent in its decision-making (Interviews 1, 2, 4, 5, 7, 10, 14, 25, 26). To be sure, there are steady consultations and exchanges of views with member states and other EU institutions at both technical and political levels. In this

[23]Based on the interview material, only Germany, the Netherlands, and Austria were clearly against OMT. Finland and Estonia usually belong to the group of "creditor" states (fiscally "conservative" or "hawkish) surrounding Germany as well, but no information could be obtained that they were explicitly against the ECB's announcement. Vice versa, there has been no indication that they were in favour of the announcement either.

way, the ECB prepares and explains its actions and takes the preferences of other actors into account. However, there is no ex-ante coordination, and no actor attempts to give instructions to the ECB—which cannot be said the other way around (Interviews 19–22, 25, 26). Before stating to "do whatever it takes", Mario Draghi had not even informed the members of the ECB's Governing Council, let alone anyone in the EU fora (Interviews 13, 15). There are only plausible presumptions about phone calls to Merkel and Schäuble, in which Draghi prepared them, explained the rationale for his measures, and made sure they would not undermine the ECB's authority after the announcement (Blackstone and Walker 2012; Spiegel 2014). At any rate, as regards the concrete case of "whatever it takes" and its timing, the German government was not informed beforehand either (Interviews 26, 27). In sum, the ECB is a formally and informally independent institution.

Given that the ECB is de jure and de facto independent, the institutional constraint attains the lowest possible value, namely full discretion by the leader (Sect. 3.4, Table 3.4). This low institutional constraint allows for very efficient decision-making by the ECB, which is especially relevant in times of crisis:

> Comparatively, decision making by the ECB is much more straightforward and fast. No parliamentary approval is required of decisions of the Governing Council, and unanimity is not required. [...] Moreover, the ECB does not have to respond to voters through elections, and its measures cause less immediate – or less visible – damage to voters. The ECB is therefore seen as the only institution that can act quickly – a characteristic that fits the dynamics of the financial markets better than slow, democratic procedures. (Beukers 2013: 1608f.)

According to the model's last theoretical proposition, and under the condition that the other two variables (power resources and preference distribution) are not to the disadvantage of the ECB, we therefore expect a strong impact and successful leadership in the case of the OMT announcement.

Given this low institutional constraint, the question arises as to whether the preference distribution assessed above played any role at all for the announcement of OMT. One could argue that the ECB could have launched OMT even if all the member states had been against it. While it is true that the ECB in theory could have done so, in practise this would have been highly improbable. In the concrete case of OMT, a launch against the will of a majority of member states would have destroyed their effect and would thus have been useless with regard to its impact, and even detrimental to the ECB's credibility and legitimacy. More generally, any action by the ECB that is not in accordance with a critical mass of member state preferences is formally possible—due to the ECB's political independence—but would do serious harm to the ECB's credibility and legitimacy in the long run. As elaborated above, a significant loss of reputation and trust in the public, or the overt withdrawal of support by a critical mass of governments, would challenge the common currency itself and thus jeopardize the ECB's existence. Therefore, the ECB—and especially its President Mario Draghi—was very careful throughout the crisis to extensively consult member state governments prior to making its decisions. Hence, it acted only once it was sure that a critical mass of actors was on its side (Interviews 1, 2, 10, 21, 22). Despite the low institutional constraint, the other actors' preferences thus still play an important role with regard to the ECB's actions and its impact on the outcomes.

In sum, all three theoretical propositions of the model's second analytical step (power resources, preference distribution, institutional constraint) pass the congruence test. If also the presumed causal mechanism applies, there must be evidence that the ECB employed its resources in one or more of the leadership strategies defined in Sect. 3.3. Such evidence would be necessary to affirm causal interference, constituting a so-called "hoop test" (Collier 2011; Van Evera 1997: 31). However, no evidence could be found that the ECB translated its resources in any of the defined bargaining strategies ("enhancing collective action"), with the only exception of "unilateral action" (see below). Moreover, there is no evidence that the other actors anticipated a negative reaction by the ECB should they not have supported OMT, and therefore backed its decision ("rule of anticipated reaction"). This indicates that the ECB, due to its political independence, refrained from engaging in power-based distributional bargaining, which distinguishes it from all the other actors examined by this work. Nevertheless, there is evidence that the ECB (1) acted as a provider of common knowledge in order to ensure acceptance for its measures and (2) relied on unilateral action which provided it with a first-mover advantage.

First, the ECB carefully prepared its measures through exchanges of views with all relevant actors, which allowed it to take the others' preferences into account, but also to explain its own course of action and thus to shape new outcomes. In particular the latter is crucial: by providing "full information" (Interview 24) as regards the state of affairs and possible outcomes, the ECB inevitably shapes the strategic preferences of the other actors involved. In particular during crisis management, ECB officials explained monetary policy and macroeconomics publicly and internally in all relevant EU fora. In this way, the ECB defined possible solutions and advocated those preferred by itself (Beukers 2013: 1581). In the concrete case of the OMT announcement, the ECB—and in particular its President Mario Draghi—were very "pro-active" in communicating with member states governments and the Presidents of the European Council, Eurogroup, and Commission (Interview 2, also 1, 10, 21, 22, 24–27). This regarded especially the German government as the potentially most powerful opponent of the ECB: Indeed, "[w]ithout compromising the ECB's independence, Mr Draghi worked informally with Ms Merkel, carefully testing what might be acceptable" (Spiegel 2014). Although the ECB thereby prepared the ground for OMT, it did not inform the other actors about its concrete plans or when to launch them.

The second strategy employed by the ECB is that of unilateral action. According to Arild Underdal, unilateral action as a leadership strategy "is exercised whenever one moves to solve a collective problem by one's own effort, thereby setting the pace for others to follow" (1994: 183). A necessary pre-condition, however, is that the respective actor occupies a dominant or preponderant position within the game in question (Underdal 1994: 183). This perfectly matches the case of OMT: the ECB solved the eurozone's most immediate problem at the time by its own effort and thereby bought time for member states to reform. As an official in the German Finance Ministry explained, the ECB took a decision which actually should have been taken in the ECONFIN Council; instead, the ECB acted unilaterally (Interview 27). An ECB official confirmed and justified the ECB's recourse to unilateral action: "There were only two alternatives: Either the ECB appearing as lender of last resort to governments or Germany moving on towards Eurobonds or Redemption Fund or something to stop the crisis" (Interview 22). Hence, by declaring to "do whatever it takes" and announcing OMT, the ECB exploited a first-mover advantage and thus modified the strategic preferences of the opponents among the member states. Although they were still against the activation of the announced bond purchasing programme, they strategically took a favourable position because otherwise they would have destroyed the effect of the announcement, thereby even increasing their *status quo* costs. As specified by Underdal, the ECB could only employ this strategy because of its paramount material power resources in the eurozone.

Results

The book's leadership model can plausibly explain the ECB's successful leadership in the case of the OMT announcement. As predicted by the theoretical propositions of the model's first analytical step, the ECB emerged as a leader because the *status quo* costs were extraordinarily high and its benefits of leading—namely, the preservation of the common currency and thus of its own existence—outweighed any costs. As regards the second analytical step, the ECB could successfully establish OMT because, as predicted by all three propositions, its power resources are extremely strong, the other actors' preferences converged on its own preferred outcome, and the institutional constraint was very low. If the ECB had not achieved the desired outcome in this case, the analytical model would have been falsified.

In sum, the ECB emerged as a leader in summer 2012 because in the light of an unprecedented fragmentation risk in the eurozone there was not only a great demand for decisive action, but also because the ECB needed to ensure its own survival. The leadership offered by the ECB was successful because it used its paramount power resources to first provide common knowledge and then to pursue unilateral action. Although there is no process-tracing evidence indicating that the ECB would have been less successful if the preference distribution or the institutional constraint had been less favourable, it appears plausible that these two factors facilitated or even enabled the ECB's impact.

Moreover, the case of OMT bears at least two further important results for the study of leadership. First, the case sheds light on the phenomenon of "*leadership by default*". Leaders by default are leaders that, although they may be very powerful actors, intervene only if there is a leadership vacuum. According to this work's theoretical model, the only reason for doing so are high costs of leading. In the case of OMT, the ECB's costs of leading were indeed very high and consisted primarily in its politicization: "An institution that was designed to be free of politics, maintaining its existence in an international environment outside the control of any one government, has become intensely politicized" (Farrell 2012). If the costs of leading are very high, potential leadership candidates act as late as possible because they hope that another actor will take the lead first and achieve the common goal in their place. However, should this not happen, they have to intervene in order to avoid the even bigger costs of *status quo* ("game of chicken"). In this way, they become leaders by default. In other words, leadership by default is costly, but driven by the fear for even higher *status quo* costs. In the case of OMT, the ECB's actions were indeed driven by the attempt to avoid the costs of non-action, namely the break-up of the eurozone implying its own institutional death (Interview 20; see also Krampf 2016: 467). Still, the ECB waited as long as deemed possible before it intervened because it hoped that the eurozone member states, and in particular Germany, would act before.

Second, and closely related, the ECB's basic interests (or meta-preferences) apparently differ from those of all other actors examined in this book. Member states as well as supranational institutions proved to be interested in the increase of their power (understood as the capacity for political influence). In the case of the ECB, however, the increase of political influence does not necessarily coincide with an increase in institutional power. The politicization of the ECB is rather a cost it faces, because it jeopardizes its political independence and makes it vulnerable to political pressure. As an ECB official, who had also been involved in the Troika activities, put it:

> In the house there is a certain unease about expanding so much the role of the ECB. I think few people are happy with the fact that the ECB had to play such an important role in the crisis management. Many people are aware of the risks that comes with it. The risk of mission creep and lack of legitimacy. (Interview 18)

Thus, although it might be argued that the ECB acted "strategically" in eurozone crisis management (Beukers 2013; Henning 2016; Torres 2013), it has not behaved like a classic power-maximizer trying to obtain its preferred outcome by employing bargaining strategies in negotiations with other institutions or member states. Instead of engaging in bargaining over outcomes or institutional power with other actors, the ECB simply reacted to functional constraints. The fact that in so doing it had to take into consideration the actions of member states does not indicate that the ECB has been a strategic player trying to maximize its institutional power. Such a claim could only be proved by evidence unveiling the ECB's bargaining behaviour in the relevant EU fora.[24] However, no such evidence could be found. On the contrary, with the only exception of the ECB's role in the "Troika", all interviewees agreed that the ECB explained the existing functional and institutional constraints on it to the member states, but refrained from using them as a bargaining chip in eurozone crisis management.

References

Altavilla, Carlo, Domenico Giannone, and Michele Lenza. 2014. The Financial and Macroeconomic Effects of OMT Announcements. ECB Working Paper 1707.

Bauer, Michael W., and Stefan Becker. 2014. The Unexpected Winner of the Crisis: The European Commission's Strengthened Role in Economic Governance. *Journal of European Integration* 36 (3): 213–229.

Beukers, Thomas. 2013. The New ECB and Its Relationship with the Eurozone Member States: Between Central Bank Independence and Central Bank Intervention. *Common Market Law Review* 50: 1579–1620.

Bild. 2008. Finanzkrise, Autoangst! Wer soll dafür blechen? *Bild*, November 17. Available online at http://www.bild.de/politik/2008/wer-soll-fuer-die-finanzkrise-aufkommen-6495460.bild.html, rev. 2016–05–18.

Blackstone, Brian, and Marcus Walker. 2012. How ECB Chief Outflanked German Foe in Fight for Euro. *The Wall Street Journal*, October 2. Available online at http://www.wsj.com/articles/SB10000872396390443507204578020323544183926, rev. 2016–05–25.

Bressanelli, Edoardo, and Nicola Chelotti. 2016. The Shadow of the European Council: Understanding Legislation on Economic Governance. *Journal of European Integration* 38 (5): 511–525.

Bressanelli, Edoardo, and Nicola Chelotti. 2018. The European Parliament and Economic Governance: Explaining a Case of Limited Influence. *The Journal of Legislative Studies* 24 (1): 72–89.

[24]The alternating sequence of action between the member states' moves in fiscal and economic policy and the ECB's moves in monetary policy (Beukers 2013: 1601) does not qualify as evidence for strategic action as the member states' actions modified the functional constraints on the ECB and thus increased its leeway in monetary decision-making (instead of constraining it). If this sequence of measures were an actual indicator for strategic interaction, there should be evidence that the ECB made respective commitments or threats vis-à-vis the member states (e.g. tit-for-tat: "if you member states decide on direct bank recapitalization, we will launch OMT"). However, no such evidence could be found.

CESifo. 2014. Ifo President Sinn Welcomes Schäuble's Opposition to ECB Bond Purchases. Ifo Institute, Center for Economic Studies (CES), Press Release, May 22. Available online at http://www.cesifo-group.de/ifoHome/presse/Pressemitteilungen/Pressemitteilungen-Archiv/2014/Q2/press_20140522_anleihe.html, rev. 2016–01–28.

Collier, David. 2011. Understanding Process Tracing. *Political Science and Politics* 44 (4): 823–830.

ComRes. 2013. Europe's Crisis Measures: A View from the European Parliament. Available online at http://www.cicero-group.com/wp-content/uploads/2013/02/eu_crisis_measures_12.pdf, rev. 2016–01–23.

Coombes, David. 1970. *Politics and Bureaucracy in the European Community: A Portrait of the Commission of the E.E.C.* London: Allen and Unwin.

Chang, Michele, and Jörg Monar (eds.). 2013. *The European Commission in the Post-Lisbon Era of Crises: Between Political Leadership and Policy Management*. Brussels: Peter Lang.

Crum, Ben. 2018. Parliamentary Accountability in Multilevel Governance: What Role for Parliaments in Post-crisis EU Economic Governance? *Journal of European Public Policy* 25 (2): 268–286.

De Grauwe, Paul. 2013. Design Failures in the Eurozone: Can They Be Fixed? LEQS Papers No. 57, London.

De Grauwe, Paul, and Yuemei Ji. 2015. Correcting for the Eurozone Design Failures: The Role of the ECB. *Journal of European Integration* 37 (7): 739–754.

Dehousse, Renaud. 2016. Why Has EU Macroeconomic Governance Become More Supranational? *Journal of European Integration* 38 (5): 617–631.

Dinmore, Guy, and Ralph Atkins. 2011. ECB Letter Shows Pressure on Berlusconi. *Financial Times*, September 29. Available online at http://www.ft.com/intl/cms/s/0/3576e9c2-eaad-11e0-aeca-00144feab49a.html, rev. 2016–01–28.

Euractiv. 2011a. Commission Buys Time on Eurobond Proposal, November 23. Available online at http://www.euractiv.com/euro-finance/concrete-eurobond-proposal-till-2012-news-509110, rev. 2016–01–22.

Euractiv. 2011b. Rehn Bids to Woo MEPs with Eurobonds Plan, June 23. Available online at http://www.euractiv.com/euro-finance/rehn-readies-eurobonds-proposal-win-meps-support-news-505880, rev. 2016–05–17.

Euractiv. 2012a. Draghi Gets ECB Backing for Unlimited Bond-Buying, September 7. Available online at http://www.euractiv.com/section/euro-finance/news/draghi-gets-ecb-backing-for-unlimited-bond-buying/, rev. 2016–05–26.

Euractiv. 2012b. Merkel on Eurobonds: 'Not in My Lifetime', June 27. Available online at http://www.euractiv.com/section/euro-finance/news/merkel-on-eurobonds-not-in-my-lifetime/, rev. 2016–05–26.

Euractiv. 2012c. Parliament Kick-Starts Frozen Eurobond Debate, April 16. Available online at http://www.euractiv.com/section/euro-finance/news/parliament-kick-starts-frozen-eurobond-debate/, rev. 2016–05–23.

European Central Bank. 2012a. Introductory Statement to the Press Conference (with Q&A), August 2. Available online at http://www.ecb.europa.eu/press/pressconf/2012/html/is120802.en.html, rev. 2016–05–24.
European Central Bank. 2012b. Technical Features of Outright Monetary Transactions, September 6. Available online at http://www.ecb.europa.eu/press/pr/date/2012/html/pr120906_1.en.html, rev. 2016–05–24.
European Commission. 2011. Green Paper on the Feasibility of Introducing Stability Bonds, COM(2011) 818 final, November 23, Brussels.
European Commission. 2012. A Blueprint for a Deep and Genuine Economic and Monetary Union: Launching a European Debate, COM(2012) 777 final/2, November 30, Brussels.
European Commission. 2014. Expert Group on Debt Redemption Fund and Eurobills. Final Report, March 31. Available online at http://ec.europa.eu/economy_finance/articles/governance/pdf/20140331_report_en.pdf, rev. 2016–01–23.
European Commissioner for Economic and Monetary Affairs. 2011. Going the Last Centimeter for Reinforced Economic Governance, June 22. Available online at http://europa.eu/rapid/press-release_SPEECH-11-468_en.htm?locale=en, rev. 2016–05–23.
European Parliament. 2011a. Draft Report on the Proposal for a Regulation of the European Parliament and of the Council on the Effective Enforcement of Budgetary Surveillance in the Euro Area, 2010/0278(COD), January 11, Committee on Economic and Monetary Affairs.
European Parliament. 2011b. Resolution of 6 July 2011 on the Financial, Economic and Social Crisis: Recommendations Concerning the Measures and Initiatives to Be Taken (2010/2242(INI)), P7_TA(2011)0331, Brussels.
European Parliament. 2011c. Report on the Proposal for a Regulation of the European Parliament and of the Council on the Effective Enforcement of Budgetary Surveillance in the Euro Area, A7-0180/2011, May 2, Committee on Economic and Monetary Affairs.
European Parliament. 2012a. European Parliament Resolution of 2 February 2012 on the European Council of 30 January 2012, P7_TA(2012)0023, Brussels.
European Parliament. 2012b. European Parliament Resolution of 15 February 2012 on the Feasibility of Introducing Stability Bonds (2011/2959(RSP)), P7_TA(2012)0046, Brussels.
European Parliament. 2012c. Report on the Feasibility of Introducing Stability Bonds (2012/2028 (INI)), A7-0402/2012, 6 December, Committee on Economic and Monetary Affairs.
European Parliament. 2012d. Report on the Proposal for a Regulation of the European Parliament and of the Council on Common Provisions for Monitoring and Assessing Draft Budgetary Plans and Ensuring the Correction

of Excessive Deficit of the Member States in the Euro Area, A7-0713/2012, May 29, Committee on Economic and Monetary Affairs.

European Parliament. 2012e. Towards a Genuine Economic and Monetary Union. European Parliament Resolution of 20 November 2012 with Recommendations to the Commission on the Report of the Presidents of the European Council, the European Commission, the European Central Bank, and the Eurogroup 'Towards a Genuine Economic and Monetary Union' (2012/2151(INI)), P7_TA(2012)0430, Brussels.

European Parliament. 2013. Resolution of 16 January on the Feasibility of Introducing Stability Bonds (2012/2028(INI)), P7_TA(2013)0018, Brussels.

European Parliament/Council. 2011. Regulation (EU) No 1173/2011 of the European Parliament and of the Council of 16 November 2011 on the Effective Enforcement of Budgetary Surveillance in the Euro Area.

Farrell, Henry. 2012. A More Imperfect Union: On the European Central Bank. *The Nation*, December 5. Available online at http://www.thenation.com/article/171596/more-imperfect-union-european-central-bank, rev. 2016-01-31.

Fasone, Cristina. 2014. European Economic Governance and Parliamentary Representation: What Place for the European Parliament? *European Law Journal* 20 (2): 164–185.

Fromage, Diane. 2018. The European Parliament in the Post-crisis Era: An Institution Empowered on Paper Only? *Journal of European Integration* 40 (3): 281–294.

German Council of Economic Experts. 2012. The European Redemption Pact: An Illustrative Guide. Working Paper 2. Available online at http://www.sachverstaendigenrat-wirtschaft.de/fileadmin/dateiablage/download/publikationen/working_paper_02_2012.pdf, rev. 2016-05-18.

Hall, Peter A. 2012. The Economics and Politics of the Euro Crisis. *German Politics* 21 (4): 355–371.

Henning, Randall C. 2016. The ECB as a Strategic Actor: Central Banking in a Politically Fragmented Monetary Union. In *The Political and Economic Dynamics of the Eurozone Crisis*, ed. James A. Caporaso and Martin Rhodes. Oxford: Oxford University Press.

Héritier, Adrienne, Katharina L. Meissner, Catherine Moury, and Magnus G. Schoeller. 2019, forthcoming. *European Parliament Ascendant: Parliamentary Strategies of Self-Empowerment in the EU*. London: Palgrave Macmillan.

Hix, Simon, and Bjørn Høyland. 2013. Empowerment of the European Parliament. *Annual Review of Political Science* 16 (1): 171–189.

Hodson, Dermot. 2013. The Little Engine that Wouldn't: Supranational Entrepreneurship and the Barroso Commission. *Journal of European Integration* 35 (3): 301–314.

Judge, David, and David Earnshaw. 2008. The European Parliament: Leadership and "Followership". In *Leaderless Europe*, ed. Jack Hayward, 245–268. Oxford: Oxford University Press.

Juncker, Jean-Claude, and Giulio Tremonti. 2010. E-bonds Would End the Crisis. *Financial Times*, December 5. Available online at http://www.ft.com/intl/cms/s/0/540d41c2-009f-11e0-aa29-00144feab49a.html, rev. 2016–01–25.

Kade, Claudia, Timo Pache, Wolfgang Proissl, Stefan Schaaf, and Peter Ehrlich. 2011. Die Front gegen Eurobonds bröckelt. *Stern*, November 24. Available online at http://www.stern.de/politik/ausland/der-weg-aus-der-schuldenkrise-die-front-gegen-eurobonds-broeckelt-3439842.html, rev. 2016–01–25.

Krampf, Arie. 2016. From Transparency to Ambiguity: The Impact of the ECB's Unconventional Policies on EMU. *Journal of European Integration* 38 (4): 455–471.

Kreilinger, Valentin. 2012. The Making of a New Treaty: Six Rounds of Political Bargaining, Policy Brief Notre Europe 32, Paris.

Krugman, Paul. 2014. Even More On Scotland. *The New York Times*, September 10. Available online at http://krugman.blogs.nytimes.com/2014/09/10/even-more-on-scotland/?_r=1, rev. 2016–05–25.

Lombardi, Domenico, and Manuela Moschella. 2016. The Government Bond Buying Programmes of the European Central Bank: An Analysis of Their Policy Settings. *Journal of European Public Policy* 23 (6): 851–870.

Ludlow, Peter. 2012. *The European Council of 30 January 2012. Between German Hegemony and 'More Europe'*. Preliminary Evaluation: Eurocomment.

Nugent, Neill. 1995. The Leadership Capacity of the European Commission. *Journal of European Public Policy* 2 (4): 603–623.

Nugent, Neill, and Mark Rhinard. 2016. Is the European Commission *Really* in Decline? *Journal of Common Market Studies* 54 (5): 1199–1215.

O'Keeffe, Mícheál, Marion Salines, and Marta Wieczorek. 2016. The European Parliament's Strategy in EU Economic and Financial Reform. *Journal of European Public Policy* 23 (2): 217–235.

President of the European Central Bank. 2012. Speech at the Global Investment Conference in London, July 26. Available online at https://www.ecb.europa.eu/press/key/date/2012/html/sp120726.en.html, rev. 2016–05–24.

President of the European Council. 2012. Towards a Genuine Economic and Monetary Union, in close collaboration with the Presidents of the European Commission, Eurogroup, and European Central Bank, December 5. Available online at http://www.consilium.europa.eu/uedocs/cms_Data/docs/pressdata/en/ec/134069.pdf, rev. 2016–05–18.

Rittberger, Berthold. 2003. The Creation and Empowerment of the European Parliament. *Journal of Common Market Studies* 41 (2): 203–225.

Rittberger, Berthold. 2014. Integration Without Representation? The European Parliament and the Reform of Economic Governance in the EU. *Journal of Common Market Studies* 52 (6): 1174–1183.

Salines, Marion, Gabriel Glöckler, and Zbigniew Truchlewski. 2012. Existential Crisis, Incremental Response: The Eurozone's Dual Institutional Evolution 2007–2011. *Journal of European Public Policy* 19 (5): 665–681.

Savage, James D., and Amy Verdun. 2016. Strengthening the European Commission's Budgetary and Economic Surveillance Capacity Since Greece and the Euro Area Crisis: A Study of Five Directorates-General. *Journal of European Public Policy* 23 (1): 101–118.

Schelkle, Waltraud. 2012. European Fiscal Union: From Monetary Back Door to Parliamentary Main Entrance. *CESifo Forum* 13 (1): 28–34.

Shackleton, Michael. 2017. Transforming Representative Democracy in the EU? The Role of the European Parliament. *Journal of European Integration* 39 (2): 191–205.

Spiegel. 2012. Merkel zur Schuldenpolitik: 'Keine Eurobonds, solange ich lebe'. *SPIEGEL ONLINE*, June 26. Available online at http://www.spiegel.de/politik/ausland/kanzlerin-merkel-schliesst-euro-bonds-aus-a-841115.html, rev. 2016–01–25.

Spiegel, Peter. 2014. If the Euro Falls, Europe Falls. *Financial Times*, May 15. Available online at http://www.ft.com/intl/cms/s/0/b4e2e140-d9c3-11e3-920f-00144feabdc0.html, rev. 2015–05–15.

Spiegel, Peter, Quentin Peel, and James Wilson. 2012. Politicians Back Draghi's Aggressive Stance. *Financial Times*, July 27. Available online at http://www.ft.com/intl/cms/s/0/a105046a-d7fd-11e1-80a8-00144feabdc0.html, rev. 2016–05–26.

Spiegel/Schulz, Martin. 2012. European Parliament President: Call for Political Union Now Is 'Dramatic Mistake', September 4. Available online at http://www.spiegel.de/international/europe/interview-with-eu-parliament-president-martin-schulz-on-euro-crisis-a-853657.html, rev. 2016–05–23.

Torres, Francisco. 2013. EMU's Legitimacy and the ECB as a Strategic Political Player in the Crisis Context. *Journal of European Integration* 35 (3): 287–300.

Underdal, Arild. 1994. Leadership Theory: Rediscovering the Arts of Management. In *International Multilateral Negotiation: Approaches to the Management of Complexity*, ed. I. William Zartman, 178–197. San Francisco: Jossey-Bass.

Van Evera, S. 1997. *Guide to Methods for Students of Political Science*. Ithaca and London: Cornell University Press.

Warren, Thomas. 2018. The European Parliament and the Eurozone Crisis: An Exceptional Actor? *The British Journal of Politics and International Relations* 20 (3): 632–651.

Warren, Thomas, Patrick Holden, and Kerry E. Howell. 2017. The European Commission and Fiscal Governance Reform: A Strategic Actor? *West European Politics* 40 (6): 1310–1330.

Waterfield, Bruno. 2012. Debt Crisis: Angela Merkel and Francois Hollande Pledge to Back Euro. *The Telegraph*, July 27. Available online at http://www.telegraph.co.uk/finance/financialcrisis/9433140/Debt-crisis-Angela-Merkel-and-Francois-Hollande-pledge-to-back-euro.html, rev. 2016–05–26.

Interviews

Interview 1. 2014. Council of the European Union, Senior Official and Administrator. Brussels, Belgium, November 6.

Interview 2. 2014. European Commission, senior official. Brussels, Belgium, November 7.

Interview 3. 2014. European Commission, DG ECFIN, official. Brussels, Belgium, November 12.

Interview 4. 2014. European Commission, DG ECFIN, administrator. Brussels, Belgium, November 13.

Interview 5. 2014. Permanent Representation of France. Brussels, Belgium, November 13.

Interview 6. 2014. European Commission, DG ECFIN, senior official. Brussels, Belgium, November 14.

Interview 7. 2014. European Council, senior official/assistant. Brussels, Belgium, November 17.

Interview 8. 2014. Council of the European Union, official. Brussels, Belgium, November 18.

Interview 9. 2014. European Commission, DG ECFIN, two administrators. Brussels, Belgium, November 20.

Interview 10. 2014. Senior EU official. Brussels, Belgium, November 20.

Interview 11. 2014. Permanent Representation of the Netherlands. Brussels, Belgium, November 24.

Interview 13. 2014. Council of the European Union, senior official. Brussels, Belgium, November 25.

Interview 14. 2014. ECB official. Brussels, Belgium, November 26.

Interview 15. 2014. Council of the European Union, senior official. Brussels, Belgium, November 27.

Interview 16. 2014. European Parliament, official. Brussels, Belgium, November 27.

Interview 17. 2014. European Commission, DG ECFIN, official. Brussels, Belgium, November 28.

Interview 18. 2015. European Central Bank, official. Frankfurt, Germany, March 9.

Interview 19. 2015. European Central Bank, senior official. Frankfurt, Germany, March 10.

Interview 20. 2015. European Central Bank, senior official. Frankfurt, Germany, March 11.

Interview 21. 2015. European Central Bank, official/official/administrator. Frankfurt, Germany, March 12.

Interview 22. 2015. European Central Bank, senior official. Frankfurt, Germany, March 12.

Interview 23. 2015. European Central Bank, senior official. Frankfurt, Germany, March 12.

Interview 24. 2015. European Central Bank, senior official. Frankfurt, Germany, March 13.

Interview 25. 2015. Federal Ministry of Finance, government official. Berlin, Germany, March 17.

Interview 26. 2015. Federal Ministry of Finance, government official. Berlin, Germany, March 19.

Interview 27. 2015. Federal Ministry of Finance, senior official. Berlin, Germany, March 23.

Interview 28. 2015. European Parliament, senior official. Brussels, Belgium, February 2.

Interview 29. 2015. European Parliament, Member of the European Parliament. Brussels, Belgium, February 4.

Interview 31. 2015. Council of the European Union, administrator. Brussels, Belgium, February 9.

Interview 32. 2015. European Parliament, official. Brussels, Belgium, February 10.

Interview 33. 2015. European Commission, DG ECFIN, two officials. Brussels, Belgium, February 11.

Interview 34. 2015. Council of the European Union, official. Brussels, Belgium, February 11.

CHAPTER 6

Evaluating Leadership: The Hard Case of the Eurozone

This chapter evaluates the findings of the book and assesses the eurozone leadership record since the outbreak of the crisis in late 2009. Section 6.1 presents the comparative results emerging from the single case studies. With regard to the emergence of leadership, it demonstrates that actors supplied leadership only if they expected individual benefits from doing so in advance. Once a leader has emerged, the chapter argues that it is the interplay of power resources, preference distribution, and institutional constraint that accounts for her impact. Moreover, the comparison yields important empirical and theoretical insights. With regard to powerful actors in the eurozone, for instance, it shows that Germany's veto power is much bigger than its actual shaping power, and that the ECB crucially differs from other EU institutions as it does *not* seek to increase its political influence when this comes at the cost of its independence. Theoretically, the chapter argues that although leadership can be a solution to collective action problems, it is no altruistic sacrifice by powerful actors. This may lead to a "leadership vacuum", but also to "leadership by default".

Extending the empirical scope of the analysis, Sect. 6.2 provides an overview assessment of the eurozone's leadership record since the outbreak of the crisis. It shows that single member states or institutions only in rare cases provided leadership. As a consequence, we can observe a shift from an unmet demand for leadership targeted at single member states to the provision of collective leadership from behind by the EU institutions. Still, with the exception of the announcement of Outright

M. G. Schoeller, *Leadership in the Eurozone*, Palgrave Studies in European Union Politics, https://doi.org/10.1007/978-3-030-12704-6_6

Monetary Transactions (OMT) by the ECB, the impact of leadership remained limited. Powerful actors like Germany or the ECB often lack the incentives to provide leadership, whereas those motivated to take the lead, such as the so-called "debtor states" or the EP, lack the necessary resources. The limited impact of leadership can be explained with the diverging preferences in the eurozone and the high institutional hurdles for reform.

Finally, the model predicts a pessimistic scenario regarding future emergence of leadership in EMU: given the lack of "push-" and "pull-factors" for powerful actors to provide leadership, the emergence of leadership appears unlikely unless a renewed flare-up of the crisis will increase both the status quo costs and the individual incentives for taking the lead. Hence, due to the heterogeneous distribution of preferences and high hurdles for institutional change, eurozone governance and reform turns out to be a hard case for the provision of political leadership.

6.1 Comparative Results

Leadership Emergence and Influence

The book's theoretical model consists of two analytical steps. The first step postulates that leadership emerges if the status quo imposes high costs on all actors involved, and, at the same time, a powerful actor expects that the benefits of leading will exceed its costs. The second step conjectures that once emerged, a leader's impact depends on the interplay of power resources, preference distribution, and institutional constraint.

With regard to the first step (emergence of leadership), the empirical analysis has shown that status quo costs were high throughout the eurozone crisis. Albeit with some variation at the upper end of the variable's range of values, status quo costs can thus serve as control variable in testing the model's first theoretical proposition (H1). Under the condition that status quo costs were constantly high, we found perfect congruence between a "leader's surplus" (=expected benefits − costs of leading) and the emergence of leadership: in all six case studies, powerful actors emerged as leaders only if they expected individual benefits from it. Hence, we can conclude that both a leader's surplus and the aggregate status quo costs are necessary conditions for the emergence of leadership.

Table 6.1 Comparative results on the impact of political leadership

	Impact of leadership (dv)	*Power resources (iv_1)*	*Preference distribution (iv_2)*	*Institutional constraint (iv_3)*
Super-commissioner	No	Medium-high	Unfavourable	High
Fiscal compact	Yes	Medium-high	Favourable	High
Eurobonds (EP)	No	Low	Heterogeneous	High
OMT	Yes	High	Favourable	Low

Source Own illustration

At the same time, we see that a strong demand for leadership (H2) alone is not a sufficient condition for its emergence: only in combination with a leader's surplus, the demand can account for the emergence of leadership. As the demand for leadership did not vary significantly during eurozone crisis management, the model's second theoretical proposition could not be tested on the basis of a cross-case comparison. However, the plausibility probes conducted in the context of the within-case analyses provide evidence for the causal effect of leadership demand.

Table 6.1 illustrates the more complex picture of the second analytical step, which accounts for a leader's impact on outcomes. As emerges from the table, only the second proposition on the distribution of preferences (H4) can be tested by means of a controlled comparison. If we compare the case of the super-commissioner with the Fiscal Compact, we see that in both cases Germany emerged as a leader, and that treaty change was required to bring about the desired results. In other words, both power resources and the institutional constraint remained stable. Hence, based on the theoretical model, we can affirm that the difference in the preferences of the followers accounts for the different outcomes. While in the case of the Fiscal Compact they weakly converged on the leader's preference, they converged elsewhere in the case of the super-commissioner. Moreover, we may speculate that the preference distribution plays a more important role for a leader's impact than the other variables. Based on this book's sample of cases, a favourable preference distribution appears as a sufficient condition for a leader's impact, independently of the values of the other variables. This would imply that if the major part of the actors agrees on the outcome preferred by the leader, there will be an impact even if the leader possesses only few power resources and the institutional constraint is high.

As regards the other two theoretical propositions concerning a leader's power resources (H3) and the institutional constraint (H5), the sample of cases does not allow for a controlled comparison. However, multiple congruence tests and process-tracing in the within-case analyses provided rich evidence for their plausibility. Moreover, the within-case analyses have shown that it is not just the value of one single variable (power resources or institutional constraint), but the interplay of all three variables, which accounts for the outcomes. Thus, the theoretical conjectures should not be applied in an isolated way, but only in the context of the entire theoretical model.

EMU Actors and Theorizing Leadership

The empirical analysis revealed further insights regarding (1) the costs and benefits of collective actors in the governance and reform of the Economic and Monetary Union (EMU), (2) these actors' characteristics and behaviour, and (3) leadership theorizing in general.

With regard to the first point, the empirical analysis reveals that the perceived costs and benefits of the German government in EMU differ systematically from those of the Commission and the EP. The costs and benefits of the European Central Bank (ECB), by contrast, fall into a third category that differs from all other actors analysed by this work.

Germany's costs and benefits in crisis management evolved around the goal of avoiding becoming EMU's "paymaster" and institutionalizing fiscal discipline, on the one hand, and calming the financial markets to stabilize the eurozone on the other. Hence, most of Germany's costs and benefits were related to material gains in a distributional conflict about economic welfare (see also Frieden and Walter 2017). To a lesser extent, the German government was also concerned with domestic costs and benefits, which in most of the cases can be translated into electoral votes.

The costs and benefits for Commission and EP, by contrast, consisted mainly in non-material power resources. It is striking that both institutional actors had almost identical rationales for action: both the Commission and the EP were primarily concerned with gains or losses in institutional and ideational resources. With regard to the latter, the EP's main concern was its legitimacy, while the Commission also took its credibility and bureaucratic resources into account.

The ECB, finally, was much more interested in its political independence and effectiveness than in gaining political influence (see also

Lombardi and Moschella 2016: 863–5). In the context of the eurozone crisis, both aspects were closely related to the ECB's survival as an institution. Moreover, the ECB's political independence is key to maintaining monetary dominance over member states' fiscal authorities.[1]

In sum, while Germany's (and arguably all other member states') costs and benefits consisted primarily in material gains and losses, the Commission and EP were more interested in non-material power resources. However, all three assessed their costs and benefits in terms of political influence, be it due to material or non-material resources. This is what distinguishes them from the ECB, which under certain circumstances faces a trade-off between its political influence and its independence. In principle, the ECB's independence outweighs an increase in political influence for the institution (see below).

Moreover, the empirical analysis allows us to draw conclusions regarding the role of collective actors in EMU governance and reform. The actor most frequently called on to assume leadership has been Germany. Being the eurozone's largest economy, its role in managing the crisis was central. However, as this book shows, Germany is not omnipotent. While it is true that Germany is a de facto veto player in EMU, its shaping power—which is crucial to create new solutions and thus to assume leadership—has clear limits. In other words, it is much easier for the German government to maintain the status quo in the eurozone than bringing about policy or institutional change in the common interest. This is certainly one reason as to why crisis management has been characterized by incremental "muddling through" rather than bold innovation. To put it even more bluntly, while Germany cannot do whatever it likes in EMU, it can block whatever it does not like. Thus, Germany provided leadership only when this involved bringing about solutions reflecting its own preferences, namely the allocation of adjustment costs at the national level through the implementation of austerity measures and the institutionalization of fiscal discipline. However, due to its limited shaping power, it did so with varying success (e.g. Super-commissioner vs. Fiscal Compact). By contrast, with the exception of

[1] Monetary dominance means that fiscal authorities adjust to the central bank's monetary policy. This is supposed to result in lower debt ratios and more price stability. In the case of fiscal dominance, instead, the central banks need to adjust their decisions to the fiscal authorities, which design their policy independently.

monetary policy, Germany successfully prevented the leadership of other actors if they promoted solutions that did not reflect its preferences (e.g. Eurobonds).

With regard to the Commission and EP, the book shows that although both actors have the same basic interest, namely the maximization of power, they face different utility functions due to their different institutional roles. Under the same external conditions, the promotion of a solution to a collective action problem in the EU may be beneficial for the EP while it is detrimental to the Commission. Although both institutions are supposed to promote the EU's common good, the EP would do so even where it stands little or no chance for success, because it can blame the executive in case the implementation of the proposal fails. As the case of Eurobonds shows, while the EP could only win by promoting a solution to the crisis, even if it was politically unfeasible, the Commission as part of the EU's executive would suffer considerable damage and therefore refrained from taking the lead on this issue. Hence, in analysing these institutions we need to consider that even if we assume the same basic interests, their rationales of action and thus their concrete policy proposals are constrained by their institutional roles.

While these insights do not challenge the rationalist assumption that both Commission and EP are power-maximizers, this does not apply to the ECB. If an increase in power, understood as capacity to influence the behaviour of others, implies distributional bargaining (e.g. compromises, package deals, commitments), the ECB tries to refrain in order to safeguard its political independence. Therefore, the ECB is no strategic player in the conventional understanding. Only if its existence is at stake, as was the case in the course of the eurozone crisis, will the ECB be ready to sacrifice (parts of) its independence and thereby become politicized. This can be seen by the fact that the activation of OMT was made conditional on an ESM programme and thus, indirectly, on the consent of member states. Nonetheless, the ECB has never made "deals" with member states, and thus managed to largely preserve its independence also in times of crisis. This insight does not mean that the ECB is no strategic player (see Henning 2016; Torres 2013)—it simply means that the ECB values its political independence higher than its political influence.

As regards the book's leadership model, finally, at least five generalizable findings emerged from the empirical analysis. First, leadership functions as a solution to collective action problems. This means that in situations in which a group faces suboptimal collective action outcomes due to incomplete institutional rules, a leader can help actors complete the institutional framework. In other words, a leader can optimize collective action. In the case of the first financial assistance to Greece, for instance, we see that not least due to a lack of leadership on the part of Germany, the eventual assistance was too little and too late. As a consequence, the eurozone as a whole was worse off as the Greek sovereign debt crisis spilled over to other member states and jeopardized the single currency. In the course of the crisis, it turned out that a limited backstop like the ESM would ultimately not suffice to calm the markets and thereby remove the immediate fragmentation risk in the eurozone. Thus, in order to suspend or even end the crisis, an unlimited backstop was needed. Eurobonds would have been such a backstop, but given that no powerful actor emerged as a leader in the issue, and the EP failed in its efforts either, the crisis continued. Only when the ECB stepped in as a lender of last resort, the eurozone's collective action problem[2] (Chapter 4) could be solved for the time being.

Second, leadership is no altruistic sacrifice. In all six cases analysed by this work, actors supplied leadership only if they expected individual benefits from doing so. In the case of Eurobonds, for instance, there would have been good normative reasons for the Commission to take the lead despite the low chances for success. However, the Commission refrained from taking the lead because it anticipated considerable losses in institutional and ideational power. The same is true regarding Germany's role in the first financial assistance granted to Greece, when pro-European arguments or values like solidarity did not suffice to make Germany emerge as a leader on the issue.

Third, the fact that also the leader needs to be better off at the end of the day can result in a leadership vacuum. In such a situation, surprisingly weak actors, which under normal circumstances would not have the chance to assume leadership, can step in and help the group achieve its common goal. This was true for the EP in the case of Eurobonds.

[2]The eurozone's collective action problem is twofold: on the one hand, a non-optimal currency union bears incentives for free-riding, which needs to be regulated; on the other hand, it requires a certain degree of redistribution. EMU lacks institutional rules with regard to both problems (Chapter 4).

However, due to their lack of resources, weak leaders will succeed only if they face a favourable preference constellation or a low institutional constraint. Next to weak leaders, a leadership vacuum can also bring about "leaders by default". In particular when the expected costs of leading are high, potential leadership candidates wait as long as possible until they supply leadership, hoping that another actor will take the lead before them. If the status quo costs are high, too, the result is a so-called "game of chicken". We can therefore conjecture that it is the actor who has most to lose in case of status quo that eventually emerges as a leader. This was the case with the ECB and its launch of OMT. Although the costs of leading were very high, the even higher status quo costs finally pushed it to take the lead. Given that the feared status quo costs consisted in the collapse of the eurozone, and thus in the institutional death of the ECB, it had even more to lose than the member states.

Fourth, the dependent variable of the first analytical step (emergence of leadership) may be better conceptualized as a continuous variable. In the theoretical model, the variable has only two possible values, which are either the presence or the absence of leadership. However, the case of the super-commissioner has shown that leaders can deliberately decide about the degree to which they provide leadership. If we compare Germany's proposal of a super-commissioner to the Fiscal Compact, for instance, we see that in the former case Germany limited itself to the provision of common knowledge, whereas it extended its engagement to the costlier employment of bargaining strategies when it came to shaping the Fiscal Compact.

Fifth, with regard to the second analytical step (impact of leadership), we find that it is the *interplay* between all three independent variables, namely a leader's power resources, the distribution of preferences, and the institutional constraint, which determines a leader's impact on the outcomes. Therefore, the single theoretical propositions apply only *ceteris paribus*. The case of the Fiscal Compact is especially insightful in this regard. If we look only at the proposition on institutional constraint (H5), which was very high, we would expect no impact. However, Germany's power resources (H3) and the favourable distribution of preferences (H4) can plausibly explain why and how the high institutional constraint could be overcome.

6.2 Leadership in the Eurozone: An Overview Assessment

This section provides an overview assessment of the eurozone's leadership record since the outbreak of the crisis.[3] The crisis' "fast-burning phase" (Carstensen and Schmidt 2018) started with Greece reaching the brink of sovereign default in the winter of 2009/2010. At the time, most eyes were on Germany as the eurozone's largest economy and most powerful member state. While a European reaction to the Greek crisis did not require the participation of each single member state,[4] it was obvious that any type of financial assistance would only be possible with the participation of Germany. This provided Germany with a de facto veto in eurozone crisis management. However, as analysed in detail in Sect. 4.1, Germany did not take the lead in the beginning of the crisis. On the contrary, it blocked the first bailout of Greece until the very last moment before Greek default (see Jones 2010). At the same time, neither the EU institutions nor other eurozone member states filled this leadership vacuum. The eurozone's first reaction to the crisis was thus characterized by the absence of leadership. As a result, the first Greek bailout came too late and provided too little in order to contain the spread of the crisis.

As opposed to later instances of crisis-management, this leadership vacuum was primarily due to the uncertainty regarding the consequences of financial assistance (vs. sovereign default) in EMU as well as unknown legal and technical issues, rather than the divergence of preferences or high institutional hurdles (see below). Still, this kind of leaderless crisis-management exercised in the case of the first Greek bailout became prototypical for the eurozone's early response to the crisis. Instead of the emergence of leadership, we find often imperfect solutions designed under the imminent threat of a eurozone collapse. Thus, the first phase of crisis management consisted in collective last-minute reactions, rather than the pro-active translation of power-resources into the achievement of a common goal by one or a few like-minded actors. The fact that solutions were agreed upon in protracted negotiations under high

[3] For concise overviews of the eurozone crisis and its management, see Copelovitch et al. (2016: 814–7) and Dyson (2017).

[4] See, for instance, Slovakia's abstention from the Greek Loan Facility.

pressure for action, giving more power and influence to Germany with the "creditor states" being the more patient actors, seems to confirm liberal intergovernmentalist expectations (Schimmelfennig 2015; see also Carstensen and Schmidt 2018: 615). According to liberal intergovernmentalists, there is not much space for leadership in EU negotiations, as all actors have the same access to information and bargaining outcomes reflect primarily the preferences of those actors with the best fall-back position (see Moravcsik 1999a, b).

To be sure, in some instances strong functional constraints helped overcome the initial resistance of veto players such as Germany, and thus led to somewhat more sustainable solutions such as the European Stability Mechanism (ESM). However, contrary to neofunctionalist expectations (Lindberg and Scheingold 1970: 128–33; Niemann and Ioannou 2015: 1999), supranational institutions did not provide successful leadership in the first phase of the crisis, but were rather circumvented by member states and, in particular, by a dominant France–German tandem. Against this background, we find almost no cases of successful leadership in the "fast-burning" phase of crisis management. The shaping of the Fiscal Compact, where successful leadership can be clearly identified (Sect. 4.3), appears as a unique exception in this regard.

A special role was played by the Franco-German tandem, which until the beginning of 2012 dominated eurozone crisis management. The close collaboration between German chancellor Merkel and French President Sarkozy even earned them the nickname "Sarkozy". Schild (2013) interprets this pattern as bilateral leadership. In hindsight, however, it is debatable whether the undeniable influence of the two biggest member states really served the interests of their "followers". Indeed, the (in)famous meeting of Deauville in October 2010, where Germany and France struck their own compromise on how to proceed with crisis management, led to strong criticism from other countries and members of the Van Rompuy Task Force, which was mandated to fulfil the same task (see below). In any case, the Franco-German dominance came to an end in spring 2012 when a new President came into office and the bilateral cooperation started to falter (Schoeller 2018).

Another early leadership candidate was the so-called "Van Rompuy Task Force". Then President of the European Council Herman Van Rompuy was mandated by the heads of states and governments to establish a Task Force and elaborate proposals on how to strengthen EMU and overcome its crisis. While the demand for leadership was obvious in this case, the provision proved to be difficult. First, the Task Force was in direct rivalry with the European Commission as agenda-setter in the EU. In preparing its proposals, a race developed with the Commission as to who would come up with their solutions first. In the end, the Commission launched six legislative proposals a few weeks before the Van Rompuy Task Force provided its final report. While the Commission thus "won the race", it can be argued that the Task Force influenced the process from behind by putting time pressure on the Commission and making it adopt much of its own proposals (Bressanelli and Chelotti 2016: 517f.). Second, as described above, Van Rompuy was ousted by the Franco-German tandem when they presented their own plans in Deauville. The pattern recurred one year later, when by the end of 2011 Van Rompuy was side-lined by France and Germany in preparing the Fiscal Compact (Sect. 4.3).

While the Commission certainly fulfilled its task as formal agenda-setter in the EU by initiating the Six-pack and Two-Pack legislation in this first phase of crisis-management, it could not provide leadership as defined by this book. In many cases, the Commission was circumvented by member states, such as with the European Financial Stability Facility (EFSF), the ESM, or the Fiscal Compact. Where it was not bypassed, it anticipated its low chances for successful leadership due to its relatively small power resources in economic governance, the unfavourable preference constellation among member states, and the high institutional hurdles for reform. In these cases, the Commission did not even attempt to come up with grand initiatives (see the example of Eurobonds, Sect. 5.1 and Hodson 2013). This changed in the second phase of crisis management, however, where the Commission teamed up with other EU institutions (see below). Similarly, also the ECB refrained from providing leadership in the beginning of the crisis. To be sure, it strongly supported eurozone crisis management with its Securities Market Programme (SMP) and Longer-term Refinancing Operations (LTRO) (see Verdun 2017). However, only with the announcement of OMT the ECB finally moved from fighting the effects of the crisis to tackling its roots by assuming the role of the eurozone's lender of last resort (Sect. 5.3, see below).

For a variety of reasons, the first half of 2012 marked a change in eurozone crisis management. The Franco-German "motor" faltered, supranational institutions assumed "collaborative leadership" in projects such as the Banking Union, and the ECB became a de facto lender of last resort by announcing OMT. In the words of Carstensen and Schmidt (2018), the "slow-burning phase" of crisis management began.

The fact that from 2012 onwards, the Franco-German strategy of "pre-negotiating" important deals largely failed (Schoeller 2018), weakened Germany and allowed for the emergence of collaborative leadership by the EU institutions. This new pattern played out most visibly in the case of the Banking Union. While the ECB assumed intellectual leadership both in the provision of common knowledge *and* political bargaining (De Rynck 2016), the Commission used its competences as formal agenda-setter to get the Single Supervisory Mechanism (SSM) on track. As Nielsen and Smeets (2018) show, it closely collaborated not only with the ECB in the agenda-setting phase, but also with the Council and its Secretariat in the decision-making phase. When setting up the Single Resolution Mechanism (SRM), instead, the Commission needed to channel its ideas through the European Council, whose president Van Rompuy could rely on the help of ECB President Draghi in keeping member state governments committed (Nielsen and Smeets 2018). The sum of the single parts delivered by different EU bodies corresponds in fact to what this book defines as leadership (Chapter 2). Apart from the extraordinary role of the ECB, however, the question remains as to how the respective contributions of single institutional actors differed from their usual job profile. From that point of view, the "Four Presidents' Report", where the President of the European Council teamed up with the Presidents of the Commission, Eurogroup, and ECB in providing a roadmap towards a genuine EMU may even be a better example of "collaborative leadership".

By contrast, the eurozone's most powerful member state, Germany, once again refrained from taking the lead in the case of Banking Union. Permanently sceptical of the idea, Germany acted as a veto player that needed to be pushed into making concessions on the establishment of the Banking Union. In this context, functional arguments on the "vicious circle" between sovereign debt and banks as well as rhetorical entrapments might have played a forceful role (Schäfer 2016). At the time of writing, Germany is still the major opponent to finalising the so-called "third pillar" of the Banking Union, consisting in a European Deposit Insurance Scheme (EDIS). As Schild (2018) has shown, also the Franco-German tandem failed to exert common influence, let alone leadership, in shaping the Banking Union.

Next to the case studies provided by this book (Chapter 4), Germany's role in the case of Banking Union raises the question of Germany's overall leadership record in eurozone crisis management. Following this book's model of leadership, where leadership emerges as a response to a collective action problem and a lack of institutions to deal with it (Sect. 3.1), Germany's leadership needed to be twofold: on the one hand, it had to complete EMU supervisory institutions combatting fiscal free-riding ("austerity"); on the other hand, it had to address EMU's distributional problem by creating institutions of financial assistance ("solidarity") (see Chapter 4). The latter function corresponds to Kindleberger's (1981) understanding of leadership ("benign hegemony"). However, as Carstensen and Schmidt (2018) put it: "If Germany is the 'hegemon' rationally calculating its interests and imposing its ideas in the eurozone crisis, it has been a highly unsuccessful one on that" (616). Putting emphasis on Germany's motivation, Bulmer and Paterson (2013) found that Germany is a "reluctant hegemon". In a more recent assessment, they come to a more differentiated conclusion, stating that Germany may have the material and ideational resources of a hegemon, but did not assume the role of a systemic stabilizer (Bulmer and Paterson 2018, Chapter 6).

In any case, the empirical record neither corroborates the picture of a "benign hegemon" nor that of leadership as conceptualized in this book. Germany may have succeeded in pushing austerity-based responses to the crisis, while blocking many solidarity-based proposals, but it did not assume a permanent leadership or hegemonic role in either material or ideational terms (Caporaso and Rhodes 2016: 8–10; Matthijs and Blyth 2011). Moreover, while the strengthening of fiscal rules and surveillance in the eurozone may be interpreted as a manifestation of ordoliberal ideas, there is little evidence that the idea of ordoliberalism has been internalized by many other eurozone countries. As a consequence, eurozone crisis management "could be viewed as lacking a benign hegemon, with Germany acting to protect its own interests rather than the general interests of all member states" (Dyson 2017: 66). Only in the rare instances where Germany's own interests coincided with the common goal of preserving the eurozone, such as in the case of the super-commissioner (Sect. 4.2) or the Fiscal Compact (Sect. 4.3), we therefore see the emergence of leadership. Not least due to its one-sided character in favour of more austerity without further burden-sharing, this type of leadership remained largely unsuccessful.

The problem of Germany's (non-)leadership in EMU is aggravated by an unfavourable incentive structure. On the one hand, Germany lacks strong "pull factors" to provide leadership. First, after multiple reforms of fiscal rules in the eurozone and all "debtor countries" having exited their EFSF or ESM programmes, the potential of austerity in the eurozone seems to be largely exhausted. Second, taking the lead on further reform may become very costly for Germany. Although fears that Germany might become the eurozone's paymaster may seem exaggerated, any stronger engagement would require concessions to France, and face considerable domestic opposition (see also Bulmer 2014). On the other hand, there are no "push factors" for Germany to take the lead. As long as the eurozone does not run the risk of collapsing, Germany benefits in many ways from the status quo and its "exorbitant privilege" (Jacoby 2015). Moreover, given that the "fast-burning phase" of the eurozone crisis is over, Germany no longer needs to find a compromise with France at any cost. Hence, at the latest since 2012, the "classic anchor stone of European integration, the Franco-German relationship, appeared to be an empty shell" (Dyson 2017: 66). These incentive structure may change if a new existential crisis erupts in the eurozone or if Germany sees a need for further integration against the background of Brexit and the retreat of the United States under Trump as reliable partner.

In the absence of German or Franco-German leadership, the ECB became a leader by default (Sect. 5.3; see also Verdun 2017). By pushing the interpretation of its mandate to the limits (Schmidt 2017), it assumed the role of the eurozone's lender of last resort (De Grauwe and Ji 2015). With a view to the common goal of preserving the single currency, the announcement of OMT ended the "fast-burning phase" of the crisis and gave member states time for reform—a situation that is still present at the time of writing. Moreover, the ECB secured its success through a large programme of Quantitative Easing (QE), which cushioned the negative effects of austerity and thus preserved the eurozone from deflation. However, as this book's case study has shown, the assumption of leadership comes with high costs for the ECB. These costs regard primarily the central bank's political independence and its legitimacy. Hence, also for the ECB there are virtually no "pull factors" to take the lead. As a consequence, we may expect leadership only if the very existence of the ECB is jeopardized.

At the time of writing, eurozone reform is largely in deadlock. This situation endures despite the need for further reform and a large array of realistic proposals (e.g. Bénassy-Quéré et al. 2018). The emergence of leadership is not in sight. The book's theoretical model provides an explanation for this leadership vacuum. As there is no manifest existential crisis for the time being, status quo costs are relatively low. This results in a weak demand for leadership. At the same time, the supply for leadership is scarce. Powerful actors like Germany or the ECB lack the incentives to provide leadership, whereas those motivated to take the lead lack the necessary resources (e.g. "debtor states" or the European Parliament (EP)).

As if things were not complicated enough, the crucial divide between "creditor states" and "debtor states" on how to reform EMU (Frieden and Walter 2017: 379–83) makes it highly unlikely for a leader to identify and promote acceptable agreements. Recent developments like the emergence of the "New Hanseatic League", a group of mainly northern EU member states with fiscally conservative views, point to the rise of new veto players rather than leaders. Potential leaders anticipate these difficulties and therefore often abstain from making a "leadership offer" in the first place. This not only explains the reserved role of the Commission (see Sect. 5.1), but also those of other EU institutions and member states. If anything, the only plausible way to overcome these impediments to leadership emergence seems to be what the literature has labelled the "collaborative leadership" of EU institutions (e.g. Nielsen and Smeets 2018). Judged by the empirical record, this worked in the case of Banking Union (see above). From a theoretical perspective, collaborative leadership enables actors to pool their power resources, thereby increasing their capacity to overcome diverging preferences and high institutional hurdles (Sect. 3.3).

In summary, only in rare cases we saw a single member state or EU institution providing leadership in the eurozone crisis or its aftermath. During the course of crisis management, the unmet demand for leadership to be supplied by Germany or the Franco-German tandem faded due to the actual provision of collective leadership from behind by the EU institutions. However, with the exception of the OMT announcement and the first two pillars of Banking Union, the impact of leadership remained limited. Based on the book's leadership model, this can be explained with the divergence of preferences between "debtor" and "creditor states" and the high institutional hurdles for EMU reform. With regard to the future emergence of leadership, the theoretical model predicts a pessimistic scenario. Despite the objective need for further reform, powerful actors lack the incentives to provide costly leadership, whereas those motivated to take the lead lack the resources. This results in the paradoxical situation that the emergence of leadership remains unlikely until a renewed flare-up of the crisis increases both the status quo costs (demand) and the incentives for taking the lead (supply) in the eurozone.

References

Bénassy-Quéré, Agnès, et al. 2018. Reconciling Risk Sharing with Market Discipline: A Constructive Approach to Euro Area Reform. CEPR Policy Insight 91, London.

Bressanelli, Edoardo, and Nicola Chelotti. 2016. The Shadow of the European Council: Understanding Legislation on Economic Governance. *Journal of European Integration* 38 (5): 511–525.

Bulmer, Simon. 2014. Germany and the Eurozone Crisis: Between Hegemony and Domestic Politics. *West European Politics* 37 (6): 1244–1263.

Bulmer, Simon, and William E. Paterson. 2013. Germany as the EU's Reluctant Hegemon? Of Economic Strength and Political Constraints. *Journal of European Public Policy* 20 (10): 1387–1405.

Bulmer, Simon, and William E. Paterson. 2018. *Germany and the European Union: Europe's Reluctant Hegemon?* London: Red Globe Press.

Caporaso, James A., and Martin Rhodes. 2016. Introduction: The Political and Economic Dynamics of the Eurozone Crisis. In *The Political and Economic Dynamics of the Eurozone Crisis*, ed. James A. Caporaso and Martin Rhodes, 1–14. Oxford: Oxford University Press.

Carstensen, Martin B., and Vivien A. Schmidt. 2018. Power and Changing Modes of Governance in the Euro Crisis. *Governance* 31 (4): 609–624.

Copelovitch, Mark, Jeffry Frieden, and Stefanie Walter. 2016. The Political Economy of the Euro Crisis. *Comparative Political Studies* 49 (7): 811–840.

De Grauwe, Paul, and Yuemei Ji. 2015. Correcting for the Eurozone Design Failures: The Role of the ECB. *Journal of European Integration* 37 (7): 739–754.

De Rynck, Stefaan. 2016. Banking on a Union: The Politics of Changing Eurozone Banking Supervision. *Journal of European Public Policy* 23 (1): 119–135.

Dyson, Kenneth. 2017. Playing for High Stakes: The Eurozone Crisis. In *The European Union in Crisis*, ed. Desmond Dinan, Neill Nugent, and William E. Paterson, 54–76. London: Palgrave Macmillan.

Frieden, Jeffry, and Stefanie Walter. 2017. Understanding the Political Economy of the Eurozone Crisis. *Annual Review of Political Science* 20 (1): 371–390.

Henning, Randall C. 2016. The ECB as a Strategic Actor: Central Banking in a Politically Fragmented Monetary Union. In *The Political and Economic Dynamics of the Eurozone Crisis*, ed. James A. Caporaso and Martin Rhodes. Oxford: Oxford University Press.

Hodson, Dermot. 2013. The Little Engine That Wouldn't: Supranational Entrepreneurship and the Barroso Commission. *Journal of European Integration* 35 (3): 301–314.

Jacoby, Wade. 2015. Europe's New German Problem: The Timing of Politics and the Politics of Timing. In *The Future of the Euro*, ed. Matthias Matthijs and Mark Blyth, 187–209. Oxford: Oxford University Press.

Jones, Erik. 2010. Merkel's Folly. *Survival* 52 (3): 21–38.

Kindleberger, Charles P. 1981. Dominance and Leadership in the International Economy: Exploitation Public Goods, and Free Rides. *International Studies Quarterly* 25 (2): 242–254.

Lindberg, Leon N., and Stuart A. Scheingold. 1970. *Europe's Would-Be Polity: Patterns of Change in the European Community.* Englewood Cliffs, NJ: Prentice-Hall.

Lombardi, Domenico, and Manuela Moschella. 2016. The Government Bond Buying Programmes of the European Central Bank: An Analysis of Their Policy Settings. *Journal of European Public Policy* 23 (6): 851–870.

Matthijs, Matthias, and Mark Blyth. 2011. Why Only Germany Can Fix the Euro: Reading Kindleberger in Berlin. *Foreign Affairs Snapshot*, November 17. Available online at https://www.foreignaffairs.com/articles/germany/2011-11-17/why-only-germany-can-fix-euro, rev. 2016–05–31.

Moravcsik, Andrew. 1999a. A New Statecraft? Supranational Entrepreneurs and International Cooperation. *International Organization* 53 (2): 267–306.

Moravcsik, Andrew. 1999b. Theory and Method in the Study of International Negotiation: A Rejoinder to Oran Young. *International Organization* 53 (4): 811–814.

Nielsen, Bodil, and Sandrino Smeets. 2018. The Role of the EU Institutions in Establishing the Banking Union: Collaborative Leadership in the EMU Reform Process. *Journal of European Public Policy* 25 (9): 1233–1256.

Niemann, Arne, and Demosthenes Ioannou. 2015. European Economic Integration in Times of Crisis: A Case of Neofunctionalism? *Journal of European Public Policy* 22 (2): 196–218.

Schäfer, David. 2016. A Banking Union of Ideas? The Impact of Ordoliberalism and the Vicious Circle on the Banking Union. *Journal of Common Market Studies* 54 (4): 961–980.

Schild, Joachim. 2013. Leadership in Hard Times: Germany, France, and the Management of the Eurozone Crisis. *German Politics and Society* 31 (1): 24–47.

Schild, Joachim. 2018. Germany and France at Cross Purposes: The Case of Banking Union. *Journal of Economic Policy Reform* 21 (2): 102–117.

Schimmelfennig, Frank. 2015. Liberal Intergovernmentalism and the Euro Area Crisis. *Journal of European Public Policy* 22 (2): 177–195.

Schmidt, Vivien A. 2017. Reinterpreting the Rules 'by Stealth' in Times of Crisis: A Discursive Institutionalist Analysis of the European Central Bank and the European Commission. *West European Politics* 39 (5): 1032–1052.

Schoeller, Magnus G. 2018. The Rise and Fall of Merkozy: Franco-German Bilateralism as a Negotiation Strategy in Eurozone Crisis Management. *Journal of Common Market Studies* 56 (5): 1019–1035.

Torres, Francisco. 2013. EMU's Legitimacy and the ECB as a Strategic Political Player in the Crisis Context. *Journal of European Integration* 35 (3): 287–300.

Verdun, Amy. 2017. Political Leadership of the European Central Bank. *Journal of European Integration* 39 (2): 207–221.

CHAPTER 7

Conclusions

This chapter answers the book's research questions and summarizes its main argument (for the specific results, see Sect. 6.1). Moreover, it points to promising avenues for future research and reflects on the broader theoretical and empirical implications of the book. The introductory chapter raised the following questions: Why and how do collective actors such as states or international institutions emerge as political leaders? Moreover, once in charge, how do political leaders manage to influence policy or institutional change? What determines their success or failure? Based on a rational-choice institutional framework, this book provides an answer to these questions.

Leaders emerge if a collective action problem and incomplete institutions create high status quo costs, and if at the same time powerful actors expect their individual benefits of leading to outweigh the costs ("leader's surplus"). While status quo costs create a demand for leadership, a leader's surplus accounts for the supply of it. In order to take the lead, leadership candidates express their preferences with regard to a change of status quo, which is supposed to serve the interests of the entire group ("common goal"). At this point, the potential leader faces opposition: if all actors had not only a common goal, but even the same preferences on how to reach it, there would be no need for a leader; they could simply move on without anyone taking the lead (see Kindleberger 1981: 243).[1]

[1] This is even true for mere coordination problems. Take the example of traffic coordination: if there were no ex-ante rule determining on which side of the road to drive, traffic

M. G. Schoeller, *Leadership in the Eurozone*, Palgrave Studies in European Union Politics, https://doi.org/10.1007/978-3-030-12704-6_7

Thus, actors take notice of the leadership offer made by the candidate, and at least some of them object to it. At this point, the emerging leader has to react by employing her resources in such a way as to reach an outcome as close as possible to the proposed change. In doing so, the actor exercises leadership.[2]

Once in charge, leaders influence policy or institutional change by translating their power resources into strategies. These can take the form of typical negotiation strategies, which help a group overcome problems caused by high transaction costs or uncertainty, or they can consist in the provision of common knowledge, which comprises the definition of problems, the presentation of innovative ideas, and their promotion as acceptable solutions. Instead of actively employing strategies, a leader can also influence outcomes by relying on the "rule of anticipated reaction" (Friedrich 1963: 199–215): followers may anticipate that the leader can use her power resources to their disadvantage if they do not behave as the leader wants them to. Therefore, they comply preventively with the leader's requests. Hence, a leader's success or failure is partly determined by her power resources. However, two further factors play a crucial role: the distribution of preferences and the institutional constraint faced by the leader. A leader's success is more likely if the preferences in the group converge on the outcome preferred by the leader, instead of being heterogeneous or even converging on some other outcome. Moreover, a leader's prospects of success increase with the leeway in decision-making provided for by institutional rules ("institutional constraint"). The more a leader has to take into account the preferences of her followers because of their decision-making rights, the less likely is her success. Hence, it is the interplay of power resources, preference distribution, and institutional constraint that determines a leader's success or failure.

The empirical analysis has shown that this leadership model can plausibly explain the (non-)emergence and impact of collective leaders in

participants would have different preferences on whether to take the right or the left side. This would result in traffic chaos. In such a situation, in which all actors have a common goal (smoothly running traffic) but diverging preferences on how to reach it (left or right side), a leader deciding for one side would be highly welcome. By contrast, if for some reason (e.g. coincidence, pre-existing rules etc.) all road users shared the same preference for one side *ex ante*, there would be no traffic chaos and no leader would be needed.

[2]Where there is more than one leadership offer, the book's model suggests that the most powerful candidate's offer will succeed.

eurozone governance and reform. Thus, rational-choice institutionalism has proven capable of theorizing political leadership, an issue so far widely neglected by rationalist scholars (see Brennan and Brooks 2014). This does not mean, of course, that *all* cases and aspects of political leadership can be explained with rational-institutionalist propositions. Most notably, non-material factors outside a rationalist framework are not captured by the leadership model. In particular regarding Germany's role in the eurozone crisis, some authors have highlighted the role of ordoliberal ideas as a crucial explanatory factor (Bulmer 2014; Bulmer and Paterson 2018; Matthijs 2016; Nedergaard and Snaith 2015; Schäfer 2016). While a discussion of these assessments would go beyond the scope of this book, it needs to be acknowledged that the theoretical model does not allow for the consideration of ordoliberal ideas in the empirical analysis. The same is true for other non-material factors such as norms, values, or identities.

Testing the model against alternative explanations of leadership emergence and impact is therefore a major avenue for future research on the topic. Such an endeavour bears a few difficulties, though. In the most controversial case of Germany's role in eurozone governance and reform, both a rationalist and an ideational approach would expect the same observable outcome, thereby making an empirical test very difficult. If we assume that Germany's behaviour is driven by rationalist cost-benefit calculations, we expect the German government to support a rule-based approach to the Economic and Monetary Union (EMU), which is based on structural reforms and fiscal consolidation (austerity) at the national level (see e.g. Frieden and Walter 2017; Schimmelfennig 2015). If we assume that Germany's role is motivated by ordoliberal ideas, instead, we predict exactly the same outcome. Also with regard to other collective actors in EMU, the logics of consequentiality and appropriateness often result in the same behaviour: the realization of an integrationist idea by the Commission frequently comes along with an increase in power for this institution; the European Parliament's (EP) efforts to increase its influence in EU policy-making go hand in hand with the norm of parliamentary representation in liberal democracies; and the ECB's fight for the common good of the euro is simultaneously a fight for its own institutional survival. One way of solving this problem of observational equivalence is to base any test of competing explanations on a careful selection of cases where rationalist and ideational propositions would predict different preferences and behaviour. Such a test is still missing at the time of writing.[3] An alternative (or complementary) way of testing competing explanations consists in careful process-tracing: even if both rationalist and ideational explanations predict the same outcome, the supposed causal mechanisms differ. Thus, specifying further the causal mechanisms leading to the emergence and impact of leadership is another important task for future research.

A second major avenue for future research concerns the increase of the model's external validity. In this book, the model is tested within the empirical scope of eurozone crisis management and reform, and with regard to four collective actors. A different empirical scope of application would not only increase our confidence in the plausibility of the book's leadership model, but also help refine and generalize its theoretical propositions. The field of International Relations appears as a promising empirical ground for that endeavour. A study of the EU as a potential leader in different fields of international politics, for instance, would be an insightful complement to this book. Given the model's generalizability, other global actors such as regional powers, international organizations, or major non-governmental organizations (NGOs) could also be the object of future studies to test and enhance the model.

Going beyond the immediate results of the analysis (see above), the book bears theoretical and real-word implications. The book's theoretical contribution consists in delivering a causal, conditional, and generalizable model explaining the political leadership of collective actors. As pointed out in the introduction, this contribution is especially relevant with regard to theories of European and regional integration. At variance with the propositions of liberal intergovernmentalism, the book corroborates the findings of Beach (2005) and Tallberg (2006) that the power of member states cannot be assessed by only determining their fall-back position or, more concretely, their relative dependence on an agreement. In addition, one has to take account of their resources. While in many cases resources may contribute to an improvement of a member state's fall-back position, there is no automatic correlation. Thus, Finland may have a better fall-back option than Germany in eurozone crisis management, as it is arguable less dependent on the survival of the eurozone. Still, there is no doubt that Germany is the more powerful actor in EMU

[3] Matthijs (2016) follows a similar logic, though.

governance due to its larger resources (Sect. 4.2), and therefore the more likely leadership candidate.

Given that in the EU resources are unevenly distributed, single powerful states can lead a group to Pareto-improving outcomes, which not only reflect their own preferences, but which would not even exist without these states' additional leadership efforts. Hence, complementing liberal intergovernmentalist propositions, the book's leadership model can help explain "irregular" outcomes such as a leadership vacuum. According to liberal intergovernmentalism, such a situation should not emerge in the context of European integration, where we would rather expect an oversupply of state leadership (see Beach 2005: 21, Chapter 1). However, as the book shows, leadership is costly and prone to failure, which is why states may refrain from leading despite the benefits of a final agreement. Furthermore, by theorizing and investigating the use of leadership strategies, the book specifies existing explanations of *how* powerful states realize their preferences.

With regard to neo-functionalist approaches and their successors, which acknowledge the role of (primarily supranational) leadership for regional integration, the book's leadership model can also serve as an insightful theoretical complement. First, it refines existing works (esp. Lindberg and Scheingold 1970) by explicating why and how national and supranational leaders emerge. Second, the model adds to existing propositions by specifying that leadership is not always an appropriate tool to further regional integration as it can also fail. Moreover, with regard to this second analytical step, the model explicates the conditions for a leader's success in the form of testable expectations. Third, the book complements neo-functionalist and supranationalist approaches by highlighting that supranational institutions do not always provide leadership in favour of European integration. As can be seen in the case of the Commission's attitude towards Eurobonds (Sect. 5.1), for instance, the promotion of pro-integrationist solutions and a supranational institution's self-interest may be at odds. According to the book's leadership model, the institution will refrain from taking the lead and safeguard its self-interest in such a case. Finally, the book confirms and refines Mattli's (1999) and Cohen's (1998) propositions that state leadership is an important explanatory factor for regional integration.

As regards the book's "real-word" implications, the detailed empirical findings were presented in Sect. 6.1. Most importantly, the analysis shows that leadership is a way of overcoming collective action problems, and that the emergence of leadership is no sufficient condition for its impact. During the eurozone crisis, some actors refrained from taking the lead, while others provided leadership with varying success. Germany, the eurozone's most likely leadership candidate, appeared in all three roles: as a veto player rather than a leader, as a failed leader, and, in rare cases, as a successful leader.[4] Eventually, it was not Germany but the ECB that managed to suspend—if not overcome—the crisis, thereby emerging as a leader by default (Sect. 5.3).

Moreover, leadership is no panacea. As its emergence and success depend on multiple conditions, it is not always appropriate to call for leadership whenever a group faces a problem. Leadership can work as a solution to collective action problems, but it is no altruistic sacrifice made by powerful actors. This implies that in times of crises it may be rational to subordinate the immediate preferences to those of the leader in order to profit from the achievement of a greater common goal. In the eurozone crisis, this happened when so-called "debtor states" accepted more stringent fiscal rules and further intrusion in their national fiscal policies through the Fiscal Compact (Sect. 4.3), and when "creditor states" around Germany refrained from proceeding against the ECB's launch of Outright Monetary Transactions (OMT). Vice versa, the book also demonstrates that leaders need to take into account the preferences of their followers if they want to succeed. Even the ECB, which can decide autonomously without the consent of member states, announced OMT only once it was assured that Germany would subordinate its actual preferences to the greater good of overcoming the crisis (Sect. 5.3). Likewise, no leader will succeed in introducing Eurobonds as long as Germany and other fiscally conservative states categorically reject them (Sects. 5.1, 5.2). As a result, each call for leadership should be preceded by a careful assessment of the relevant conditions in order to find out from which actor we can reasonably expect the provision of successful leadership. The leadership model proposed by this book provides some criteria for such an assessment.

Finally, leadership is not a tool to make everyone happy. Even the final achievement of a common goal does not mean that all actors agree with the way this was done. In none of the cases analysed by this book did all actors agree with the solution proposed by the leader. This implies

[4] This demonstrates that leadership is an issue-specific phenomenon.

that despite the presence of a leader there are always relative winners and losers. One can even argue that if all actors not only share a common goal, but also the same preferences of how to reach it, there is no need for a leader. These implications confirm what Charles Kindleberger wrote already in 1981: "[...] leadership to provide the public good of stability, properly regarded, misunderstood as exploitation, or sniped at by free riders, seems a poor system, but like democracy, honesty, and stable marriages, is better than the available alternatives" (252).

The EU's current "polycrisis" (e.g. Dinan et al. 2017; Falkner 2016), the rise of populist radical right parties, and the increasingly eurosceptic climate in almost all member states does not seem to allow for a "leadership surplus" when it comes to the pending completion and deepening of EMU. However, in the light of still uncorrected institutional design failures, persisting macroeconomic imbalances and striking inequalities between eurozone member states, leadership remains as needed as ever before in the eurozone.

References

Beach, Derek. 2005. *The Dynamics of European Integration: Why and When EU Institutions Matter*. Basingstoke and New York: Palgrave Macmillan.

Brennan, Geoffrey, and Michael Brooks. 2014. Rational Choice Approaches to Leadership. In *The Oxford Handbook of Political Leadership*, ed. R.A.W. Rhodes and Paul 't Hart, 161–175. Oxford and New York: Oxford University Press.

Bulmer, Simon. 2014. Germany and the Eurozone Crisis: Between Hegemony and Domestic Politics. *West European Politics* 37 (6): 1244–1263.

Bulmer, Simon, and William E. Paterson. 2018. *Germany and the European Union: Europe's Reluctant Hegemon?* London: Red Globe Press.

Cohen, Benjamin J. 1998. *The Geography of Money*. Ithaca, NY: Cornell University Press.

Dinan, Desmond, Neill Nugent, and William E. Paterson (eds.). 2017. *The European Union in Crisis*. London: Palgrave Macmillan.

Falkner, Gerda (ed.). 2016. EU Policies in Times of Crisis: Mechanisms of Change and Varieties of Outcomes. *Special Issue of the Journal of European Integration Research* 38 (3).

Frieden, Jeffry, and Stefanie Walter. 2017. Understanding the Political Economy of the Eurozone Crisis. *Annual Review of Political Science* 20 (1): 371–390.

Friedrich, Carl J. 1963. *Man and His Government*. New York: McGraw-Hill.

Kindleberger, Charles P. 1981. Dominance and Leadership in the International Economy: Exploitation Public Goods, and Free Rides. *International Studies Quarterly* 25 (2): 242–254.

Lindberg, Leon N., and Stuart A. Scheingold. 1970. *Europe's Would-Be Polity: Patterns of Change in the European Community*. Englewood Cliffs, NJ: Prentice-Hall.

Matthijs, Matthias. 2016. Powerful Rules Governing the Euro: The Perverse Logic of German Ideas. *Journal of European Public Policy* 23 (3): 375–391.

Mattli, Walter. 1999. *The Logic of Regional Integration: Europe and Beyond*. New York: Cambridge University Press.

Nedergaard, Peter, and Holly Snaith. 2015. 'As I Drifted on a River I Could Not Control': The Unintended Ordoliberal Consequences of the Eurozone Crisis. *Journal of Common Market Studies* 53 (5): 1094–1109.

Schäfer, David. 2016. A Banking Union of Ideas? The Impact of Ordoliberalism and the Vicious Circle of the EU Banking Union. *Journal of Common Market Studies* 54 (4): 961–980.

Schimmelfennig, Frank. 2015. Liberal Intergovernmentalism and the Euro Area Crisis. *Journal of European Public Policy* 22 (2): 177–195.

Tallberg, Jonas. 2006. *Leadership and Negotiation in the European Union*. Cambridge and New York: Cambridge University Press.

Index

M. G. Schoeller, *Leadership in the Eurozone*, Palgrave Studies in European Union Politics, https://doi.org/10.1007/978-3-030-12704-6

The manufacturer's authorised representative in the EU is Springer
Nature Customer Service Centre GmbH, Europaplatz 3, 69115 Heidelberg,
Germany. If you have any concerns regarding our products, please
contact ProductSafety@springernature.com

Printed and bound by CPI Group (UK) Ltd, Croydon, CR0 4YY
30/09/2026
02225443-0003